Hon Alpheus Felch,

Saginaw,

with Regards and
Compliments of
The Author

July 1873

TEUCHSA GRONDIE:

A

Legendary Poem.

BY

LEVI BISHOP.

SECOND EDITION.

TO WHICH ARE ADDED

MISCELLANEOUS POEMS,

BY THE AUTHOR,

NOT BEFORE PUBLISHED.

ALBANY:
WEED, PARSONS AND COMPANY.
1872.

The following work was composed in such leisure hours as could be spared from the engagements of a laborious profession, and I now, with many misgivings, and fully sensible of its many defects, venture to send it forth, to stand or fall by the verdict of a discriminating but just and generous public. L. B.

DETROIT, May, 1870.

INDEX.

PRINCIPAL ACTORS.

Actor	
WA-WON-AIS-SA; or, Whippoorwill, (SIX GENERATIONS,)	Teuchsa Grondie Indians.
JOSSAKEED; a Prophet,	
CHE-TO-WAIK; the Plover,	
KEN-NA-BECK; a Serpent,	
MUS-KO-DA-SA; the Grouse,	
ISH-KO-DAH; the Fiery,	
WA-BE-NO-KA,	
KAH-GAH-GEE; the Raven,	
KO-KO-KO-HO; the Owl,	
SUB-BE-KAH; the Spider,	
SHAU-GO-DAH; a Boaster,	
TA-TO-KEE,	
WA-WA-TAY-SEE; the Firefly,	
PEZ-HE-KEE; the Bison,	
LE VAREAU; a Franciscan Monk,	French.
JENOCAIRE; a Jesuit Missionary,	
BOURDELAIS; a Jesuit Missionary,	
DUROC,	
TAI-GO-NE-GA,	Huron Chiefs.
KAN-NE-TOW,	

ME-SHI-NAU-WA, a Pipe Bearer, Mohawk Chief.

WA-BAS-SO; a Rabbit, Ottawa Chief.

Actor	
KA-GO-GEE,	Iroquois; or, Ho-dé-no-sau-nee.
DO-KA-TEE,	
O-TO-QUOT,	
TANG-GU-SHIN,	
KI-SAN-KO-SEE,	Illinois; or, Chic-ta-ghicks.
NI-KAN-NO-KEE,	

NI-NI-VAY; a Miami Chief.

NO-NE-YAH; a Pottawattamie Chief.

TEUCHSA GRONDIE.

CANTO I.

THE VILLAGE.

A. D. 1565.

PREFATORY NOTE. History informs us that when the present site of Detroit was first visited by Europeans, it was occupied by an Indian village called Teuchsa Grondie. The Indian word Wa-won-ais-sa signified Whippoorwill; and it is proposed to trace the family of Whippoorwill through several generations, for the purpose of illustrating, in some measure, the totemic order of descent in the female line. The name So-wan-na signified the great Master of Life, who presided over the place of departed spirits, in the distant Southwest.

I.

MY gentle Muse! Awake and sing—
Of wigwam, tomahawk and quiver!
Abroad thy sweetest echoes fling,
Of western forest, lake and river:
Of fairy tale and fairy scene;
Of war paint and of bark canoe;
Of winter bleak and summer green;
Of spirit of the Manitou:
Of pioneer in wilderness,
Where darkest perils oft beset;

Of bold adventures numberless;
    Of magic power of calumet:
Of struggles of heroic brave,
    In raging storm on every side,
His hunting grounds and home to save,
    Against an overwhelming tide:
Of chieftain roaming thro' the West;
    Of war-whoop and the victor's shout;
Of fiercest passions in the breast;
    Of strong battalia in the rout:
Of nations in the balance tossed;
    Of superhuman strength and skill;
Of dearest rights forever lost;
    Of Wa-won-ais-sa, Whippoorwill.

II.

Beside that broad but gentle tide,
Where navies of the world may ride;
    Whose waters creep along the shore,
    Ere long to swell Niag'ra's roar;
Here quiet stood an Indian village,
    Unknown its origin or date —
Algonquin huts and rustic tillage,
    Where stands the City of the Strait.
Upon the sloping bank it stood,
And yet extended from the flood,
    Towards the forest, circling nigh,
    That rose majestic to the sky.
From dark antiquity it came,
    In myths and dreamy ages cast;

And Teuchsa Grondie was its name—
Proud relic of forgotten past.

III.

The huts of bark on every hand,
Neat, conical in form,
In happy, artless order stand,
A shelter from the storm.
The cabin door of scanty size,
The central fire, are there;
Above, the graceful smoke may rise,
And shoot to outer air.
The floor with mats is neatly spread;
The winter stores are over head;
And, round about in every space,
Weapons of war and of the chase

IV.

No chairs or sofas there are found,
Or tables, as in courtly life;
No plates or cups or table cloth:
The guests are seated on the ground;
The finger serves as fork and knife;
The hand or wooden spoon for broth.
No costly vases — curious cast;
No spices that the taste incite;
No dainty viands — rich repast,
To tempt a pampered appetite:
No fiery drinks of drug malign,
As yet have cursed the nation;

Pure, crystal water serves for wine
And for devout libation:
And, heedless if the common dish,
Be owl, or bear, or dog, or fish,
The eager circle quickly share
The pottage and the scanty fare.

V.

The tidy dress from waist to knee,
Of skins or braid of bark or grass,
Was simplest of simplicity,
Save when it noted rank or class.
The plaited leaves of ash or oak,
Might well supply the janty cloak;
And often, when the summer shone,
The dress of nature served alone.
But when the sterner season came,
And winter suns were crouching low,
The richest furs of captured game,
Were proof to frost and driving snow.

VI.

Then gathered round the cabin fire,
The mother, pappoose and the sire;—
The young beside the older folks,
With hearty laugh for ready jokes.
The chief would tell his wondrous tale,
Of war-path and of forest game;
And eager youth would deep inhale
The love of glory, love of fame.

The necromancer, too, would tell,
To listeners held as by a spell—
    Of trees that walked in masquerade;
    Of birds that spoke like charming maid:
Of pigmies that, with potent charm,
Could doughty warriors disarm;
    Of heroes in the magic dress;
    Of wayward child in wilderness:
Of sorcerer in lonely glen;
Of manitous in shape of men;
    Of maidens, in the mystic grove
    With spirits, melting into love:
Of chieftain turned to beast, and then
The savage beast to warrior men:
    Of ghost and gorgon, seen afar,
    In lands towards the evening star:
Of sights and sounds of fearful wonder;
Of voices like the crashing thunder;—
    Till frighted children quick would glide,
    By instinct, to the mother's side.

VII.

Around this ancient Indian village,
In artless form was Indian tillage;
    Where, in their season might be seen,
    The corn, the vine, the squash and bean.
And there, laborious, bending low,
Was gentler sex, with rustic hoe;
    Nor haughty brave, from cabin shade,
    Would condescend to lend his aid.

The ground prepared, she dropped the seed,
She watched the springing blade;
She pulled away the thrifty weed,
For vines the arches made.
And when approached the harvest day,
With ever watchful eyes,
She drove the thieving birds away,
With motions and with cries.
And hers the task, the summer o'er,
To gather in the autumn store;
To guard it with a prudent care,
And thus supply the winter fare.

VIII.

The fearless hunter, roaming far,
In quest of savage game,
Was bred to bold, relentless war,
To fields of worthy fame.
In wilderness that circled round,
The chase, its trophies, quickly found:
The deer, the partridge, fox, and bear,
The turkey, squirrel — all were there.
In bark canoe, with line and hook,
Rare sport with profit well partook;
The angler seldom turned about,
Without his bass, or pike, or trout.
The rivers teemed with finny race,
That would a royal table grace;
And when the winter store was spent,
The waters an abundance lent.

IX.

And in the center of the place,
For councils, dances, and for play,
Was left a square — an open space,
Like *Champ de Mars* of later day.
The mother, here, beneath the sky,
In cadence wild sung lullaby;
Or, caught the yell resounding far,
Of chieftain from the distant war.
And here the young, as moon was bright,
Would from the dingy cabin rove;
And, in the flying hours of night,
Would breathe the gentle words of love.

X.

For great occasions, hall of bark,
Of ample, stately form would rise,
To grace the lovely central park —
An arch beneath the arching skies.
And here, in circles, on the ground,
In solemn mood, in thought profound,
Were held the councils of the State;
To hear ambassadors from far,
To deep advise of peace and war,
To listen to the stern debate.
The chieftain, here, in lofty strain,
Would all his burning wrongs maintain,
Yet meet a calm, an iron stare;
The fiercest passions of the breast,
Tho' deeply moved would seem at rest,
Nor leave a sign of vengeance there.

But when the firm resolve is ta'en,
They execute, with might and main;
    They sweep like rolling, rushing tides;
Of charging foe they meet the shock,
Like Dover Cliff or Ocean rock,
    Or sturdy ship of iron sides.

XI.

Here warrior to his standard flew,
    Not knowing what his future doom;
And, calling on his Manitou,
    Would plunge into the forest gloom.
And when from war-path he returned,
    Besmeared with paint and blood of slain—
From wigwam rudely sacked and burned,
    His clan received him here again.
The war song cheered him as he went,
On deeds of high ambition bent—
    The chieftains' ever pure delight:
The dance of death upon the green,
Must now present its dismal scene—
    Appalling, sickening, horrid sight!
Good heavens! the hapless prisoner's lot!
The ghastly wound, the arrow shot;
    The crushing stone, the cruel blow,
    The fires that round the victim glow;
The taunting jeer, the yell accurst,
The stoic nerve that braves the worst;
    The heavy drops of clammy sweat,
    While ebbing life may linger yet;

The death song, grimly murmured low,
From fierce, unutterable woe;
    The stifled groan, the gasping sigh,
    Dear tokens that the end is nigh;
To dogs the mangled body cast,
Or eaten as a rich repast;
    The dance around the gloomy den:
    And these we call a race of men!

XII.

To brighter scene we turn the eye —
To dance beneath autumnal sky.
    The hunter from the summer roam,
    Is welcomed to his rustic home.
The ears of corn are neatly strung;
The venison, dried, in cabin hung.
    The forest in its golden sear,
    Bespeaks the winter drawing near;
And yet the "Indian Summer" day
Is lovely as the blooming May.
    On every hand Dame Nature smiles,
    And every pain of earth beguiles.
The clear, refreshing air is bland,
Like atmosphere of fairy land.
    The buoyant spirits freely rise,
    Like incense from the sacrifice,
And calmly float upon the air,
As if their native home were there:
    Oh, is not this a sweet prelude,
    To heavenly home — beatitude!

XIII.

Now comes the autumn jubilee:
The happy people, gay and free,
With stranger, present, or by chance
Or by design, from far away,
Would have a merry, festal day;
Would revel in the village dance.
Loud chime the reed, the horn, the shell,
With human voice in wildest yell;
The forest echoes back the sound;
Their active limbs the dancers ply;
They fling their arms against the sky;
They whirl the rapid — giddy round.
Like swelling, undulating tide,
They sweep the square from side to side;
They form the circle hand in hand:
They shout, they swing around amain;
They vow their friendship to maintain,
'Gainst every foe of every land.

XIV.

And such was Teuchsa Grondie then,
A pleasant Indian town;
Unknown to other race of men,
Yet full of high renown.
Its annals, tho' obscure, might trace,
The prowess of Algonquin race;
Its many heroes were its boast,
Whose names are now forever lost.

The charm that its location lent,
    Its free access and central station,
Attracted here a continent;
    Fit capitol for mighty nation.

XV.

And now approach the shades of night;
    The troubled clouds a terror shed·
The silent hours to couch invite;
    The ready mat and skin are spread.
The inmates of the cabin's nest,
Are lost in sleep and dreamy rest;
    Save Wa-won-ais-sa, wakeful still,
    To soothe her infant Whippoorwill,
    And quell to rest a fevered brain,
    With lullaby and cabin strain.
The measured numbers softly tell,
    Like mellow sound of distant horn;
And deep enhance the midnight spell,
    Beneath the cabin roof forlorn.

CABIN SONG.

1.

How slow the wakeful hours,
  That creep along so weary,
Beneath the rustic bowers;
  How heavy and how dreary.

2.

The hunter from the chase,
  That he pursued so fleetly,
Now rests from hardy race,
  Upon his mat so sweetly.

3.

The warrior from afar,
  Repeats his bloody story;
Wild, fierce, relentless war,
  His life, his soul, his glory.

4.

From snow and chilling rain,
  The pappoose in the cabin,
Awaits till come again,
  The spring-time and the robin.

5.

I love the wigwam home,
  Its brands so cheerful burning;
Wherever I may roam,
  I love the sweet returning.

6.

And when this life shall end,
  When calls the great So-wan-na,
Southwestern shall I wend,
  To roam the great Savanna.

XVI.

As Wa-won-ais-sa sweetly sung,
The babe that to her bosom clung,
    Had lost, in quiet sleep, its pain,
    And all was dark and still again.
The mother in her sleeping plight,
    Addressed a prayer to Manitou;
The owl rung out the hour of night,
    That quiet reigned, and quickly flew.

TEUCHSA GRONDIE

CANTO II.

TO HON. ALEXANDER D. FRASER,

OF THE DETROIT BAR:

My highly esteemed friend, by whose kind encouragement I have been induced to persevere in the accomplishment of this work, and by whose friendly criticisms I have been much benefited therein, this Second Canto is, with his permission, most respectfully dedicated by

THE AUTHOR.

TEUCHSA GRONDIE.

CANTO II.

THE PUBLIC GAMES.

A. D. 1585.

PREFATORY NOTE. It was customary among the American Indians, to hold annual festivals, in the fall of the year, celebrated by public games. In the Indian tongue, Da-hin-da signified bullfrog: Ad-hec, reindeer: Kit-ta-coin-si, one that climbs: Mah-nah-be-zee, swan: Ke-no-zha, pickerel: Mas-ke-nozha, pike.

Michabou was the great presiding Manitou of the Northern lakes, having his headquarters at Mackinaw. Ghosts, spirits, and hobgoblins were familiar objects among the Indians, and the fairy scene above the river, is designed as a picture of a branch of the Indian mythology.

It will be noticed that the red men had already become alarmed at the approach of Europeans, although none of that race had as yet visited this section of the country.

I.

HOW rich the fields of human thought,
In myriad paths as yet untrod!
How vast the range that may be sought,
Empyrean, round the throne of God!
Tradition but obscurely lends,
Its light from far along our way;
Yet if we walk where nature tends,
Tradition blazes into day.

Though history be not our theme,
We skirt its ever shining page;
And though our song be but a dream,
It boldly paints heroic age.
Imagination's utmost range,
Invites our footsteps far and wide:
At every step a pleasing change,
And sweet wild flowers on every side.

II.

The morning stars proclaim the day;
The nightly shadows melt away.
The rising sun with smiling mien,
Displays the "Indian Summer" sheen;
A day for sports and public games,
In mem'ry of heroic names:
For well may Teuchsa Grondie boast,
Of honored names a mighty host.
The people take their early fare;
They sally out to public square;—
A motley band of young and old,
Of women and of chieftains bold;
In paint and plumage—bright array,
With expectations high;
And eager for the grand display,
The boldest feats to try.
Among the gay and happy throng—
A wife, her mother living still—
The wakeful child of cabin song,
Now honored as the Whippoorwill.

III.

And first, the umpire, all agreed,
Should be the prophet, Jossakeed:
His word is law in every strife;
His nod, that day, is death or life.
The way is cleared. Upon the lawn
With bison's shoulder blade,
Or tomahawk, a line is drawn:
A circle now is made.
"Who from the line shall farthest leap,"
The umpire loud proclaims;
"The prize—an eagle's wing—shall keep:
Begin the festal games."
Away they fly as on the wind,
Afar they eager spring;
Da-hin-da leaves them all behind;
Applauses loudly ring;
The victor strides with lofty air;
The prize he places in his hair.

IV.

"Stand forth, two men," said Jossakeed;
Upon their heads he placed a reed:
"Now one by one your muscle try,
And run and spring as for the sky;
Who passes o'er and touches not,
The hawksbill prize shall be his lot."
Then swift they fly apast the stand,
And each and all the prize demand;

For all have leaped in one procession,
And scaled the reed in quick succession.
Aratto, now—the light and fleet,
Ambitious yet,
Flies o'er the reed and turns complete,
A summerset:
And loud and long the shouts arise;
The victor proudly takes the prize.

V.

The race was next. Upon the lawn,
Far to the rear the line was drawn.
"That is the goal; from river start:
Quick, on the signal, all depart."
Then Jossakeed sends forth the cry,
And up the slope they wildly fly:
Swift as the roe upon the plain,
And eager all the prize to gain.
Loud swells a shout on every side,
As pours along the sweeping tide;
And while they nearly keep abreast,
Ad-hec, the reindeer, leads the rest.
He leaps the goal with flashing eyes,
And loudly claims the worthy prize.
The prize, a curious braided sash,
Of grass and bark of mountain ash.

VI.

Said Jossakeed, "The willows bring,
And twist them to a perfect ring,

Like bison's rolling eye;"
Said Jossakeed, "Your arrows bring,
A hundred paces let them sing,
Your skill and strength to try;
A painted arrow is the lot,
Of each whose arrow hits the spot."
At once a hundred bows they drew;
At once a hundred arrows flew;
And many could the prizes boast,
While many erring ones were lost.
Just then, a shadow from the sky,
Was seen athwart. The upward eye,
Beheld a hawk of largest size,
Well poised upon the air;
Instinctively each sought the prize,
Which tempting circled there:
And as he floated on the wing,
A hundred arrows flew;
Unerringly they upward sing,
And pierce him thro' and thro'.

VII.

Beyond the cornfields in the rear,
Majestic stood the oak and elm;
Now richly clad in golden sear,
The kings and queens of forest realm.
"Go mount;" cried Jossakeed aloud:
A murmur ran thro' all the crowd.
"We can not do it," they exclaim;
"And can not, now, is not a shame:

Unworthy feats we will not share;
Shall we compete with cat and bear?"
Then Kit-ta-coin-si from the rest,
Stood forth, and thus his mind expressed:
"Who says he cannot, need not try;
Who says he will, may even fly:
Who thinks him weak, is weakly still;
Success, is in determined will:
And no one knows what in him lies,
Until with all his might he tries."
With that, like flash of sabre stroke,
He sprung, elastic, to the oak;
Like wild cat to the top he went,
While shout on shout the welkin rent.
But what is that! a horrid sight!
That chills the blood with sudden fright!
Upon a sturdy branch there lay,
To watch the sports of festal day,
Black, grim, and fierce, in all his pride,
A monarch of the forest wide.
A surly growl! quick preparation,
To hurl intruder from the station.
Retreat cut off, for deadly strife,
Brave Kit-ta-coin-si, draws his knife.
Such battle field was never seen;
Unequal was the war, I ween.
No re-enforcements can they call,
And one must quickly die and fall.
Fierce terrors dart from bruin's eyes:
I can, I will, the other cries.

They grapple, now, in deadly throe:
The frighted oak sways to and fro:
While down upon the distant plain,
Wild fears and hopes alternate reign.
As bruin snaps a brawny part,
His eyes a burning glare,
The knife is driven to his heart,
And deadly rankles there.
He soon unlocks his rigid clasp;
He quickly draws a mortal gasp.
Down, down he tumbles with a bound,
A worthy trophy, to the ground.
Hold, victor, hold! your balance keep,
Upon the dizzy height:
In vain, in vain! thou, too, must leap,
Perhaps to endless night.
The quick re-action in his brain,
Sent him down plunging to the plain;
Yet he, tho' whirling round complete,
Like wild cat, landed on his feet.
He proudly strides to waiting square,
And throws his pond'rous trophy there.
The crowd survey with eager eyes;
A belt of wampum is the prize.

VIII.

The husband, this, of Wa-won-ais-sa's charms;
His pappoose sees the battle fray;
His wife receives him proudly to her arms,
The hero of the festal day.

IX.

"And now make ready, one and all,"
Said Jossakeed, "for game at ball;
In fury, on the level plain,
Let mimic war resound again."
At once two painted stakes are set,
Three hundred yards or more apart:
Between, the rival parties met,
The flying ball to strike—to dart.
To drive it past the stake amain
Of hostile party in the strife,
That was the point for each to gain—
To seek it as for very life.
The party wolf is at the west,
The party beaver at the east;
And wild will be the furious test,
Like beast against ferocious beast.
At signal, promptly, they engage,
With shout and shriek and deafening yell;
And stern, heroic, battle wage;
And both assail, and both repel.
Like rushing clouds along the sky,
Like surges on resounding shore,
Wher-e'er the ball is seen to fly,
There fiercely, madly, do they pour.
If either party seems to gain,
The other hurls them back amain;
And if the game approach the stakes,
It soon a counter current takes.

At last the ball a chieftain throws,
As on the wing, with lofty bound;
And past the western stake it goes:
The beavers rend the air around.
Upon the spot, from umpire's hand—
The worthy Sachem, just and grave,
The wampum flies to victor band,
As ever brave reward the brave.

X.

"The navy, now," says Jossakeed,
"A prize demand for skill and speed.
Start from the strand the other side,
And row across the crystal tide.
The first to touch the hither shore,
Shall win the prize, a polished oar."
At once there shot like solar beam,
A hundred skiffs across the stream—
As light as fleecy clouds of air,
Although a stalworth man was there.
Now, ranged along the distant land,
They wait the signal—wave of hand.
At once a hundred paddles fly;
No lack of nerve the rowers know;
They pull as worthy pull the brave;
They toss the spray against the sky,
And breast to breast the shallops go;
They lightly skim along the wave.
The manly strokes full rapid tell,
And fiercely shout the eager band;

The shores hurl back resounding yell;
　　The sight is thrilling—truly grand.
The trees around, in watchful mien,
Bend forward to behold the scene;
　　Nor inattentive to the view,
　　The water spirit—Michabou.
At Teuchsa Grondie, crowded strand,
All, breathless, wait the first to land.
　　Nor was it long; a modern fleet,
　　Might there have suffered a defeat.
Old pickerel—Ke-no-zha bold,
　　The rest a trifle led;
And in he came, as was foretold,
　　A half a length ahead.
Upon the spot the prize is paid—
　　The oar of mountain ash;
Shout peals on shout like cannonade,
　　Or mighty thunder crash.

XI.

Said Jossakeed, "Your skiffs aside,
　　And let their worthy crew,
Dash in and swim the sweeping tide,
　　The prize—a bark canoe."
A moment and a lengthened line,
　　Of dusky figures brave,
On farther shore expect the sign,
　　To plunge them in the wave.
They go—like frogs into the deep,
　　When danger may be nigh;

Their brawny arms in order sweep,
And strongest efforts ply.
The way is quickly measured o'er;
The goal is seized with eager eyes;
And soon they reach the hither shore:
Proud Mah-nah-be-zee wins the prize.
And yet no voice is heard aloud,
In all that terror stricken crowd;
For Michabou, with jealous eye—
The watchful guardian of the main,
As man invades his watery reign,
At once resolves a chief shall die.
The god can smile upon his chosen race,
When in a pleasant vein;
But terrors gleam upon his frowning face
When anger swells again.
And as the racers shoot toward the goal,
With fierce ambition burning in the soul,
Sir Pike—proud Mas-ke-no-zha, on his heel,
Sharp feels a grip as firm as hook of steel.
He tries to call. Alas! his voice is dumb:
Alas, he knows his final hour is come.
He gasps, he struggles, in a deadly throe;
He sinks forever to the shades below.
At once each mind with gloom is overcast:
The gay excitements of the day are past.

XII.

Then slowly, calmly, Jossakeed arose;
His solemn voice was heard;

"The gods are angry and the games I close;
The dance shall be deferred."

XIII.

The sun has set beneath the west,
Tho' not arrived the hour of rest.
Thro' hazy clouds above the river,
The stars look down as bright as ever.
The gentle waters glide along,
Sweet emblem of mellifluent song.
The clear, the bracing autumn air,
Sheds lovely charms of evening there.
The people on the sloping hill,
Calm, listen to the whippoorwill.
No other voice the silence breaks,
Till Jossakeed prophetic speaks.
"The stranger landed on the eastern shore,
In vast canoe, with flying clouds unfurled—
I dread his coming, as I deep deplore;
He bodes no good to this our western world.
In every breeze I snuff the coming storm;
The trees, the very skies are stained with blood;
Destruction to our race in every form—
See! Mas-ke-no-zha! with an angry god!"
All gaze intent upon the circling wave,
Where late the gasping, struggling, hero sunk;
And darkly there, and gloomy as the grave,
Arises grim, his melancholy trunk.
Beside him stands dread Michabou the great,
Dark as the blackest caverns of the night;

Tremendous, fierce, and frowning stern as fate,
In terrors clad, and majesty and might.
They rise obscurely on the misty deep;
Those on the shore the deepest silence keep,
With eyes in horror firmly set;
And as the phantoms float upon the air,
By slow degrees a myriad host are there,
In shades of death together met.
The owl whoops out a doleful note,
The frighted curs in terror whine,
No more sweet Wa-won-ais-sa sings;
Unnatural wolf howls wildly float,
The evening star forgets to shine,
The pappoose to its mother clings.

XIV.

At first the spectres circle round and round,
The god and Mas-ke-no-zha, in a dance;
Their music, sighs—a melancholy sound,
Dreamy as whispering breezes, in a trance.
And quick, and quicker yet the action grows;
In one dim undulating mass they move;
The glassy stream is rippled as it flows;
The fleecy clouds are gently stirred above.
The frighted mist at length has slowly fled;
The night looks down upon the spectral dead.
It is a sight the coursing blood to chill—
That spirit world in evolution still.
A crowd of Manitous, on every hand,
In silence gaze upon the fairy band.

Nor is the curious moon unmindful then,
Of these that fix the eyes of gods and men.
Slowly she rises on the forest gloom,
To see the sign of swiftly coming doom.
Her step is silent. Silent is her train.
She mildly peers above the wide domain.
To view, and not disturb, her sole intent;
Again she ne'er may see the like event.
She sees, and tho' with calm and smiling mien,
Her look is fatal to the gorgeous scene.
The Chief and Michabou, with lightning haste,
A refuge take beneath the watery waste.
The troubled fairies hie themselves away,
As from the light and terrors of the day.
The spectres melt into the lightsome air:
To eyes intent—a vacancy—is there.

XV.

"In this dread scene I clearly read,
Our fate and doom," says Jossakeed;
"A woe upon our kind:
Like these our race shall pass away,
At some not distant future day;
Nor leave a trace behind."

XVI.

And now, amid the balmy air,
The people to their huts repair.
The lowly couch is quickly spread;
The evening prayer is quickly said.
Silence resumes his awful reign;
And Teuchsa Grondie sleeps again.

TEUCHSA GRONDIE

CANTO III.

To Hon. AUGUSTUS S. PORTER,

Now of Niagara Falls;

Formerly of the Detroit Bar,

And member of the Senate of the United States for Michigan:

Under whose patronage I commenced, and under whose guidance I in part pursued, that course of legal and other studies which has resulted in whatever of professional success and reputation I have attained as a member of the Bar of Michigan, this Third Canto is, as an expression of esteem and gratitude, respectfully dedicated by

THE AUTHOR.

TEUCHSA GRONDIE.

CANTO III.

THE EXPLORATION.

A. D. 1610.

PREFATORY NOTE.—It will be remembered that the Pinta was a vessel of Columbus. The expeditions of Cortes, Scott, and Maximillian are those supposed to have been led by Ambition to Montezuma's Hall. For the purposes of euphony I place the accent on the first and last syllables of the word Ottawa. The word Niagara is derived from the Indian word O-ni-ag-raah. Ca-da-ra-qui was an ancient name for Lake Ontario. It is estimated that the Falls of Niagara have been seventy thousand years in receding from Lake Ontario to their present position. Hé-no was the Iroquois name for thunder, which was supposed to be a great Manitou, having his abode under the Falls of Niagara, and who required the sacrifice, by going over the falls, of at least one human being every year. The nether cave —Cave of the Winds, so called at the falls. In the use of the words *follow* and *valhalla*, I have been compelled, in order to retain the sense, to violate the rule of rhyme. In reading this Canto the following dates should be remembered. In 1565 the Spaniards settled at St. Augustin, in Florida. In 1607 the English settled at Jamestown, Virginia. In 1608 Champlain founded Quebec. In 1609 the Dutch settled at Manhattan, now New York. The expedition related in this Canto commenced in 1610. In 1620 the Puritans settled at Plymouth, Mass.

I.

PROPITIOUS Muse! of wild Ambition sing,—
The star malignant round the throne of God;
Of untold crimes an ever active spring;
To hapless man a fierce avenging rod.

Ambition plows the seas and braves the storms,
And faces danger in a thousand forms.
Ambition freezes in the polar snows,
And melts in deserts whence the Nilus flows.
Ambition bravely walks the battle plain;
And heaps the earth with mountains of the slain.
The brightest hopes of men, in freedom bred,
Are lost beneath Ambition's crushing tread.
When servile path to thrift Ambition sees,
Crouching, it licks the hand of power to please:
Proud independence, then, it flings away,
For one blest smile upon a festal day.
The lofty pyramids Ambition raises,
And on triumphal arch in sculpture blazes.
Ambition builds the proud imperial dome,
That makes the modern rival ancient Rome.
To swell the pomp of power with aliment,
The daring Pinta to the west is sent:
And, thrice obedient to the silent call,
Ambition leads to Montezuma's Hall.
Ambition, too, with ensign proud unfurled,
        Explores with eager hand,
The lakes and forest of this western world,
        As of a promised land.

II.

The Dutchman, on Manhattan Bay,
    On high his tattered banner threw—
The morning star of rising day,
    Of nation springing into view.

The Spaniard, on the Everglade,
One feeble settlement had made.
    The Briton only one could boast,
    Upon the wide Atlantic coast;
For restless puritanic stock,
Had not yet seen the Plymouth rock.
    Thro'out the north and boundless west,
    Unmindful of the stranger guest,
And still the master of his home,
The red man could a monarch roam.
    To seize the prize—a continent,
    The Gallic king a squadron sent.
He draws a line thro' friend and foe,
From Labrador to Mexico:
    The *fleur de lis* is flung on high,
    With flaming cross, against the sky.

III.

At first, as by a natural law,
They thread the rapid Ottawa.
    Around its tumbling cataracts,
    They lug their skiffs and heavy packs;
And, guided by the northern star,
    Beside the "Upper Lakes" they rally;
They push their searches westward far;
    They reach the Mississippi valley.
Meanwhile, vague rumors darkly told,
  Like distant echoes from the past,
    Of O-ni-ag-raah's thundering way;

And where the devotee so bold,
To place his life upon a cast,
And search it out without dismay?
An active monk, of humble spirit,
No vain ambition in his heart,
Franciscan, yet of signal merit—
A beggar, dared the noble part.
Le Vareau was his modest name,
Now blazoned on the rolls of fame;
The mighty Lake's resounding shore,
Shall waft it on forever-more.

IV.

Two yawl boats were his humble fleet,
To venture far from land;
Twelve chosen men the crew complete—
An Argonautic band.
To guard against a jealous foe,
And unseen dangers none could know;
To bear the peaceful calumet,
And guide where obstacles beset;
To lead upon the trackless wave;
Pipe Bearer, Me-shi-nau-wa brave—
A Mohawk chief, his service lent,
Upon a bold adventure bent.

V.

A chant they sing; adieus they take;
An unknown heathen world their aim:
They pass proud Ca-da-ra-qui Lake—
The Lake Ontario now the same.
They land upon the western shore;
They hear Niagara's distant roar:
They see its cloudy, rolling spray:
Eight stalworth men the navy bear;
The baggage is the others' care;
The tangled portage they essay.
And up the steep they onward press,
Amid a darksome wilderness.
Upon projecting points they tread,
Above the rocky, fearful bed.
Le Vareau walks the narrow way;
In terror does he often shrink:
If but a step were set astray—
Ye horrors, what a frightful brink!
They wend their way to "Table Rock"—
Deep rent by frost and heaving shock;
High poised, and ready to be hurled,
With crashing sound to nether world.
The sun is in the western sky;
He casts his beams against the spray;
The rainbow bursts upon the eye,
And cheerful smiles at parting day.

The forest trees upon the ledge,
    Stand high above the iris bow;
Peering at times beyond the edge,
    Into the yawning gulf below.
They gaze upon that awful scene—
    That God-created battlement,
That boiling surge of deepest green,
    That never-ending swift descent.
They note that one eternal roar;
    They mark those misty, fleecy tears,
That speak from still receding shore,
    Of seventy thousand flying years.
Those widely gaping, thirsty jaws,
    Although long fed by rushing flood,
Insatiate still, can know no pause,
    In this stupendous work of God.

VI.

The party sought a lonely grot,
In which to spread an humble cot;
    And where a ledge, tho' wild in form,
    Might shelter from a threatened storm.
By those that gnawing hunger feel,
Is soon dispatched the evening meal;
    And all are seated on their mat,
    To have a social evening chat.
Awhile they sit in thought abstract,
Before that rushing cataract.

On high the rolling mist is hurled,
As from a subterranean world:
And though they sit upon a rock,
They feel the mighty ocean shock.
At length Le Vareau silence breaks,
And reverent thus he calmly speaks:

LE VAREAU.

This awful gorge, this mighty, rushing flood,
Declare the works, the majesty of God.
The vast cerulean arch above he flung,
And whirling planets to his glory sung.
He formed the earth, the ocean, and the lake;
And at his voice their deep foundations quake.
The spring—his smile; the flying cloud—his breath;
His pardon—life: his frown—eternal death.
At his command, the rivers to the main
Their courses keep, and n'er return again.
He holds his seat above the vaulted sky,
And, though unseen, is yet forever nigh.
Thro' sweeping time, as ere the world begun,
He rules and reigns, Eternal—Three in One.
He is the God that on the lightning soars:
His is the voice that here forever roars.

ME-SHI-NAU-WA.

Na, na; at once replies the Mohawk chief;
Give ear whilst I relate the true belief.
Beneath that shooting flood, a vacant space;
And there the sullen Hé-no holds his place.

His throne is there. On adamantine rock,
That firm resists the mighty torrent shock,
He watchful sits—the guardian, ever true,
Of this wild realm;—dread Gitchie Manitou.
Of lofty frame—collossal is his size;
Like balls of living fire his rolling eyes.
His locks, his color, are of deepest green;
His aspect stern; majestic is his mien.
This constant spray—the vapor of his breath;
This roar—his moan, as of the pang of death.
And when, in anger fierce, he sallies forth,
He chills the air like gale from icy north.
The lightning streaks, that dart athwart the sky,
Are but the flashes of his gleaming eye.
The pealing thunders that above us roll,
Are but the howlings of his troubled soul.
His giant sons are ever at command,
To roam and howl and thunder thro' the land.
He annual craves, I tremble to recite,
A human form to sate his appetite.
Perhaps, e'en now, in council there below,
He meditates for us a fatal blow.
For this invasion of his rightful reign,
One, if not all, may be untimely slain.

VII.

The chief was silent. Silent all,
Except that deafening water fall.
 The chief, to custom ever true,
 Invoked his guardian Manitou.

Le Vareau then his vespers sung:
The cross upon a bramble hung.
For incense—burning leaves instead;
The wafer—slips of moldy bread.
Yet where the heart is right within,
The simplest offerings cleanse from sin:
The merit is the good intent;
There all is well where well is meant.
When each had thus his prayer expressed,
With leaves and blankets piled around,
The party sunk at last to rest,
And sleep and darkness reigned profound.

VIII.

Meanwhile, beneath the plunging flood,
The heralds of the thunder god
Reported strange intruder near—
A stranger bold and void of fear.
"And who," stern Hé-no quick replied,
"Has thus my ancient realm defied?
Go forth, arouse the raging storm,
In fiercest terrors, blackest form."
Abroad at once the heralds went,
Upon their midnight errand bent;
And soon the rolling thunder cloud,
Spread, far and wide, a gloomy shroud.
The winds let loose from "nether cave,"
Drove mists above the angry wave.

The sweeping blast an effort made,
To level low the forest shade.
Down poured a flood of drenching rain,
That, surging, rushed to river main.
The Manitou leaped up on high,
And bared his frontlet to the sky.
His gleaming eye was vivid flame;
His thunder shook the starry frame:
Loud echoes bellowed thro' the air,
As if the gods were warring there.
Near by, upon a sturdy oak,
Went crashing down a thunder stroke:
The heavy, deafening, earthquake shock,
Let loose a mass of "Table Rock,"
Which, leaping—went, in ruin hurled,
Like wreck of a dissolving world.
As peal on peal upon them broke,
The Frenchmen and the chief awoke;
The chief, a statue, stood appalled,
The others on the Virgin called.
The angry Hé-no, one could see,
Fierce raging thro' the sky
The others, awful majesty—
The Majesty on high.
They stood and gazed. The vivid flame,
Alternate with the dark extreme,
As quick it went and quickly came,
Was frightful as a horrid dream.
And then that dread abyss below,
That lightning flashes quick reveal—

It yawns like pits of darkest woe,
 That damnéd spirits deep conceal.
At last the thunders die away;
 The disappointed Manitou,
 Beholding all his terrors vain,
 Withdraws into his darksome den;
And tho' the distant lightnings play,
 The sulky winds, with much ado,
 Returning to their caves again,
 Leave sweet repose to weary men.

IX.

As early woke the smiling morn,
The lightsome fleet was quickly borne,
 Above the rapids, sweeping by,
 Like time to long eternity.
The morning meal, at once prepared,
Among the hungry crew was shared.
 The boats were loosened from the strand;
 Aboard was now the little band.
The oars were ready at the sides;
Le Vareau and the chief the guides.
 Up rose a sailor—stout La Coste;
 He stept and quick his balance lost;
A moment reeled from side to side,
Then fell into the sweeping tide.
 He lightly rises on the wave;
 All hands are quickly stretched to save.
No one can reach him: on he goes,
Deep fraught with overwhelming woes.

An oar is reached for him to clutch;
The oar is just beyond his touch.
He goes, he goes! O, all is lost!
Farewell forever, brave La Coste!
He rushes down the rapid stream,
Like wingéd thought or solar beam;
Nor can his struggles aught avail,
When rocks and dashing waves assail.
Le Vareau lifts his voice on high,
To God of mercy in the sky—
To pardon, bless, and kindly save,
A mortal rushing to the grave.
The Mohawk sees, above the flood,
The Manitou—the angry god,
Enraged, that terrors of the night,
Have not the strangers put to flight.
A fearless gull he seems to roam:
And now he dips the dashing foam;
Anon he screams with wild delight,
So soon to sate his appetite.
The victim rises on the surge;
He sends a loud, despairing cry,
That swells above the deafening roar;
It is his last;—his funeral dirge,
It rolls along the vaulted sky;
It echoes from resounding shore.
Ah, now the two from sight are lost!
Amid the surging, plunging main;
The pioneer—the brave La Coste,
On earth shall n'er be seen again.

The first white man that met his doom,
In that insatiate, dread valhalla;
How many since have sought its tomb!
What myriads yet are there to follow!

X.

With heavy heart the little crew,
Applied the oar and onward flew.
Beneath the morning's rising beam,
The navy cut the glassy stream.
The frighted duck from danger fled;
The wild goose circled over head.
The shooting pike would oft display,
His form above the dashing spray.
The floating sedge apast them flies;
A broad expanse before them lies.
On either side—the forest green,
Enchanting to the view;
The tufted islands rise between,
The homes of Manitou.
The balmy air and nature smile,
While songs the heavy hours beguile.

XI.

The river passed, upon them breaks,
Another of the mighty Lakes.
They onward press a day or so;
They pass the head-land Abino.

For Long Point now they ply the oar,
And soon they reach the sandy shore.
The line is drawn with steady hand;
A sturgeon flounders on the strand;
    Which, soon dispatched, and on the fire,
    Is all that hunger can desire.

XII.

The blazing orb of summer day,
    Beneath the glowing west is set:
For blessing on the distant way,
    The crew at evening prayer are met.
"Spirit of Life," the Mohawk cries,
"May thy protection here arise;
    Oh smile upon this desert shore!"
Le Vareau with uplifted eyes,
Invokes the Power above the skies;
    "To Whom all praise forever-more."

TEUCHSAGRONDIE

CANTO IV.

To Dr. ZINA PITCHER:

One of the pioneers of Detroit, and one of its highly esteemed and distinguished citizens; who, in an hour of misfortune and deep distress, kindly extended to me his personal and professional assistance, and by whose counsel and advice my attention was turned to the law as a profession, this Fourth Canto is, with his permission, gratefully dedicated by

THE AUTHOR.

TEUCHSA GRONDIE.

CANTO IV.

THE DISCOVERY.

A. D. 1610.

PREFATORY NOTE. In reading "The Evening Call" it should be remembered that the early French explorers of this country were from Normandie, on the Lower Seine.

Mah-nah-be-zee, the Swan, an ancient name for the Island called by the French *Ile au Cochon,* and now known as Belle Isle, in the Detroit river. At-ti-ca-me-gue was the Indian name for the whitefish. In this, as well as in other Indian names, I presume I have varied from the proper Indian accent and pronunciation. It is almost impossible, after the lapse of two hundred and fifty years, to determine the proper pronunciation of words in a language which had no alphabet, and which was first written by Europeans. Our exploring party are still on Long Point, in Lake Erie, at the opening of this Canto.

I.

AS night advanced, upon the shore,
The waves prolonged a gentle roar,
In soothing murmurs low;
The weary party soundly slept,
No danger nigh no vigil kept,
Secure from every foe.

And whether on the rural cot
We quiet sleep; or in the grot
On bed of evergreen;
Or in the pampered city life;
Or on the ocean's angry strife;
Or 'neath a sky serene;
Or, pioneer, in chilling rain,
Or, soldier, on the battle plain,
Upon the reeking ground;
Or on the trail of savage game;—
Refreshing sleep is much the same
Wherever it is found.

II.

When scarce the hour of two was past,
Le Vareau rose, and round him cast
A cassock; and, the cross in hand,
He sallied forth upon the strand.
Tho' chill and humid was the air,
The summer reigned in glory there.
Above—the stars and milky way;
Around—a waste of waters lay.
No white man e'er before had been
Upon this solitary scene.
Such lonely spot, at dead of night,
Was fit abode for anchorite.
With folded arms Le Vareau stood,
Amid the shades of night unfurled,
And gazed upon the darksome flood—
Fit emblem of a sinful world.

And while he stood in thoughtful mien,
Emerging from the waste was seen
 The morning star—a brilliant gem;—
The herald of the coming day,
Like John, in lonely desert way,
 Of coming Star of Bethlehem.
And one by one the sister train
Arose above the watery main—
 Bright sapphires in the eastern sky;
They soft unfold the morning light,
While slow retire the shades of night
 From arching canopy on high.
And now the East is all aglow;
The light mounts upward, steady, slow;
 With darkness wages deadly war:
Reflected beams upon the wave,
Like wingéd hope above the grave,
 Proclaim returning life afar.
In turn the starry train is dim,
As creeps above the water's brim,
 That glowing ball of fiery red:
The vision sweeps the waste anew;
Creation springs again to view,
 As springs again to life the dead.

III.

Le Vareau lifts his eyes on high,
The cross upheld against the sky;
 And thus is calm devotion paid:

"Oh thou eternal, gracious God!
That rules the storm and raging flood;
  By whom the ocean lakes were made;—
Oh, guide us in this desert way;
Extend to us, from day to day,
  Thy mighty, all-protecting care;
Go with us to the heathen land,
That we may plant, with holy hand,
  Thy standard cross forever there."

IV.

The crew are up. The tent they strike,
  With rising of the morning sun;
They breakfast on a lusty pike,
  And soon the journey is begun.
The sky is bright, and calm the lake,
  While soft the gentle zephyrs blow;
The oars the glassy waters break;
  They leave the point for "Westward Ho!"
No forest birds are there to sing,
  The echoes of the morn to wake;
And yet the sea gulls dip the wing,
  And welcome to the stranger speak.
The laden boats, on steady tack,
Leave far behind the widening track;
  The ripples from the plying oar
  Are felt upon the distant shore.

V.

The jolly crew, to while away
The lengthened hours of summer day,
    Their oft-told stories tell again,
    Nor as a pastime tell in vain.
Nor is the Mohawk silent then;
    His tales forbid the quiet sleep;
He tells of ghosts and murdered men,
    And "Spirits from the vasty deep."
And songs are there in order due;
If old they please, they please if new:
    The songs that tell of distant home,
    Will touch the heart wher-e'er we roam.
And Duroc sings "The Evening Call,"
    In full and rich and lively strain,
So often heard by one and all,
    In dear Normandie on the Seine.

THE EVENING CALL.

1.

Come, ride upon the Seine to-night;
  Your many friends are waiting there;
Their hearts are light, their smiles invite;
  Come, take the fresh—the evening air.

2.

The stars above are wooing thus;—
  The queenly moon so fair and bright;
Come, have a pleasant chat with us,
  Upon the lovely Seine to-night.

3.

Now glides the boat with easy grace,
  And songs abound, and repartee;
And one and all, with jolly face,
  Are reveling in felicity.

4.

The redbreast and the whippoorwill,
  May chant their sweetest roundelay;
But we will sing yet sweeter still,
  Our carols of the closing day.

5.

And now the evening shades are set;
  The hours have run their rapid flight;
To-morrow eve do not forget
  To sail again: Adieu—good night.

VI.

As died the mellow sounds away,
And milder shone the evening ray,
    Le Vareau sunk to gentle sleep,
    In that frail barque upon the deep.
The crew respect his quiet slumbers;
The oars relax their steady numbers.
    Delicious breezes fan his brow;
    His cares are all forgotten now.
And yet, tho' sleeping on the lake,
His active mind is still awake;
    Yea, nothing to disturb its ken,
    Still clearer is its vision then.

It rolls upon his enterprise,
That should its leader canonize:—
Its purpose, spirit and intent;
Its aim—a boundless continent;
Its scope—a deep concocted scheme
Of vast imperial sway;—
Are thus portrayed, in fitful dream,
Upon the watery way.

LE VAREAU'S DREAM.

1.

The martial genius of the Gaul arose,
With that of Albion,—ever jealous foes;
Both grasping for a wide dominion:
Europe for ages they had drenched in blood,
And stained with crimson every ocean flood,
For power, or freedom of opinion.

2.

Upon the western world they cast their eyes,
Both eager to possess the worthy prize;
The right was in the first possession:
And while the Briton held Atlantic coast,
An artful circumvention France could boast,
By prior claim, or by aggression.

3.

The genius, too, of Papal Rome arose;
The olive branch extending to the foes,
That bowed to her supreme relation;
Yet flamed the sword as flamed the holy cross,
To purge the faithless as unworthy dross,
In every land and every nation.

4.

Then rose the genius of the mighty West,
With every clime and untold riches blest,
With grandeur, power, beyond expression;
The Gaul this wide dominion would secure;
To Roman faith the heathen must enure;
To one, to both, a vast possession.

5.

An humble monk, with rosary and sash,
On enterprise as bold as it was rash,
Then rose upon his troubled vision;
His was the task in this, a heathen world,
To bear aloft the standard thus unfurled;
To glory bound, or just derision.

VII.

A yell from distant forest broke;
The dreamer from his dream awoke:
A hunter spied the little fleet,
And, ready any foe to greet,
The signal to his comrades gave;
His voice resounded o'er the wave.
Again the crew apply the oar;
Nor court acquaintance with the shore.
And quiet thus the days are passed;
No accident a gloom to cast.
Dried meat the food, and fish and bread,
With water dipt from fountain head.
And thanks are paid, as ever due,
To God above, and Manitou.

They skirt along the northern shore;
Its bays and rivers they explore.
At night they anchor to the strand,
And guard against a foe at hand.

VIII.

They reached, ere long, *La Pointe Pelée;*
Where, to prevent a night surprise,
The sentinel in secret lay:
A wise precaution n'er despise.
And here they raised a shelter tent;
In social chat a time was spent:
When, as the hour of rest was nigh,
A flight of arrows whistled by;
And as the singing weapons erred,
A fearful war-whoop shout was heard.
The French with terrors were beset;
The Mohawk raised the calumet;—
That emblem true—that admonition,
Of friendship and of peaceful mission.
The skulking stranger knew it well;
Obeyed it as a magic spell:
Discomfited, he slunk away,
Like wild beast, cheated of his prey.
The danger past, the mats are spread;
The thankful vespers now are said.
The stars shoot forth their evening beams,
That gleam along the watery plain;
The crew are lost in pleasant dreams,
And night resumes his silent reign.

IX.

The gilded morn unfolds the day;
The crew, refreshed, are on their way.
Then far toward the west serene,
A lightsome bark canoe is seen;
That glides, beneath the bending oar,
From islet to the distant shore.
A chief it bears, of gleaming eye,
And manly arm and breast;
And shady plumage waving high,
In proud and noble crest.
With hopes to banish idle fear,
And lure a friendly stranger near,
The calumet is quickly sent
Toward the azure firmament.
Evasive, like a flitting ghost,
As if in wild affright,
The stranger seeks the distant coast,
And vanishes from sight.

X.

At length the color of the deep,
The floating sedge the surface bore,
The action that was felt below;
Bespoke a current's rolling sweep,
An inlet from an unknown shore,
That soon its welcome should bestow.

And soon these indications true,
Presented to the opening view,
That river, clear and broad and bland,
The charm of all this western land.
Its lucid waters quiet rolled,
Its gem-like islands seemed to float,
Its heavy forests bloomed on high,
Its grasses waved beneath the sun;
Its pendant vines on every hold,
Its winding banks like rising moat,
Its wild game flapping in the sky;
Its whole—a paradise begun.

XI.

On, boldly pulled the little crew;
The gulls above in circles flew.
Upon the shores the feathered game,
Unnatural, chanted wild acclaim.
And in the forest, too, were there,
With furtive look of coming peril,
The wolf, the deer, the surly bear,
The fox, the raccoon, and the squirrel.
Nor beast alone was witness then
Of this invasion bold displayed;
Among the trees astonished men,
Were peering, skulking in the shade.
As push the boatmen up the stream,
From tree to tree their figures gleam.
The Mohawk shows the calumet,
As if by mortal foes beset;

Le Vareau lifts the cross on high,
As if infernal sprites were nigh.
And prayer is heard. In wild surprise,
To Michabou the Mohawk cries:
The Frenchmen call on heavenly power,
To guard them in the trying hour.

XII.

Arrived below a grassy isle,
That could no lurking foe conceal,
The party stop to rest awhile—
Prepare and take the hasty meal.
They anchor to the thrifty grass;
The blooming shores are full in view;
A fire of coals is quickly struck;
They artful hook the sombre bass,
And luscious at-ti-ca-me-gue:
The arrow brings the dainty duck.
The teeming lakes, in nature's plan,
Of vast extent from shore to shore,
Shall furnish food for hungry man,
From age to age for evermore.

XIII.

Refreshed and rested, on they go,
Against the current's gentle flow.
A broad expanse before them lies,
And verdant banks to charm the eyes.

At times the curling smoke is seen,
    That floats upon the dusky air;
And tells of hut in forest green,
    Perhaps of foeman lurking there.
No nets are seen for finny race,
    Or windmills on projecting land;
Yet nature, in her native face,
    Is truly pleasant, truly grand.
They reach an angle in the stream;
    They onward still their way pursue;
When bursts upon them, like a dream,
    Fair Teuchsa Grondie full in view.
Toward the left the village lies,
    Like coquette, wooing, on the strand;
A spot to charm the ravished eyes,
    A fairy scene in fairy land.
Far up, as seen in purest air,
A mirror glitters—Lake St. Clair;
    And on the eastern shore serene,
    Are forest robes in richest green.
And in the central stream, apart,
That master-piece of nature's art,
        Where beauty sets her seal;
The Mah-nah-be-zee, Swan its name;
The *Ile au Cochon*, all the same;
        The same the fair Belle Isle.

XIV.

In solemn mood Le Vareau bent;
On high his thanks devout he sent;
With firmest vows of zealous life,
In all the woes of earthly strife.
The distant channel first they made,
For fear of crafty ambuscade;
But while their boats are drawing nigh,
And calumet is held on high,
The pipe of peace is clearly seen—
The token of sincere good will,
At Teuchsa Grondie on the green,
Where Jossakeed is prophet still.

XV.

The boats are quickly on the pebbly strand;
The natives, wondering, all surprise conceal;
The chiefs to huts conduct the stranger band,
And Whippoorwill prepares the evening meal.

TEUCHSA GRONDIE.

CANTO V.

The Reception.

To Hon. DANIEL GOODWIN,

Of the Bar and Judiciary

of Michigan:

To whose instructions I was indebted for a large share of my legal education, and for whose learning, ability and integrity I have always entertained a high esteem, this Fifth Canto is, with his permission, respectfully dedicated by

THE AUTHOR.

TEUCHSA GRONDIE.

CANTO V.

THE RECEPTION.

A. D. 1610–11.

PREFATORY NOTE. Jeebi were a species of mythological hobgoblin. The hoot or whoop of the owl inspired a peculiar dread among the Indians. Champlain, at the head of a party of French and Hurons, attacked and defeated a war party of Mohawks on the western coast of Lake Champlain, in 1609. It is said, that the first horses ever seen at Teuchsa Grondie, or Detroit, were taken from General Braddock, by the French and Indians, at the battle near Fort Du Quesne, in 1755.

I.

THE summer morn, beside the western lakes
Inspires a mild, but sweet exhilaration;
And happy he who with the dawn awakes,
And walks abroad for healthy recreation.

II.

Le Vareau from unquiet rest awoke,
And took a stroll about the public square;
On every side the village well bespoke,
That savage life in rudest form was there.

The cabin was a shelter from the storms,
Where mat and skin their easy comfort lent;
But, stretched upon the ground, were lazy forms,
With shades of night for cover well content.
The bee was humming to the blossom wild;
The robin warbled from adjacent tree;
The mocking bird the early hour beguiled;
And nature breathed her sweetest melody.

III.

The plain repast was early spread,
And Teuchsa Grondie quickly fed;
The strangers, too, were well supplied,
With Mohawk chief—the crafty guide.
No questions e'er the silence broke,
As "Why you visit us perforce;"
The words were few that either spoke,
And dignified the intercourse.
And yet the urchin, skulking round,
And peering from behind the sire,
In stranger costume subject found,
Whereof to wonder and admire.
In shady nook and humble station,
He gazes oft in admiration—
At Vareau's robe in shining dross;
At rosary and flaming cross.
When youth we thus can deeply move,
To first incline and then approve;
Though not an effort be exerted,
The coming age is half converted.

IV.

When dangers threaten or beset—
When difficulties round us press,
Bold action triumph may beget;
Audacity may bring success.
Le Vareau, slowly, from his tent,
With solemn and imposing air,
Upon the square for worship went—
To boldly raise his standard there.
A thrifty maple lent its shade,
The center of the promenade;
The altar there he raised:
Upon the cross the dying Lamb;
Beside it waved the Oriflamme:
"Let God be ever praised."
In graceful festoons, overhead,
An arch of evergreens he spread;
Upon a mat he kneeled:
The Avés floated on the air;
The Lord of Hosts was worshiped there,
To western world revealed.
The vast cathedral's awful dome,
At London, Paris and at Rome,
Inspires the true sublime;
And yet the dome of vaulted sky—
The work of God, may well defy
All else of earth or time:
And whether we believe or not,
That service holds us to the spot,
By soft attractive charms;

Its solemn grandeur calmly tells,
Like mellow sound of distant bells,
And prejudice disarms.
The red man close attention lent,
In silent, deep astonishment,
As if to wonder prone;
He there beheld a living light,
That shone upon a dismal night
Upon the dread unknown.

V.

From day to day, in open air,
The parties mingled on the square,
In social conversation;
The weeks and months in quiet flew,
Each day presenting something new;
No vapid relaxation.
At times the Frenchmen used the quiver;
The rapid race the natives run;
Both parties angled on the river;
They danced beneath the setting sun.
And when the winter evenings came,
In cabin, by the central flame,
Le Vareau, versed in sacred laws,
And always true to holy cause,
Unfolded to the savage mind,
By gloomy superstition bound,
The destiny of human kind,
That learned sages may confound.

He tells of mighty Lord above,
That rules the vast, mysterious train
Of works of nature multiform —
In bee that hums the song of love,
In bison roaming o'er the plain,
In fierce resounding thunder storm.
He tells how first creation rose;
Of tempter, and of sinful man;
Salvation and the earnest call;
Of refuge for rebellious foes;
Of judgment and the final ban;
Of paradise for one and all.

VI.

The Mohawk listened, stern and cold,
As to a wonder often told;
For missionaries, long before,
Had told the story o'er and o'er,
As truth divine, without alloy,
In cabins of the Iroquois.
And Jossakeed, with dark suspicion,
The living type of many more,
Received the heavenly admonition,
As worthless legendary lore.
To him the stranger guest appeared,
A pioneer of deadly foe;
In every act and word he feared,
A messenger of coming woe.
And yet there opened to his view,
As more and more he daily scanned,

Resemblance of his Manitou,
    Descriptions of his spirit land.

VII.

The female heart will quicker move,
        Than that of sterner sex,
At tale of suffering, tale of love;
        And less of doubts perplex.
As Vareau told, in fervent strain,
The story of a Saviour slain;
    Of woes and tears of heavenly Dove;
    Of cross and never dying love;
Of cries and groans in dying hour;
Of tyrant Death's relenting power;—
    One plastic mind in blooming youth,
    Was deep impressed with solemn truth.
'Twas Wa-won-ais-sa, Whippoorwill,
    The heir of Kit-ta-coin-si brave;
Whose mother then was living still,
    Whose father slept in honored grave:
The two the female line prolong,
Of her that sung the cabin song.
    Young Whippoorwill had often sat,
    In deep reflection, on her mat,
And heard Le Vareau calm explain
The truth of God's eternal reign.
    Amid conflicting hopes and fears,
    Her very soul was moved to tears.
In paradise, in angel band,
She saw her own dear spirit land.

By faith she saw, and clear and calm,
For woes of life the healing balm —
The sovereign cure, that sets its seal,
Where nothing else on earth can heal.
And in the priest she saw the friend,
Enchained to her by magic power;
Whom she would faithfully defend,
In danger and the trying hour.
And yet, with prudence past her age,
Like Mary acting wiser part,
She kept her thoughts a hidden page,
And pondered deeply in her heart.

VIII.

The active leav'n, in kneaded flour,
To agitation moves the whole;
And truth, inspired by heavenly power,
Will vibrate thro' the human soul.
The acorn on the prairie thrown,
In forest pride shall upward soar;
And truth divine, when once 'tis sown,
Shall live and bloom for evermore.
The sluggish, gloomy, savage mind,
With wayward thoughts of Deity;
With shreds of truth, yet truly blind;
With dreams of sweet felicity; —
Is heaved upon tempestuous throe,
In dark vibration, to and fro,
By glimpses of an opening day; —

Vibration that shall onward float,
From age to age, as yet remote,—
Till race itself shall flee away.

IX.

And thus the evening hours were spent;
And thus the winter came and went;—
The winter with its crystal air,
And scanty snows that cumber there:
Good cheer beguiled the chilling blast;
And weeks and months in pleasure passed.
And sport was rife, on hunter's trail;
The huts with meat were well supplied,
From deer and turkey, partridge, quail,
And brave Sir Bruin in his pride.
No horses graced that paradise,
For servitude or proud review;
And hence, no "Running on the ice,"
Or racing "On the Avenue."
The active children sport and play,
Upon the river's frozen side;
No schools to take their time away,
No mistress there to watch and chide.
On Sabbath morn no chiming bell,
Inviting to the house of prayer;
And yet the chants in grandeur tell,
From altar in the open air.
By intercourse, from day to day,
Reserve, suspicion, wear away;

Of scenes of love we, too, might tell,
Between the guests and *mademoiselle.*
The French incline to social life;
The red men, spite the scalping knife,
To peace and honest friendship tend;
And thus the races quickly blend.

X.

While thus upon the surface reigned
A universal calm,
Beneath, a gloomy soul retained
The spirit of alarm.
The dark, perverse and rigid mind,
Of Jossakeed, was all suspicion;
He feared the worst; nor aught could find,
In stranger guest but admonition.
He saw approach, with rapid pace,
The darkest woes for all his race;
He firm resolved in coldest blood,
To nip the danger in the bud.
He first consulted Whippoorwill —
The widowed mother, living still;
She, seeing how his mind was bent,
In silence yielded her consent.
The secret labored in her mind;
She would prevent the fearful slaughter;
And, like a whisper on the wind,
She darkly hinted to her daughter.

XI.

The Mohawk, though a trusty guide,
Was blood of the Algonquin race;
And Jossakeed, in speech aside,
Could well a vengeful spirit trace.
The fortunes of a bloody war,
Had sunk him to the prisoner's ban,
To perish or his race abjure;
He rose at once an Iroquois:
It changed his name and changed the man;
For savage grace may thus enure.
Champlain the Mohawks late assailed;
Before him proudest chieftains quailed.
Some wildly fled with fiercest yell;
Some nobly fought and bravely fell.
A smothered vengeance, dark and dread,
Still raged in Me-shi-nau-wa's breast;
"Death to the French," he calmly said;
"I guide the viper, yet detest."

XII.

Six trusty braves were in the plot—
Six braves—of demon world begot;
Fiends, that in darkness love to walk,
To wield the knife and tomahawk.
"To perpetrate the bloody deed,
Choose darkest night," said Jossakeed;
"And of that night the darkest hour,
To end the strangers' hated power."

At length arrived the dreadful night—
The dark assassin's pure delight.
    The French were lost in slumbers deep;
    Or feigned, at least, profoundest sleep.
No voice is heard, or even breath;
Their tent is like the house of death.
    Abroad the chieftains quiet steal,
    Their fatal, vengeful blow to deal.
They creep along the darksome way,
Like tigers crouching for the prey:
    And soon the war-whoop yell will ring,
    The prelude to the deadly spring.

XIII.

But first they cautiously survey,
The waiting scene for bloody fray—
    A reconnoissance wisely made,
    To guard against an ambuscade.
Below the hanging canvass door,
An open space, an ell or more,
    Was left by chance, or by design;
Low stooped the leader—Jossakeed,
To see if aught could there impede—
    To see if all to sleep incline.
A chilling horror quickly stole,
Upon his grim and troubled soul;
    His eye was met by ghostly stare;
A smothered brand, a fitful blaze,
Reveals to his affrighted gaze,
    A dismal phantom standing there.

Its dim outline is scarcely seen,
And yet it has imposing mien,
Like spectre in a horrid dream;
Its moan is that of deepest woe;
Its eye is on the crouching foe,
With steady anger flashing gleam.
Condemned, like statue, there to lie,
The chief can neither speak nor fly,
Or rise or turn aside the view;
The jeebi seems, in terror's eye,
A spirit from an angry sky,
Or vengeance-dealing Manitou.
The stillness of the awful hour,
Is like unknown, supernal power,
That petrifies the wicked mind;
The heaving breath is like the sound,
Of stifled groan from under ground;
And expectations grimly bind.
To add to the unbounded fright,
And swell the terrors of the night,
The owl whoops out his yell agen;
Up spring, as from a thunder blast,
The dread conspirators aghast,
And scamper to their darksome den.

XIV.

As whispers to the forest trees
The ever restless autumn breeze,
Young Whippoorwill obscurely told
Le Vareau of the plot so bold;

And as the fatal hour drew near,
She trembled with unwonted fear:
She feared, for him, the reeking blade;
And for herself, if once betrayed.
Fore-warned, fore-armed: On the alert,
The French for dreaded worst prepare;
Their deepest skill they now exert,
To wisely do and bravely dare.
To save a life at any cost,
Would ever be a worthy boast;
To every peaceful means exhaust,
Le Vareau played the spectre ghost.
If this should fail to check the foe,
The fearful strife would quickly tell;
And blow upon redoubled blow,
Would sound a dreadful funeral knell.
The stratagem was all success;
The plot was quickly laid aside;
The phantom left its deep impress,
Upon the red man's vaunted pride.

XV.

The shadows of the night are darkly set,
As deeply colored by a murd'rous deed;
Its dreadful scene the chiefs can n'er forget,
And slumber flees the eyes of Jossakeed.

XVI.

If gentle woman cannot secret keep;
If from her indiscretions many weep;

If all her inmost thoughts at once are read,
And thro' a tell-tale world are quickly spread;—
How many grave mishaps does she prevent,
By sly suggestion, admonition lent!
How oft, when direst woes are near at hand,
She glides a guardian angel thro' the land.

TEUCHSA GRONDIE.

CANTO VI.

To the OLD SETTLERS,

And to the Summer Colony,

At Grosse Point:

Who have so many opportunities to observe the beauties and attractions, a description of which is herein attempted, this Sixth Canto is, with much regard and esteem, respectfully dedicated by

THE AUTHOR.

TEUCHSA GRONDIE.

CANTO VI.

OT-SI KE-TA.

A. D. 1611.

PREFATORY NOTE. Ot-si Ke-ta was an ancient Indian name for Lake St. Clair. For the story of Equa Monido and Isk-wan Dai-me-ka, see Schoolcraft's Hiawatha Legends, page 213. The lodge of Isk-wan is supposed to have been at the present site of the Grand Trunk Railway Depot, on the Canada side, at the out-let of Lake Huron.

I.

SEASON of birds! Thou lovely spring!
Make haste, abroad thy odors fling!
Let nature's grateful incense rise,
A tribute to benignant skies:
The swelling bud, the flower display,
In robes of green for summer day;—
To shade the hunter in his roam;
The prelude to the harvest home.

II.

The sun ascends the vernal skies;
Its tenants, now, the cabin spurn;
The soft—the balmy winds arise;
Aquatic birds to North return.
No mountain torrents here, from melted snow,
To dash and thunder to the plains below:
The even tides of mighty lake and river,
Like rolling years, roll steady and forever.
The sparkling waters, in their vast extent,
Reflect the glories of the firmament.
Unbounded plains in gorgeous verdure shine:
Oh, Mighty West! True majesty is thine.

III.

The rosy fingered morn awoke serene,
The birds their carols sung so merrily;
The rising day, arrayed in richest green,
Walked thro' the land a bright divinity.
Each kept the secret of that dreadful night,
Nor question made of what the other knew;
The French no dark suspicion would invite,
The crafty Mohawk would his craft renew.
Artful the speech, the mien, the studied air,
That each observed, tho' often frank and bold;
And oft the eye would meet unguarded stare,
That quick betrayed, and all the secret told.

IV.

Though raging storm may die away,
And leave, serene, the blazing day;
Though dashing torrents may subside,
And slow abate the surging tide;
Yet angry rolls the turbid stream,
So lately in commotion tossed;
Like soul awake from horrid dream.
Or mind in recent fury lost.
Although in stoic calmness all appears,
The fiercest passions of the human soul —
Hate, disappointment, ire and mingled fears,
Rage in the red man's breast without control.
If once the gloomy Jossakeed should learn,
That dreadful ghost was but the monkish sire,
And he a dupe, his vengeance fierce would burn,
To priest and men an all-consuming fire.
Le Vareau sees it all; and yet is blind
To all he sees and knows. His self-possession,
His kindly Christian heart, his prudent mind,
The danger meet and baffle all aggression.
'Tis sure destruction now and here to falter,
And every look and step is firm and bold;
The service, more imposing, at the altar,
Its ringing chants a solemn awe unfold.

V.

Enjoyment in its purity,
Must feel a calm security.

A mutual fear with cold distrust,
Will generate a deep disgust:
And weary is the daily life,
And full of inward grief and pain,
Where dark, suspicious dread is rife,
With empty pride and high disdain.
They poison every cheerful ray,
That beams on life's tempestuous way;
And formal signs of kindness made,
Are but deceptive masquerade.

VI.

The haunted mind, in every form,
Suggests a rising thunder storm.
Dark indications, every day,
In silence call — away, away!
The very curs the call enhance,
By surly growl and look askance.
The pappoose on the mother's arm,
Is instinct with a dread alarm.
The troubled clouds of summer night,
Are filled with terror and affright.
The hoot of owl at midnight hour,
As of a trusty sentinel,
Bespeaks the rise of dreaded power —
Of tomahawk and savage yell.
"Away," Le Vareau says, "away;
We perish if we longer stay;
Prepare the boats while yet we may;
Be calm, and yet — away, away!"

Says Jossakeed, "Do not prevent,
　　But urge, assist them to depart:"
"Away," the Mohawk cries, still bent
　　On vengeance rankling in his heart.

VII.

The lightsome tent at once is struck;
　　The boats are floating at the strand;
Aboard is placed the scanty truck;
　　The oars and helm are ready man'd.
Le Vareau chants the Te Deum,
　　At holy altar on the square;
He goes, for parting hour is come,
　　But leaves the altar standing there.
Le Vareau's love for heathen band
　Invokes a blessing from above,
　　Upon them all—the young and old,
　　　Like pastor on his little flock;
The chiefs accept extended hand,
　But hate return for kindly love;
　　Adieus are silent, grim and cold,
　　　And stern as from a mountain rock.
The boats move up the crystal tide;
With easy grace they calmly glide:
　　The gazing crowd, upon the shore,
　　Will see this hapless crew no more.
And now, upon the air so still,
　Is heard, in rising numbers sweet,
　　And richest notes, the wild refrain—
　　　The soul depressing, parting song;

Brave Duroc and the Whippoorwill,
Alternate from the strand and fleet,
The swelling symphony maintain;
The shores the melody prolong.

THE PARTING SONG.

DUROC.

Farewell, thou lovely, charming spot,
That nature formed with choicest art;
To leave thee thus, oh, hard the lot;
And yet, farewell, we must depart.

WHIPPOORWILL.

Stranger, adieu! you lately came,
Unheralded by friend or foe;
And yet did whispering birds proclaim,
The pioneers of coming woe.

DUROC.

We came not like the flitting bird,
That leaves no footprints on the air;
The song eternal ye have heard,
Undying faith is planted there.

WHIPPOORWILL.

Nay, nay; before you disappear—
Before the sun shall set to-day,
All vestige of your coming here,
In vengeance shall be swept away.

DUROC.

Yet plastic mind shall firm retain,
The emblem of the cross, unfurled;
And soon the standard, sent again,
Shall wave above the western world.

WHIPPOORWILL.

It may be so; the human will,
Enraged—determined to be blind,
Recurs to hated dogma still,
And hate enchains it on the mind.

DUROC.

Adieu, adieu; though ills beset,
To unknown lands we onward press;
The flying past we soon forget,
We brave the distant wilderness.

WHIPPOORWILL.

You rest upon a broken reed;
Take warning—from the danger flee;
The coming of the vulture heed,
Beware the storm and treachery.

VIII.

The sounds upon the waters died:
The fleet shot up the islet side.
The playful wave, from bending oar,
Was lost upon the sandy shore.
Then loud was heard upon the strand,
Of Jossakeed, the stern command:
"Throughout the town, in every place,
Their hated footprints deep erase;
Not e'en the holy altar spare,
That blazes on the public square."
The work, upon the spot begun,
Was finished ere the set of sun.
The ashes of the stranger's tent,
They scatter with determined will;

They madly snuff the very scent,
    That of the guests may linger still.
Yet, till his death, old Jossakeed,
    With all the bravery he could boast—
With stoic pride and stoic creed,
    Could n'er forget the dreadful ghost.
The cross, upon the maple tree,
    Which Vareau cut in living bark—
That emblem—in symplicity,
    Is covered—a detested mark.
But deep impressions, left behind,
Upon the thoughtful, savage mind,
    Among the race ere long shall tell;
From vilest worm that walks the sod,
The spirit of the living God,
    Assenting faith will soon compel.

IX.

The oar beneath the swell was bent;
The little fleet was onward sent.
    It followed in the gentle wake
    Of pioneer—a stately drake.
To soothe the rage of hostile clan,
The calumet was in the van;
    To lure a guardian angel nigh,
    The cross was lifted to the sky.
The Mah-nah-be-zee, swan, they pass,
        In blooming, bright, array;
They skirt the fields of waving grass;
        The river floats away.

They enter on that smiling lake,—
The Ot-si Ke-ta fair;
No chafing winds the surface break,
Of much admired St. Clair.
No swelling sails the vision grace,
For pleasure or for gain,—
To fright the game or finny race,
Or vex the placid main.
And yet in ages not remote,
A mighty commerce here shall float—
To outward world shall soon extend,
And with the ocean traffic blend.

X.

The scene is charming to behold;
Like sweet elysium, often told:
The pebble on the strand appears,
In polish of a thousand years.
The forest on the sloping side,
Is mirrored in the crystal tide;
And though beneath the shady green,
The peering native oft is seen,
And curling smokes the hut bespeak,
No yells upon the silence break.
Wild flocks in purest waters lave,
And circle far above the wave.
Beneath, the at-ti-ca-me-gue,
The sturgeon and the bass pursue
Their lazy life, with nimble pike;
A paradise for all alike.

And speed and grace the trout combines;
His gilded robe in glory shines:
He moves as if by will alone,
A monarch on his watery throne.

XI.

By counteracting forces held,
Fierce heat and cold are here repelled.
Intensest beams of summer day,
Are mellow as the autumn ray.
Unbroken plains of waters vast
Attemper winter's chilling blast,
And mitigate the tempest's rage;
Spring clothes the banks in richest green;
The golden autumn smiles serene —
Bright emblem of the golden age.
The waters, to the distant eye,
Are blended with the azure sky;
The two as one — an ocean seems;
Light, fleecy clouds, and here and there,
Are floating on the buoyant air,
The chariots of the land of dreams.
Seek ye a paradise below,
With cool and sweet refreshing air?
Go draw the breath the walks bestow,
At Ot-si Ke-ta, Lake St. Clair.
Seek ye a lovely rural home,
Where land and water well combine?
No farther need than here to roam;
Here, calm contentment shall be thine.

XII.

Away the little navy flies;
The coast is mingled with the skies.
The ripples from the dipping oar,
In murmurs lap the distant shore.
At length the meadow plains appear,
The winding channel intricate—
The "flats" that vex the engineer,
And mariners exasperate.
They wind along the crooked way,
The waving grasses ever nigh;
Wild duck their nautic skill display,
The blackbird charms the summer sky.
And up they wend that noble stream,
The same—St. Clair, its honored name;
Whose banks with richest verdure teem;
Whose forests teem with noble game.

XIII.

As river islands past them glide,
Up speaks the surly Mohawk guide:
"To legend lend attentive ear,
The scene of which is drawing near.
Upon the distant 'Sleeping Bear,'
A mother would her daughter spare;
Nor would the bridal hand bestow,
Of lovely Equa Monido.
She hides the maid by night and day,
Within an ark upon the Bay.

The water-spirits multiform,
In anger raise the driving storm.
The girl is swept, a lightsome freight,
Thro' Mackinaw—the narrow strait,
To Huron's outlet flood afar—
The lodge of Isk-wan Dai-me-ka.
Old Isk-wan guards the rapid shoot,
And dares who will the maid dispute:
He takes her as his lawful wife;
The spirits yield the dreadful strife.
The mother, in her wild despair,
With lamentations rends the air.
In turn the spirits lend their aid,
To swift return the hapless maid.
Another storm they soon prepare,
That sweeps the maid to 'Sleeping Bear;'
Nor will the raging storm abate,
Till Isk-wan feels their settled hate.
By fiercely driving wind and tide,
The lodge of sand, from side to side,
They shake and heave, in disarray,
Till shapeless mass is borne away.
The fragments, that the tempest fled,
In these fair islands raise their head:
Beneath them, in the watery deep,
The bones of Isk-wan quiet sleep.
The many islands found below,
To shores of rolling Erie far,
May also thank the Monido,
And vanquished Isk-wan Dai-me-ka."

XIV.

And now behold the Huron flood,
Where, thro' the narrow bracing gate,
The current swiftly rushes out;
The guardian Manitou's abode—
Old Dai-me-ka, as grim as fate;
The paradise of shooting trout.
On either hand the oak and pine,
And stately ash: The pendant vine,
Its grateful shadow lends.
From ocean lake the cooling breeze,
In whispers thro' the forest trees,
A cordial welcome sends.

XV.

The sun is sweeping down the western sky;
The hour of rest and sleep is drawing nigh:
The boats are hauled upon the sandy beach;
A grove of pines for shelter soon they reach:
A tent is set; the hook and line are cast;
And soon is spread the traveler's rich repast.
The prayers—the solemn vespers said again,
And night resumes his solitary reign.

TEUCHSA GRONDIE.

CANTO VII.

To the MARINERS

Of the Great Northern Lakes:

A class of generous men, who, in an important branch of industry and public service, not unfrequently brave the storms and encounter the waves of Lake Huron, a partial description of which is herein attempted, this Seventh Canto is respectfully dedicated by

A LANDSMAN.

TEUCHSA GRONDIE.

CANTO VII.

EQUABAW.

A. D. 1611.

Prefatory Note. Ca-ni-a-ta-re, was a general Indian name for Lake Huron. Qua-to-gie, also signified Huron, whether applied to a lake, river or nation. The "Great White Rock," in Lake Huron, was an object of much interest and even of superstition among the Indians of the Northwest. Equabaw, the end of deep waters, an ancient name for Saginaw Bay. This, and several of the following Cantos, afford an opportunity to present some prominent features of the Indian mythology.

I.

HAIL, ancient Ca-ni-a-ta-re!
Proud Huron, noble Qua-to-gie!
Thy flood, a sea — an ocean makes;
Majestic Queen of Northern Lakes!
Thy ample robes, in freedom cast,
Are playful sport for sweeping blast!
Thy darksome caverns, dread, sublime,
Are fed by wrecks and spoils of time.

As night devours the evening beams,
And thus divided reign maintains;
Thou drinkest in a thousand streams,
That murmur from a thousand plains.
Beneath thy bosom many sleep,
Where manitous their vigils keep;
There myriads yet their life shall pay,
Before the final judgment day.
Roll on, majestic Huron wave!
Let wind and water fret and rave:
Let billows lash resounding shore;
Roll on, proud Huron, evermore!

II.

And now the rays of morn awake;
The early meal the party take.
The tent is struck at rising sun,
And soon the journey is begun.
The boats, like swimmers, hardy seem;
They labor up the rapid stream.
The plying oars, on either side,
Are bent beneath the sweeping tide.
A dog the crafty Mohawk craves,
To soothe the sleepless river god;
He kills it, throws it in the waves;
Le Vareau gives assenting nod.
Great Michabou assistance lends,
And up the little navy sends.

They enter that extended sea,
Far rolling Ca-ni-a-ta-re.
The rising sun is clear and bright —
In gorgeous panoply of light.
The placid lake a mirror seems,
That flashes back the morning beams.
And yet ere long will storm awake;
The coast the lashing tempest feel;
The earth to her foundation shake;
Sublime the volleyed thunder peal.

III.

They pass along the western shore,
That rises boldly to the view;
Its bays and cliffs and streams explore,
And onward still their way pursue.
To right — a waste of waters mild;
To left — unbounded forest wild; —
As wild — its roving habitant,
With soul and will of adamant.
They sail beside the shady pines,
Beneath the oak's extended arm;
The summer in its glory shines,
And fragrant odor swells the charm.
The view that far and wide extends,
To Duroc inspiration lends:
His notes a measured cadence keep,
With bending oar beneath the deep.

SONG.

1.

Upon the lake the shallop flies,
Beside the forest green;
The Qua-to-gie a mirror lies,
That deep reflects the azure skies;
Enchanting is the scene.

2.

As farther still away we roam,
Upon the western plains,
We oft recur to early home,
Around the old cathedral dome,
Where happiness remains.

3.

But what, in distant wilderness,
May now for us delay?
Yea, what may be our deep distress—
What horrors may around us press,
In this the desert way?

4.

May He that reigns above the sky,
Eternal and alone,
Though distant, be forever nigh;
And, like the apple of His eye,
In mercy guard His own.

IV.

For ambush or for battle fray,
The red men skulk along the way;
And pipe of peace is kept in sight,
With flaming cross—celestial light.

To feed and rest the weary band,
The fleet is moored upon the strand.
The baited hook is quickly cast,
And soon is spread a rich repast.

V.

That temple of the Manitou —
The "Great White Rock," was full in view;
It boldly stood a beacon light;
It proudly shot above the wave,
The wind and raging storm to brave;
A trusty guide by day or night.
Beneath its ever hallowed shade,
Devout libations oft were paid,
To jeebis in their deep recess;
And from its lofty, dizzy view,
Brave chieftains prayed to Manitou,
The foe to curse, the friend to bless.
The water spirits, grim and dread,
Would march in fierce and horrid tread,
Upon the raging flood below;
And then would hurl from ocean shock,
The dashing spray above the rock,
To paint the smiling iris bow.
In presence of the little band,
The Mohawk mounts the lofty stand;
And, in apparent deep contrition,
He silent prays great Michabou,
Of Northern Lakes the Manitou,
To send them all to swift perdition.

VI.

While thus the surly chieftain prayed.
    A fairy form they dimly see;
She whispers from the sylvan shade:
    "Beware the storm and treachery."
The party onward press: The coast,
A rough — a rocky bed can boast.
    The hidden, far-projecting reef,
    Is shun'd by wary pilot chief,
Of wreck and ruin fraught. They reach
A desert shore — a sandy beach;
    A point they turn, and smiling lies
    An ample bay before their eyes.
Its ancient name was Equabaw —
        The end of waters deep;
Its modern, Bay of Saginaw,
        Where dangers rarely sleep.

VII.

Though oft in calm serenity,
It was a rolling — troubled sea.
    The gathered tempest on the lake,
    Would thro' the narrow passage break;
And then, in turn, the forest side,
Would refluent hurl the windy tide.
    Alternate gales, thus sweeping by,
    The billows toss against the sky.
The foaming surges, on the shore,
Prolong a heavy, distant roar;

Nor laden yawl or bark canoe,
In safety, then, can venture through.
The countless wrecks, in every form,
Far scattered on the strand,
Are trophies of the raging storm,
Like tempest now at hand.

VIII.

Great Michabou had heard the prayer,
The Mohawk whispered on the air:
He hushed the eager winds to peace;
He bid the troubled water cease.
Inviting was the placid tide,
But treacherous as the crafty guide;
And vultures, circling on the air,
Foretold disaster lurking there.
Le Vareau said: "The passage o'er,
Is narrow, from the shore to shore;
Speak, shall we fearlessly essay,
And speed us on the shortest way?"
"We shall," the Mohawk quick replied;
"We soon may run the glassy tide
In perfect safety." Dire advice!
Destruction to the crew the price.
He trusted to his lusty arm,
When angry wave should roll,
To save him from the raging storm,
And bring him to the goal.

IX.

The preparations ready made,
To try the shorter way,
A voice was heard in forest shade,
In melancholy lay.
It floated on the mellow air,
To Vareau and the rest,
As if an angel warbled there,
Or spirit of the blest.
The party lend a ready ear,
To catch the sweet refrain;
The stanzas echo soft and clear,
The chorus swells again.
"Ye rest upon a broken reed;
Take warning, from the danger flee;
The coming of the vulture heed;
Beware the storm and treachery."
When once again the voice is still,
They recognize the Whippoorwill.
The chief she knew; the storm foresaw,
Upon the restless Equabaw.
Her earnest warning to repeat,
She followed, long, the little fleet:
By wave of hand she bid adieu,
And back to Teuchsa Grondie flew.
The Mohawk hears, with silent rage,
The calm, prophetic voice;
The others at the oars engage,
And make the fatal choice.

X.

The boats are pushed from off the strand,
And swift retires the hazy land.
    The oars a steady cadence keep;
    A glassy swell is on the deep.
One-half the anxious passage o'er,
They dimly see the farther shore.
    Arises now the frowning god;
    He strides upon the troubled flood.
A vivid flame—his darting eye;
His thunder rolls along the sky.
    He bids the sleeping winds awake,
    And sweep along the narrow lake.
The clouds to darker fury grow;
And black as fate the floods below.
    Relentless as the god, and strong,
    Wave chases rushing wave along—
Surmounted by the snowy crest,
An instant foaming, then at rest.
    The Manitou applies the scourge;
    The boats are dashed upon the surge.
As massive oak and lofty ash,
Are rent by volleyed thunder crash,
    They shiver: Light, the ruins lie,
    All playful dancing to the sky.
The monk, the crew, the crafty guide,
        Amid the fearful strife,
Are hurled into the angry tide,
        To battle there for life.

The Manitou has marked their home,
By stern, unbending law;
He cuffs them with the dashing foam,
Of furious Equabaw.
In hapless, hopeless, wild despair,
They rise and gasp for vital air;
No hand is there to save:
In vain is now their stalworth might;
They sink, exhausted, out of sight,
In overwhelming wave.
And there, like foeman deadly foe,
Upon the battle plain,
They grapple in a mortal throe,
In fierce, convulsive strain.
And Michabou is near at hand,
His destined victims to demand,
With shrill, exultant yell:
They perish, one and all, in brief,
Save Duroc, Vareau and the chief:
Devoted band, farewell!

XI.

Brave Duroc, hopeful to the last,
Seized Vareau's cassock firm and fast;
Le Vareau, in his wild despair,
The Mohawk grappled by the hair.
No time was there for vain debate,
No time to stop and think;
The chief must save detested freight,
Or with it quickly sink.

Two "vessels" thus he took "in tow,"
Forlorn in friendless hour;
Nor should the "salvage trip" be slow,
With such a motive power.
Nor did the chief a question ask,
Or chaffer as to pay;
He quick addressed him to the task,
That plain before him lay.
His brawny limbs he firmly plied,
Like steady sweeping oar;
He dashed the rolling flood aside,
He "pulled" for farther shore.
And fierce the Manitou may rave,
In deep chagrin and grief;
He now must stay the wind and wave,
Or take his crafty chief.
Like shattered frigate of the main,
That anchors in the bay;
The Mohawk touches land again,
With those he would betray.
And now the Manitou may flee,
To roam upon the Qua-to-gie;
And there to watch for other prey,
Perhaps to come another day.

XII.

As set the sun in western sky,
And clouds in purple shone,
A feeble voice sent forth a cry,
In melancholy tone.

It first repeats the warning voice
Of anxious Whippoorwill,
Against the false — the fatal choice:
The echoes deeply thrill.
"You rest upon a broken reed;
Take warning, from the danger flee;
The coming of the vulture heed,
Beware the storm and treachery."
AND THEN:
"The red breast and the Whippoorwill,
May chant their sweetest roundelay;
But we will sing yet sweeter still,
Our carols of the closing day."
Brave Duroc, weary, faint and chill,
In distant wilderness,
Could warble forth his music still,
Tho' horrors might oppress.
In stranger land, however far,
Whatever dangers may beset,
Wherever in the world we roam;
However fierce malignant star;
We never, never can forget,
Familiar songs of early home.

XIII.

The sounds upon the waters die away;
The chilling dews of evening heavy fall;
Soft melts the twilight of departing day,
And gloomy darkness soon envelops all.

While baffled winds are sighing on the deep,
  And sulky waves are moaning on the shore;
The three, exhausted, sink to welcome sleep,
  To dream their many weary troubles o'er.

TEUCHSA GRONDIE.

CANTO VIII.

Thunder Bay.

To FRANCIS PARKMAN:

From whose historical writings I have drawn many facts, and much of the inspiration of the present work, and for whose exhaustive researches and attractive descriptions of Indian life and character, and of western scenery, the country, and especially the West, are much indebted, this Eighth Canto is respectfully dedicated by

A CO-WORKER

IN THE SAME FIELD.

TEUCHSA GRONDIE.

CANTO VIII.

THUNDER BAY.

A. D. 1611.

PREFATORY NOTE. Cannibalism was not unfrequent among the North American Indians. Wa-bas-so signified the rabbit, or the nimble-footed. Keneú was the great war eagle, representing, among the Algonquins, the Manitou of thunder; and Thunder Bay, on Lake Huron, is deemed an appropriate locality in which to distinguish the Algonquin ideas of thunder from those of the Iroquois, as presented in the Third Canto. It will be remembered that the Ottawa is one of the great rivers of Canada.

I.

WHEN darkest clouds beset our way,
And shafts of death around us play;
When life is on a moment cast,
And each fond breath may be the last;—
In fierce excitement of the hour,
We rise as by a hidden power;
We calmly hear the tempest roar;
We seem above ourselves to soar.

Reaction comes. The scene of danger fled,
We seem as if but risen from the dead.
The nervous system sinks from wild excess,
And all the horrors of the past oppress.
And yet the spirits rise upon the wing
Of purest thankfulness. We joyful sing.
Devotion from the grateful heart aspires —
Pure emanation from celestial fires.

II.

As morning light invades the skies,
From troubled lake the vapors rise;
    But as the sun displays his beams,
    They flee like unsubstantial dreams.
The waves that late the navy tore,
Now gently murmur to the shore:
    In mournful symphony they blend,
    With sigh and moan for perished friend.
Although the tempest fierce beset,
The Mohawk saved the calumet;
    But oh, irreparable loss!
    Le Vareau missed the holy cross.
And yet he soon the loss forgave;
    For by it, as from pious care,
An altar rises 'neath the wave,
    To purge the souls that wander there.

III.

Upon the bark of thrifty beach,
As high as lifted arm could reach,

The priest, devout, a cross engraved;
The *fleur de lis* beside it waved.
In lowly reverence then he bowed;
A gloom the forest shed;
In solemn tone he sung aloud,
The requiem for the dead.
"Sleep on, dear friends, beneath the flood;
All men to death are born;
Rest, troubled souls, in peace of God
Till resurrection morn.
And we, great God! we onward press,
As mercy Thou hast shown;
Thy witness, in the wilderness;—
In dangers yet unknown."
The chief, apart, in forest shade,
With dripping vapors wet,
In deep chagrin, devotion paid,
On vengeance firmly set.
"Thanks for myself, to Michabou,
For safety from the wave;
But why, oh, why! great Manitou!
Have two escaped the grave.
And why was I the instrument,
To drag them from the deep descent?
One wish, one only wish, I cherish —
That both, accursed, may quickly perish."

IV.

With neither bow, or food or boat,
With succors far and goal remote,

The future way is dark indeed;
And yet the trio onward speed.
But how shall hunger find supplies?
Can roots or leaves or bark suffice?
Or will the ravens, as of yore,
Supply with bread the desert shore?
Enough, beneath a gentle sky,
A guardian angel hovers nigh;
And, in the faith of gloomy chief,
The Manitou will bring relief.
In trying hour, a sure defense,
Is found in trusted Providence.
The storm that raged the night before,
A lusty sturgeon high had cast,
In rocky pool upon the shore,
Where still it lived, a rich repast.
The flint, selected from the strand,
Struck on the knife emits the spark;
Combustibles are near at hand,
In withered leaves and tinder bark.
With simple culinary care,
The coals perform their proper share.
The luscious meal is quickly spread;
The unforgotten grace is said.
The feast they eagerly divide,
And appetite is satisfied:
A part is saved for future day;
The trio speed them on the way.

V.

The path was desert, wild, forlorn;
Deep shaded by the fir and pine;
Beset with bush and cruel thorn;
Thick interlaced with limb and vine.
The Huron dashed resounding tide,
Against the rock-bound forest side;
Or rolled upon the sandy shore,
In one harmonious, constant roar.
Upon the waters, clear and bright,
The gull was never out of sight;
And high above the sylvan green,
The hawk and eagle oft were seen.
Throughout the land's unbounded space,
Were noble trophies for the chase;
Vexation sore and heavy cost,
To him that had his weapons lost.
The party wandered on, so dreary,
Till on the third revolving day,
They sat them down, forlorn and weary,
Upon the shore of Thunder Bay.

VI.

Since first the three were left alone,
A sombre brow the chief had shown;
For deep design, upon the life
Of other two, was always rife;
And therefore one a vigil kept,
Alternate, while the other slept.

But now, beneath a noon-day sky,
Untold the listless moments fly;
The forest lends a grateful shade,
And slumbers heavy eyes invade.
The chief is wakeful. Night and day
He watches to destroy his prey.
"Now is the time," he calmly said,
"To send the living to the dead:
Great Michabou, the others take,
Nor I will drag them from the lake."
He softly creeps upon the strand;
He grasps a stone in either hand;
Like crouching cat, with gleaming eye,
He glides to where the sleepers lie.
The trophy scalp, so highly prized,
Will here be proudly realized;
And, borne to cabin whence he came,
Will swell a wide extended fame;
The spirits of the victims far
Shall wander — to the evening star.
He grinds his teeth in very rage;
He now will read a bloody page.
The massive stones are lifted high;
Sweet, sweetest vengeance now is nigh.
An instant and unerring throw,
Will thunder down the crushing blow; —
The sleepers perish on the spot,
Their fate unknown, their names forgot.

VII.

He gave a fiendish — ghastly yell;
He sprung his length into the air;
He yelled again and lifeless fell,
And lay a bloody trophy there.
A lurking foe, unknown, unseen —
He too, with savage, vengeful art,
From deeply shaded, bushy screen,
Had sent an arrow to his heart.
In doubt if friend or foe beset,
Le Vareau rose in wild amaze:
He raised the peaceful calumet;
Another met his eager gaze.
And soon, emerging from the shade,
A lofty savage form he saw:
The sign of recognition made,
Revealed the friendly Ottawa.

VIII.

The Mohawk chief, on bold foray,
In desperate war of former day,
Amid the northern blast;
The brave Wa-bas-so's friend had slain,
And vengeance called for blood again —
Atonement for the past.
And, in his cabin home afar,
Upon the rapid Ottawa,
From bloody strife at rest;

Wa-bas-so, rabbit, lately knew,
Of expedition had in view,
Toward the distant West:
And that the Mohawk, in his pride,
Pretentious, as a trusty guide,
Would act the crafty role;
And on the unsuspecting French,
Would try, in fatal hour, to quench
The hatred of his soul.
As lion rouses from his lair,
Wa-bas-so quick resolved to dare,
The dangers of the way;
Le Vareau and his crew to spare,
Their never ending peril share,
And blood for blood repay.

IX.

With tomahawk and calumet,
And trusty bow and ready blade,
And plumage for his coronet,
He plunged into the forest shade.
He traced the well known Ottawa,
He passed the Nipissing;
He struck for distant Mackinaw,
Like eagle on the wing.
To pass the lake, now full in view,
He soon constructs a bark canoe;
He steals along the rugged coast,
Like jeebi, or the flitting ghost.

He turns the point of Thunder Bay,
With ever watchful care;
He distant sees, upon their way,
The weary trio there.
He crouches in a friendly shade,
To see what may impend;
He silent lies in ambuscade,
To strike, or aid a friend.

X.

The Mohawk, with a fevered brain,
Suspicious, darted gleaming eye
To every nook on either hand,
And startled at each rustling sound;
Nor could his stoic calm maintain,
As conscious of a foeman nigh,
Or prowling, skulking warrior band,
From rampire thicket soon to bound.
He feels, nor savage can disdain,
The gnawing worm of guilty Cain;
Nor can his fierce, unbounded hate,
The terrors of the hour abate.
No smiling Manitou is seen,
The traitor's damning guilt to screen;
Nor yet his murd'rous arm uphold:
The rest we have already told.

XI.

Though all unknown the stranger guest,
His presence and his mien attest,

That for the French there grew apace,
The friendship of Algonquin race.
Nor shall the growing, bitter hate
Of conquering Iroquois abate,
As whispering birds the news convey,
Of murdered chief at Thunder Bay.
Nor fine distinction will they draw,
Between the French and Ottawa;
For both, as swells their fiercest rage,
Shall feel their wrath in future age.

XII.

Kind salutations quickly said;
Of what should a repast be spread?
The Ottawa had brought his bow;
And baited hook could quickly throw
Into the calm — inviting Bay,
And darting pike or trout essay.
A pouch of corn he also bore,
And scraps of meat in scanty store —
A diet that might well content,
Ascetic days of rigid Lent.
The skipping fly shall quickly tell —
Ah, flounders up the pickerel!
And now it writhes upon the fire,
While quivering life is there;
The odors from the flames aspire,
A perfume on the air.

XIII.

"Come," said Le Vareau, "share the dainty dish,
That well might grace a royal tent;
Come, let us dine upon the noble fish,
By Providence so kindly sent."
"Not I," Wa-bas-so quick replied; "I make
My supper of a well selected steak,
Yet fresh and bleeding, palpitating, rare,
From hated Mohawk chief that welters there."
Le Vareau, Duroc, raise their eyes on high,
To throne of Virgin Mother in the sky:
Yet prayer nor calm entreaty aught avails;
The gleaming knife the fallen foe assails.
The fierce Wa-bas-so sates his appetite;
The others sicken at the horrid sight.
The mangled corse is cast upon the shore,
In sorry plight to what it was before;
When, ere its fall, the battle plain it strode,
Majestic in its form;
In spirit, air and strength a demi-god,
Relentless as the storm.

XIV.

Le Vareau graved upon a pine,
The *fleur de lis* and cross divine;
A sign to wanderer there by chance,
Of Papal Rome and Royal France.

XV.

The burning heat of summer sun,
Another daily course has run.
    The forest shades of parting day,
    Are cast upon the smiling Bay.
Upon the shore in open air,
For rest the trio now prepare.
    Beside the fragrant sylvan shade,
    Of leaves the scanty bed is made.
But rising clouds obscure the sky;
A storm the ruffled waves descry.
    The gleams of distant lightning play;
    Roll, threatening echoes, far away.

XVI.

Says Duroc: "O-ni-ag-raah's Manitou —
    That terror-hurling deity,
May come to take the fiery vengeance due,
    For murder of his votary."
Le Vareau says: "The God that reigns on high,
    His righteous law can here maintain;
His thunderbolts may any instant fly,
    In vengeance on this second Cain."
Wa-bas-so stood, as lightning round him played,
And crashing bolt — an awful cannonade,
And while each dreadful peal might be his last,
As if his frame were solid iron cast.
No sign of fear appeared upon his face,
And one, e'en there, a playful smile might trace.

"Nor Manitou of distant plunging flood,"
He cries, "Nor anger of Le Vareau's God,
This scene magnificent; — this blazing sky:"
Then raising to the clouds his gleaming eye:
"See! See! Upon the lofty mountain's crest,
Above the storm, imperial keneú's nest!
See! Robbers now! his nestlings there disturb!
Ah, naught on earth his furious rage can curb!
His lightnings flash athwart the firmament!
His foes, in fragments, on the gale are sent!"
Redoubled, now, awakes the storm again;
Pours down, in sluicy floods, the drenching rain.
Fierce from on high the fiery bolts are hurled,
And rolling thunder shakes the solid world.

XVII.

The storm abated, quiet calm
Is like the genial, healing balm
 To rankling wound, or troubled breast;
 Or frighted dreamer sunk to rest.
And welcome now the shades of night,
For weary toils to rest invite.
 The air is sweet and all is still,
 Save whistle of the whippoorwill.
The waters ripple notes of love;
The sky flings out its gems above.
 Around the leafy — dewy bed,
 The evening orisons are said.
But thoughts are wandering far away,
To Equabaw — the fatal Bay;

And farther still, beyond the main,
The mem'ry lingers on the Seine.
Ah, ere his wakeful eyes would close,
Brave Duroc's voice impromptu rose;
And sweetly sung the verses o'er,
In silv'ry strain on desert shore.

1.

"You lean upon a broken reed;
The warning take, the danger flee;
The coming of the vulture heed;
Beware the storm and treachery."

2.

"The redbreast and the whippoorwill
May chant their sweetest roundelay;
But we will sing yet sweeter still,
Our carols of the closing day."

TEUCHSA GRONDIE.

CANTO IX.

To the RESIDENTS

And the Summer Colony

Of Mackinaw:

Who will be able to judge of the correctness of the following descriptions far better than the author, and who may more fully appreciate the beauties of the Island of Mackinaw, which was celebrated among the Indians beyond even their own traditional recollections, not only as a locality possessing many attractions, but as being the headquarters of the great Manitou of the Lakes, and a central rallying point of innumerable spirits and hobgoblins of the Indian mythology, this Ninth Canto is respectfully dedicated by

THE AUTHOR.

TEUCHSA GRONDIE.

CANTO IX.

THE GREAT TURTLE.

A. D. 1611.

Prefatory Note. It is well known that, at a little distance, the Island of Mackinaw has the appearance of a great turtle; and, as its name signifies, it was so called by the Indians. Tei-o-dan-do-ra-gie, was also one of its ancient Indian names. The great Manitou of the Lakes was supposed to have his home there; and the Island was also supposed to be infested with jeebis, spirits, okies, demons and hobgoblins, that often made night hideous with their revels, dances and combats. A cave, which had served as a deposit for human bones, but of which tradition could give no account, was discovered on the Island at an early day. The clear and brilliant setting suns of the northern lakes are familiar to the tourist of that part of the continent.

I.

WHEN fierce beset with dire alarms,
And terror bravest hearts disarms;
If stranger spring upon the sight,
It fills us with renewed affright.
And yet, by some mysterious law,
The friend will recognition draw;

In every look, in air and mien,
The friend or foe is quickly seen.
And when true friendship thus appears,
Sincere and in its purity,
We quickly banish groundless fears,
And feel a firm security.

II.

Wa-bas-so and the Frenchmen slept,
Without a thought of danger near;
Nor was the weary vigil kept;
Till rose the morning sun to cheer;—
Effulgent from the watery field,
In grand diurnal march again;
Like glories of Achilles' shield,
Effulgent on the Trojan plain.
The morning beams above the Bay
Have chased the floating mists away;
And yet upon the forest green
The sparkling gems of dew are seen.
In silver veil the whole appears—
A simile we borrow,
Like maiden smiling in her tears,
With mingled joy and sorrow.

III.

The baited hook brings up the pike;
A fire the flint and tinder strike;
The scalping knife dissects the fish;
The coals must serve for cooking dish.

For table and the ready plate,
Fresh strips of bark are adequate;
    And soon, with neither salt or bread,
    The grateful lenten meal is spread.
If gnawing hunger fierce intrude,
The rudest means are amplitude;
    And, once the urgent call is met,
    The inconvenience we forget.

IV.

The bark and fibre lend their aid;
With nautic skill a boat is made:
    It dances on the darksome wave,
    Like buoyant hope above the grave.
The paddle bends. They shoot away,
Around the point of Thunder Bay.
    A desert waste before them lies;
    The distant waters touch the skies.
In shade of fir, and birch, and sycamore,
They pass along the steep, uneven shore.
The mossy rocks their firm foundations keep,
And brave the bluster of the angry deep.
Behold the hawk, the crow and stately crane;
The gull and duck disporting in the main:
Among the trees behind the bushy screen,
The strutting turkey and the deer are seen.
The owl at night will raise the hooting note;
    The cuckoo make the forest ring;
The howl of wolves upon the air will float,
    And wa-won-ais-sa gaily sing.

And now the skiff may speed with lifted sail,
    Now cut the tide with plying oar;
And yet beware the frequent rising gale,
    The waves that lash resounding shore.

V.

Above the distant forest screen,
A graceful curling smoke was seen:
    It mingled with the azure sky;
    It spoke the hut of stranger nigh.
And practiced eye might clearly see,
Like skulking cat from tree to tree,
    In plume and paint — a full display,
    The ever warlike Chippeway.
His home was in the dreary north;
From whence he oft would sally forth,
    And range the milder southern plain,
    The chase or war-path to maintain.
With piercing eye he quickly saw,
Displayed by friendly Ottawa,
    The token red men ne'er deny —
    The peaceful calumet on high.
"Pass on, in peace," he calmly said;
    "No danger now for brave and bold;
Pass on, the Mohawk chief is dead;
    Loquacious birds the whole have told:
The deeply hated Iroquois,
    That ventures to this western world,
On errand, or of peace or war,
    To certain doom shall quick be hurled.

I hate him for my kindred slain,
I hate him for Algonquin race,
I hate him for his vaunted power;
I hate him for his wide domain,
I hate him in his every place,
I hate him now and evermore."
With that a bleeding fawn he threw
Into the trembling bark canoe,
A feast, for hunger, to provide;
Le Vareau waved the thankful hand,
Then pushed the shallop from the strand,
Upon the sparkling, crystal tide.
Wa-bas-so, with a deafening yell,
Then swung his trophy scalp on high;
The Chippeway sent back the swell;
The forest echoed to the sky.

VI.

They quiet cut the glassy plain,
Amid the bracing northern air,
Unvexed by wave or gusty flaw;
They soon a distant view attain,
Of Tei-o-dan-do-ra-gie fair —
The far-famed Isle of Mackinaw.
Upon the Lake it seems to float,
A Turtle of enormous weight;
It stands a strong — eternal moat,
To guard the passes of the strait.
Its rugged cliffs are lifted high;
Its tree tops mingle with the sky:

We fresh inhale upon its coast,
The purest air the world can boast.
The gleaming pebbles, on the strand,
Seem emeralds of fairy land.
The waters that its base invade,
Have many wizard grottoes made.
Those waters, in the solar beam,
The clearest, purest crystal seem;
And 'neath the tide we clearly see
The trout preside in majesty.

VII.

The skiff is on the islet strand;
Its prow is buried in the sand.
The baited hook for eager trout
Is thrown; the captive flounders out.
Secure the boat and scanty freight,
With guarded step and air sedate,
To cliff the trio make their way:
They there behold the setting day.
The sky is clear, the air serene;
No clouds obscure or intervene.
From glances of the setting rays,
The mighty West is all ablaze.
The sun, a central ball of light,
Is sinking to the shades of night;
But as he sinks he upward flings,
The flashes of a thousand wings.
The pensive drake, to islet bay,
His little navy leads away.

The muskelonge leaps up on high,
To see these glories of the sky.
The nighthawk and the gull aspire,
And seem, to natural sight,
To circle through the liquid fire,
As if in pure delight.
The central ball below has fled,
And yet a sky of gorgeous red,
Is looming from the watery plain,
Like burning Moscow seen again.

VIII.

And now the flint is struck, the fire is made;
The trout and tender fawn, with ready blade,
Are quickly dressed; the joints and slices fry
Upon the burning coals; a rich supply.
A day of hardy life will early bring
The gnawing appetite; and rudely fling
To pampered city life, affected choice,
That rings thro' dining hall stentorian voice.
The evening grace, with sign of cross, is said;
And then the meal, with neither salt or bread,
Is shared among the three; delicious meat!
That peers and kings without a blush might eat.
The feast is ample, full enough and more,
And yet Wa-bas-so from his private store,
For rich dessert, in calmness can essay,
A slice from fallen chief at Thunder Bay.

IX.

The night was coming on apace,
And where should be the resting place?
    Upon the strand in open skiff,
    Or 'neath the oak upon the cliff?
Perhaps a shelter might be found
Beneath a rock, or under ground;
    Perhaps a manitou or bear,
    A friendly cave or den might share.
A hasty search at once they ply,
And in the twilight shade espy
    A darksome figure, grim and spare,
    That seems a demon moving there.
The form is bent like aged friar;
The eyes are piercing balls of fire.
    The floating hair is thin and gray;
    The wrinkled skin bespeaks decay.
Her only dress — a tattered rag;
A staff sustains the withered hag.
    Her voice is like the hollow wail,
    When ghosts the frighted night assail.
To arching cave, for nightly rest,
She beckons now the stranger guest;
    Nor longer there prolongs her stay,
    But like a shadow glides away.

X.

The lonely vault, in deepest gloom,
Suggests the pit of final doom.

The air is heavy, close and dread,
As in the chambers of the dead;
Or like the dismal catacomb,
Along the ways of ancient Rome.
And yet the three, with troubled breast,
At once compose themselves to rest.
The bed is hard and rough indeed;
And yet in times of pressing need,
Kind sleep will close the wakeful eye,
And consciousness will quickly fly.
The surfeit of the evening meal,
A fevered indigestion bred;
And troubled slumbers quick reveal
A goblin host around the head.
The demons of the nether world,
With shady banners high unfurled,
Arose to war, in hideous night,
With spirits of the upper light.
The two in mystic ranks arrayed,
Their helms and shining arms displayed;
And fierce the airy battle rose,
Of manitous with demon foes.
Opposing shields are in the sky;
Arms flash in horrid circles high.
The lance a thunderbolt is sped,
To call the living to the dead.
And ghastly wounds are gaping wide;
And blood, an overwhelming tide,
In torrents flows; and heavy moan
Is mingled with the dying groan;

While all around, the heaps of slain
Obscure the wide extended plain.
    At length the blows and struggle cease;
    The scene proclaims returning peace:
    The warior phantoms melt away,
    Nor leave a sign of battle fray.

XI.

The restless trio, in their sleep,
A constant, painful vigil keep,
        In terror and in dread;
They draw a heavy, stifled breath,
As in the grim embrace of death,
        In mansions of the dead.
And now appears a fairy scene,
Upon a lawn of brightest green,
        Beneath a charming grove;
The trees — a varied colonade,
With mingled hues of light and shade —
        Sweet bowers for gentle love.
And music steals upon the ear,
As from the distant waters clear,
        A soft — enchanting sound;
And breezes on the senses tell,
With Araba's delightful smell,
        Where sweetest flowers abound.
And now the graceful fairy train
Comes pouring on the shadowy plain,
        In dazzling bright array;

Their fleecy robes are airy light,
Begemed with stars of autumn night,
Like robes of milky-way.
They dance among the smiling trees,
They gently stir the evening breeze,
They quaff a pure delight;
With every grace beyond compare,
They seem to float upon the air,
As if in mystic rite.
And now, a rapid movement lent,
The forest mingles by consent;
The stars the call obey;
The sleepers draw a heavy sigh,
At once their pleasant visions fly;
The fairies hie away.

XII.

Nor yet the dreamy night is o'er;
Another scene is yet in store;
The monarch of this haunted shore,
Will now his right reclaim:
His birth was in this cabin shade;
The northern lakes by him were made;
No mortal can his might evade;
Great Turtle is his name.
He rises slowly to the view---
The dread — the mighty Michabou —
Of watery realm the Manitou,
In this his ancient cave:

Beneath his eye and frowning face,
Intrusive stranger, in his place,
May well despair of saving grace,
    If coward or if brave.
A grinning skeleton his guise;
Deep sunken are his glassy eyes;
He gloats in human sacrifice,
    In fiery furnace cast:
Gigantic is his horrid form;
Around him sprite and jeebi swarm;
His anger is the raging storm;
    His voice the howling blast.
His bolt can rive the knotty oak,
And split the hoary headed rock;
The islands feel his thunder shock—
    The terrors of his hate:
He strides around the darksome den;
His rattling joints resound agen;
He seems to tread on living men,
    With crushing, deadly weight.
And now the native form is seen:
The Manitou, in Turtle screen,
Now hides himself. The ocean green,
    Is now his robe of state:
Upon the rocky bed he glides;
Upon extended claws he rides;
Stern, fixed decree, his will abides,
    And dark, impending fate.
He stands erect upon the end;
His heavy limbs elastic bend;

To monster size his parts distend;
His armor and his head impend;
He meditates his fall:
The sleeping trio pant in vain;
In vain they sweat in drops of rain,
Or gasp a stifled groan of pain;
Fate holds as by eternal chain:
An instant crushes all.
Like judgment from an angry sky,
Impending death is poising high;
Nor can the tortured victims fly,
Nor utter an imploring cry,
Nor horrid bed forsake:
Down; down he comes! with rushing sound,
To grind the trio in the ground;
They start and spring with lofty bound;
Their loosened voices wild resound;
And quickly all awake.

XIII.

The morning sun is rising on the wave;
The twilight dim reveals the gloomy cave,
With damp, and chill, and heavy air;
Of rough and pointed stones, the sides and bed;
One vast projecting rock is over-head;
A score of men might harbor there.
The feast—the surfeit of the night before,
Of trout and fawn and ready private store,

Might bring the night-mare to this desert shore,
With demon sprite and horrid groans;
Yet clearer light at once displays to view,
On every hand, a grinning, ghostly crew,
That all the terrors of the night renew—
A CHARNEL HOUSE OF HUMAN BONES.

TEUCHSA GRONDIE.

CANTO X.

TO THE MEMORY OF

FATHER BONAVENTURE,

A PRIEST OF THE ORDER OF

ST. FRANCIS:

Who served as a missionary on the Detroit Station in the forepart of the eighteenth century; who gave the name of St. Anne to the French Parish at Detroit; and also to the old French church which long stood, a venerable relic of a former age, on the site of the present French church; and who, according to tradition, was not an unworthy successor of our Franciscan — Le Vareau — this Tenth Canto is dedicated by

One who can, in some degree,

Appreciate the piety, labors and

Sufferings of the early French

Missionaries in North America.

TEUCHSA GRONDIE.

CANTO X.

THE HURON MISSION.

A. D. 1626.

PREFATORY NOTE. Jean Brébeuf, Isaac Jogue, Antoine Daniel and Gabriel Lallemand are historical characters, who came to this country as Jesuit missionaries in the forepart of the seventeenth century, and all of whom perished as martyrs among the Indians. There are between thirty and forty rapids in the Ottawa river. The Manitoulin is a large island in Lake Huron. The Matchedash river was the same as the present river Severn, the outlet of Lake Simcoe; and the Matchedash Bay, which now bears the same name, was an arm of the present Georgian Bay in Upper Canada. In 1626 the Huron Mission on the Matchedash was a central point of French missionary effort in this country. In reference to the last line of this Canto, see the last line of the Iliad.

I.

AN equal balance is the end,
  To which the laws of nature tend.
    A flood in one direction set,
    Will soon a counter-flood beget.
The torrent from the mountain high,
Returns in vapor through the sky.

The rushing wind across the plain,
Is soon replaced by wind again.
Disturbing forces may assail,
With unrelenting hate;
But order will at last prevail,
The raging storm abate.
In human nature, here below,
The law will hold the same;
A thousand hostile currents flow,
And ebb to whence they came.
The social and religious states,
A kindred story tell;
The fierce excitement soon abates,
The calm succeeds the swell.

II.

A thousand years of one consent,
In gothic age, their sanction lent,
To mould the Christian faith in one,
From rising to the setting sun.
And yet nor time nor creed can bind,
The active, free, immortal mind.
From lofty hierarchic sway,
Masses by millions break away:
But, as the flood is rushing by,
A counter current we espy.
The order of the jesuit,
In rigid compact, firmly knit;
Implicit in the one belief;
Obedient to the ruler chief; —

Springs up to meet, to bold withstand,
The mighty shock in every land.

III.

A school of strictest self-denial;
Obedient unto every trial;
Invincible and calmly bold,
A social problem to unfold:
In vigils long; in rigid fast;
Beneath the scourge in penance cast:
With constant, never failing zeal,
That all the woes of man can feel:
With self-sustaining fervor blest,
That long devotions well attest;
With deep, enthusiastic glow,
That blazes in the polar snow:
With master policy refined,
To rule the world of human kind;
In closest league with royal state,
Wide conquests to accelerate:
With grasp of universal plan,
Embracing every race of man;—
Such was the order shrewdly sent,
To seize the western continent.

IV.

The meek Franciscan pioneer,
Who first the work begun,
Must from the labor disappear;
His haughty rival shun.

The Jesuit obeys the call;
High duties on him press;
He lands in lovely Montreal,
To brave the wilderness.
Jean Brébeuf, to heathen land,
Was leader of a worthy band:
His solid virtues calmly shone,
Or when in public or alone.
His robe—a heavy, bristling sack;
The lash, applied to naked back,
His penance told. While others slept,
His vigils long he nightly kept.
Ecstatic visions blest his eyes;
Yet foulest fiends would oft arise,
To terrify the sleepless hour,
With ever dread, infernal power.
Unclouded peace was in his soul,
Which, like the needle to the pole,
In darkest day of earthly race,
Would vibrate to the throne of grace;—
And if or weal or woe might come,
He sought the crown of martyrdom.
A worthy trio round him stand—
Père Daniel, Jogue and Lallemand.

V.

Amid adieus and parting tears,
And hopes with mingled doubts and fears;
Amid the sound of Te Deum,
And prayers of fervent Christendom;

With Huron escort for a guide,
They launch upon the broken tide
    Of rushing, tumbling Ottawa,
    And from a gazing world withdraw.

VI.

The forest gathers o'er the way,
        In rich, luxuriant bloom;
And oft obscures the blaze of day,
        In sylvan twilight gloom.
The shaded waters darkly flow,
        In eddying circles boil;
And every noxious taint they owe,
        To sun-forsaken soil.
Around the numerous waterfalls,
        Canoes and packs are borne;
At night a dismal shade appalls,
        The couch is cold, forlorn.
Three hundred leagues the way is rough;
        The food is poor and scant;
The escort, too, are sour and gruff,
        With hearts of adamant.
And yet the earnest jesuit,
        No suffering can depress;
Their every vow they calm acquit,
        In frightful wilderness.
The vespers and the solemn mass
        Are daily sung or said;
As if they all might quickly pass
        From living to the dead.

VII.

Arrived upon the Nipissing,
On high a song of praise they fling.
Arrived upon the Matchedash,
They chant beneath the oak and ash.
And while they note the Indian village,
And, round about, the Indian tillage;
Surprised they note, on bark and moss,
The *fleur de lis* and holy cross.
"Ah, who the messenger of grace,
Has seen this wild and desert place;
And here engraved, with pious hand,
These emblems of our native land!
Has mother Church a mission sent,
Some other fearful way?
Has France her royal banner lent,
A conquest to essay?"

VIII.

While thus Brébeuf, in anxious frame,
Inquires, in doubt, from whence they came;
And none can answer; none can tell,
The source of traces known so well;
Deep from the sylvan, twilight shades,
A tuneful voice the ears invades.
The soft vibration calmly tells,
Like tones of distant evening bells:
The vocal forest joins the strain,
And sends its echoes back again.

The song, the tune, familiar seem,
Like serenade in pleasant dream.
They hear the lovely "Evening Call"—
That mem'ry cherished, sweet refrain,
So often heard by one and all,
In dear Normandie on the Seine.
"The redbreast and the whippoorwill,
May chant their sweetest roundelay;
But we will sing yet sweeter still,
Our carols of the closing day."
As die the sounds upon the ear,
Behold a stranger drawing near!
And tho' his mien and savage dress,
Denote his home the wilderness;
His form, his color and his face,
Proclaim the proud Caucasian race.
The mystery is quickly told,
By worthy stranger, brave and bold.

IX.

Escaping from the Turtle's paw,
In charnel house at Mackinaw;
Emerging from the dreadful cave,
Like mortals rising from the grave;
Le Vareau, on a lofty rock—
Beneath the hanging moss—
That feels the waves' eternal shock,
Engraved the holy cross.
And by its side, its constant aid,
The gallic banner flamed;—

The tokens of a conquest made,
And heathen world reclaimed.
As morning sun displays his beams,
"Away," the trio said;
"From demon haunts and goblin dreams,
And mansions of the dead."

X.

With brave Wa-bas-so for a guide,
They shot across the Huron tide.
Gay songs the heavy hours beguile:
They reach the Manitoulin Isle;—
Another haunt of demon ghosts,
That swarm upon the northern coasts:—
A place to shun, with rapid flight,
Before approach the shades of night.
Wa-bas-so sees with clearest vision,
The spectres in the forest shade—
The jeebi train. "Fly, fly!" he cries,
"This dread abode—this goblin den:"
Le Vareau holds him in derision,
With all his ghostly masquerade;
And calm his crucifix applies:
Then swiftly darts the skiff agen.
With weary limb, but thankful joy,
They pass the Bay of Iroquois—
Of later times the Georgian Bay,
Where summers fly in haste away.
They land beside the Matchedash,
Beneath the shade of birch and ash.

The evening meal is quickly spread,
And soon prepared the scanty bed.
In heavy sleep the Frenchman lies;
The breezes sigh along the shore;
Wa-bas-so steals away and flies;
Le Vareau never sees him more.

XI.

Since then the rolling years had flown;
The stranger old and gray had grown:
And yet his features, voice and frame,
Tho' changed, bespoke him still the same.
And while his tale he calmly told,
A stalworth chieftian, brave and bold,
But grim and taciturn and gruff,
Among the party of Brébeuf;
Recalling, from his early day,
A stirring scene at Thunder Bay;
And goblin sprites of horrid dream,
That still upon his mem'ry gleam;
Which he and others, frighted, saw,
In dismal cave at Mackinaw; —
This chieftain — brave Wa-bas-so — springs
As if amid alarms;
In shout the name of Duroc rings;
He clasps him to his arms.

XII.

And Duroc yet pursues the story —
A tale of missionary glory:

For many long and weary years,
In toil and sorrow, hopes and fears;
The meek Le Vareau calmly stood,
A messenger of grace,
In social bands of brotherhood
Among the Huron race.
In diet, habit, smoky den,
He played the Indian role,
To change the faith of heathen men,
And save the human soul.
It was a living martyrdom,
Well worth a happy life to come—
Well worth a paradise;
To live in filth, and eat it too,
In rags, among a brutal crew,
And curs and fleas and lice.
With here and there a noble trait,
The Huron was a reprobate,
With instincts vile and low;
Nor sense of shame he ever knew;
We "give the devil all his due,"
Nor calumny bestow.
Suspicion, too, in fiercest blast,
Le Vareau's life had often cast,
Upon the fearful brink
Of fiery torture. Yet he stood,
Undaunted, in sublimest mood,
The bitter cup to drink.
"And I," says Duroc, "often read
The growling storm above my head;

But I, in song — in roundelay,
Could charm the evil hour away."

XIII.

Like sturdy ship that waves assail,
Whose energies ere long must fail;
The human frame will yield at last,
Beneath the burden on it cast.
The hardships of the wilderness
Have brought disease and deep distress,
And yet Le Vareau, calm and clear,
Encounters death devoid of fear.
The neophytes around him wait,
And every want anticipate.
He peaceful dies; as die the just;
His dust returns to kindred dust:
His spirit mounts on angels' wings,
To meet, on high, the King of kings.
In tears brave Duroc tunes the lyre,
To chant the praise of worthy sire.
A cross is set in forest shade,
With pious care, to sanctify,
And mark the spot the monk is laid,
In future age, to passer by.

XIV.

The solemn story told; the monk — Brébeuf —
In pensive mood exclaims, "Enough, enough!
The pioneer — the lost, whose name has rung
So long, is dead: His requiem now be sung."

And soon a graceful arch of evergreen,
Above the grave, adorns the sylvan scene.
The altar, soon, with crucifix, is there:
Majestic is the mass in open air!
The massive trunks of trees, in order nigh,
Are proud cathedral columns lifted high.
Inlaced above, the boldly branching arm —
Cathedral arches that beholders charm.
The blooming foliage of the forest dome —
The gorgeous vault of Lateran at Rome.
On high, ethereal frame — sublime effect! —
No art can rival, and no architect.
The swelling chants thro' hollow shades resound,
And men devout, and angels, list around.
The neophytes bewail with sobbing groan;
The French lament with heavy, tearful moan.
The requiem for the dead the priests rehearse,
And fame is echoed thro' the universe.
Such were the solemn rites the throng display'd;
And peaceful slept the pious Vareau's shade.

TEUCHSA GRONDIE.

CANTO XI.

To the Memory of

MY FATHER AND MOTHER;

Who Lived Respected,

And Died Lamented:

In a sequestered, rural home, which was also the home of my childhood and youth, among the wild, mountain scenery of the west of New England; upon the frequent and pleasant visits to which, in later years, where rapid changes, and some of a melancholy character, were visible on every hand, many of the following lines and descriptions were suggested, this Eleventh Canto is reverently inscribed by

THE AUTHOR.

TEUCHSA GRONDIE.

CANTO XI.

THE RETURN.

A. D. 1639.

Prefatory Note. Nah-ma Se-pee, Sturgeon River, the Thames. The dream of Tai-go-ne-ga is supposed to have taken place on the spot where the celebrated chief Tecumseh was slain. In reading this part of the Canto, the following dates and events should be remembered: In 1649 the Huron nation on the Matchedash was destroyed by the Iroquois, as related in the twenty-third Canto. In 1755 General Braddock was defeated and slain by the French and Indians near Fort Du Quesne. In 1759 the French and Indians were defeated by General Wolfe on the plains of Abraham. In 1763 the Pontiac war took place, in which Detroit, though assailed by all the power of the foe, was one of the few exposed places that escaped destruction. In 1790 General Harmer was defeated by the Indians near Fort Wayne; as was General St. Clair, on the Wabash, in 1791. In 1794 General Wayne defeated the Indians near Maumee Rapids; and General Harrison defeated them in 1811, at Tippecanoe. In 1813 Tecumseh was killed in the battle of the Thames, fought by General Harrison and General Proctor.

I.

WHEN early youth has passed away,
And from parental roof we stray;
And intervening years are cast
Into the swift receding past;

And days of sweet felicity
Are fading from the memory;
    And stormy life's tempestuous wave
    Is wafting onward to the grave;—
How pleasant, wheresoe'er we roam,
To see again our early home.
    The blooming vale, the brook, the hill,
    The forest—all are lovely still.
And yet, alas! however fair,
A melancholy lingers there;
    For change is written on the page
    Of every living—flying age.
The younger trees are larger grown;
The aged trunks are overthrown;
    The mansion house of former day
    Has felt the hand of swift decay;
Perhaps the spot we now recall,
By ancient well or cellar wall.
    Our little playmates, cherished then,
    Are grown beyond the shrewdest ken.
The youth to distant parts are fled;
The aged and infirm are dead;
    And in their place and proper station,
    A new—an unknown generation.
    Strange faces meet us everywhere;
    We scarcely feel our home was there.

II.

For years Le Vareau faithful toiled;
    And Duroc, too, his service lent;

Till every garment was despoiled,
Save what the chase in mercy sent.
The masses told the morning hour;
Religious teachings were bestowed;
The chants rung out in rustic bower;
Intense religious fervor glowed.
And thus were spent the weary years,
In toil, privation and distress—
With fondest hopes and darkest fears,
Amid a howling wilderness.
Yet all in vain: The news of grace,
The faithful pioneer had sown,
Upon the rigid, savage mind;
Was like the seed in stony place,
Which to a sickly plant had grown—
The sport of every flitting wind:
Or like the seed upon the rock,
In burning solar ray,
To be devoured by hungry flock,
Or quickly blown away.

III.

From daily practice, weary long,
A rich—a priceless benefit—
Brave Duroc spoke the Huron tongue,
And could instruct the Jesuit.
And he, loquacious, often told
Of navigation long and bold;
Of swift Niag'ra's wild array;
Of brave La Coste the castaway;

Of Teuchsa Grondie, Equabaw;
Of Thunder Bay and Mackinaw;
  Of manitous and goblin ghosts,
  That swarm upon the northern coasts;
Of Mohawk chief, and Jossakeed;
Of Ottawa in time of need;
  Of hunger and the polar chill;
  Of Wa-won-ais-sa, Whippoorwill.
These, with unnumbered incident,
To winter eve attraction lent;
  Nor Oriental Thousand Nights,
  Could tell such wonders and affrights.

IV.

But long had been the weary stay,
  Upon the rapid Matchedash:
And active duty called away,
  To far explore, however rash.
The village on that charming river,
  Of which loquacious Duroc told—
Fair Teuchsa Grondie, fair forever,
  The missionary would behold.
Four men the party should compose;
And first, among the rest arose,
  To worthy do and bravely dare,
  The pious, fearless Jenocaire:—
A firm—devoted Jesuit,
For any distant service fit;
  He burned, the living faith to spread,
  And raise to Christian life the dead.

The standard cross he now unfurled,
For conquest of the heathen world.
And Duroc next, with good intent,
His service to the party lent:
To see again that lovely strait,
What man of taste could hesitate?
With Duroc, too, there lingered still,
Bright visions of the Whippoorwill.
A third the proud Wa-bas-so makes:
To guide, to guard he undertakes;
Nor perils of the battle fray,
Or death or tortures will he heed,
To see, before he pass away,
The aged prophet Jossakeed.
The fourth, a worthy Huron chief,
Tai-go-ne-ga, the young and bold;
With leaning to the new belief,
Yet, doubtful, clinging to the old.
And this the brave, devoted band,
To deep explore a desert land;
To trace a dangerous path afar,
In wilds toward the evening star.
The chapel rings with solemn rite,
And heavy sigh and moan arise;
The priest and monk and neophyte,
Invoke the blessing of the skies.

V.

"Away, away;" the Huron said;
"Away," Wa-bas-so calm replied;

The chieftains to the forest led,
  With form erect and lofty pride.
Each one his scanty luggage bore—
  The scrap of meat, the pouch of corn,
The bow, the hook, the knife in store:
  The sash and plume the whole adorn.
The friends in long procession wend,
  To border of the forest shade;
On high a parting shout they send;
  And there the last adieus are paid.

VI.

With calumet and cross on high,
Defying foes that may be nigh,
  And every danger and distress,
  The party brave the wilderness.
Like dreamy shadows of the night,
The unknown way may well affright.
  Discouragements are often met;
  A thousand obstacles beset.
A fallen tree will here intrude,
And there a tangled vine exclude;
  Here boldly stands a frowning ledge,
  There brambles or a bristling hedge;
A frightful swamp must here be passed,
And there a mountain range is cast.
  A torrent here obstructs the way;
  A windfall there will long delay.
Here cheerful smiles the forest sheen;
There sombre frowns the evergreen.

Of heat, to-day, they loud complain;
To-morrow of the chilling rain.
Their food is fish and forest game,
Precarious the supply;
Their nightly rest is but the name,
Beneath a frosty sky.

VII.

They come upon the Qua-to-gie,—
The queenly Ca-ni-a-ta-re.
A storm is raging on the lake:
Upon the beach in fury break
The rushing waves. One constant roar
Is heard along the rugged shore.
The Huron chief, in distant view,
Can see an angry manitou;
But in the eye of Jenocaire,
The elements are warring there;
And on the waters, tossing high,
He sees the sovereign Deity.
The sweeping tempest to evade,
They plunge into the forest shade;
Beneath the dripping, chilling rain,
Pursue their weary path again.

VIII.

In passing thro' a narrow glade,
Beside a grove of tamarack,
That well might screen an ambuscade,
Of foeman on the foeman's track;

An arrow whistles from the leaves,
The brave Wa-bas-so is its aim;
The Huron's arm a scratch receives;
Enough his vengeance to inflame.
He sends the war-whoop to the skies,
His tomahawk is in the air;
Toward the skulking foe he flies;
Swift retribution hovers there.
Beneath his piercing, gleaming eye,
A Mohawk springs upon the view;
Fly, fly for life! your muscle try;
No laggard foe will now pursue.
The Mohawk flies like fleeing hind —
Like mortal terror on the wing;
The Huron darts as on the wind,
Fierce vengeance nerving every spring.
Nor one the safe retreat can make,
Although for very life the race;
Nor can the other overtake,
In this unrivaled, thrilling chase.
Among the trees they stream along;
Their yells re-echo far and wide;
They still the even race prolong;
What umpire shall the strife decide?
The Mohawk stumbles, plunges low;
Upon him springs his nimble foe.
Their eyes are gleaming balls of fire;
And hate and vengeance well conspire.
Like wildcats in the rocky glen,
They grapple at each other's throats;

Their yells and screams resound agen,
    The din of battle wildly floats.
His knife is in the Huron's hand;
    It gleams on high like winged dart;
Nor Mohawk can its force withstand;
    The Huron drives it to his heart.
Young Ka-go-gee, the Mohawk, dies;
    The scalp is quickly torn away;
And back the victor rapid flies,
    His trophy proudly to display.
Ah, fatal triumph! Vengeance dread,
    Ere long shall seek retaliation;
The Iroquois, with crushing tread,
    Shall fall upon the Huron nation.

IX.

This lively scene was near the place,
So fatal to Algonquin race
    In later age. A river there,
    That swells the tide of Lake St. Clair.
Its name, among expressive names,
        With scarce a parallel —
The Nah-ma Se-pee, River Thames,
        Where sturgeon love to dwell.
As sinks the sun beneath the west,
The party lay them down to rest,
        Beside that gentle river —
That speaks a bright historic page,
And carries on, from age to age,
        Tecumseh's name forever.

Presentiment! Its hidden laws?
Ah, what the silken cord that draws,
To future, dire event?
We often see, and feel, and know,
What no one yet has seen below—
Some great misfortune sent.
Without a guard or vigil kept,
The weary party soundly slept;
All but the Huron brave;
From him, excitement of the day,
Drove rest and quiet far away,
And burning fever gave.
His wakeful mind, in rapid pace,
Ran o'er the fortunes of his race,
Through many ages past;
And future, too: His restless brain
Would roll upon the battle plain,
Till final die was cast.

DREAM OF TAI-GO-NE-GA.

1.

At length the Huron fitful sleeps;
A dismal vision o'er him creeps;
Unconsciously he sighs and weeps,
And breathes a stifled moan:
The terror-dealing Iroquois,
Fierce wage exterminating war
Upon his cabin home afar,
Where helpless victims groan.

2.

A smile lights up his troubled face,
As Braddock falls in deep disgrace,
And glory crowns Algonquin race,
Before the fort Du Quesne:
And then reverses darkly tell;
Before that lofty citadel,
The hostile shouts of triumph swell,
On Abrahamic plain.

3.

Again, in fiery, dismal track,
Beneath the eye of Pontiac,
There gleams a universal sack,
Save Teuchsa Grondie fair:
Light lingers yet. The forest braves,
In war dance 'round their fathers' graves,
Hurl back detested name of slaves,
To Harmer and St. Clair.

4.

The vision deepens — dark and dread;
Malignant stars are fiery red,
As gallant men are bravely led
By Harrison and Wayne:
And yet the war-whoop's thrilling blast,
Re-echoes from the mighty past,
And loud demands a final cast,
Upon the western plain.

5.

A worthy chieftain now appears;
His brother — prophet, onward cheers;
Each clan the summons gladly hears;
To right the wrongs of flying years,
The western forest quakes:

"To arms!" the leader fiercely calls;
Loud ring the vaulted council halls;
The war-whoop's frightful din appalls;
A yell, and brave Tecumseh falls:
Tai-go-ne-ga awakes.

X.

"Ah, is it thus! And must we perish?"
He cries, with bitter sigh and moan,
"From this dear land we fondly cherish?"
The forest echoes back his groan.

XI.

As morning springs upon the East,
The party on a sturgeon feast;
And then with ever cheerful air,
They skirt the placid Lake St. Clair.
The breeze bestirs the grassy plain,
Like graceful waves of ripened grain.
The ripples lap the sandy shore,
And soft prolong a gentle roar.
The water fowl, with welcome cry,
In circles cut the azure sky.
The robin, on the blooming tree,
Pours forth the richest melody.
Their steps the four accelerate:
They soon behold that lovely strait,
Whose isles, and banks, and gentle flow,
Will charm or if we come or go.

Fair Mah-nah-be-zee, on the tide,
Like floating swan, they stand beside.
The overhanging forest green,
Presents a charming river scene;
While sloping down the farther strand,
Beneath the summer day,
Is Teuchsa Grondie — fairy land,
In smiling, bright array.

XII.

"Here rest we for the coming night,"
Says pious Jenocaire —
"Till peaceful token us invite,
The village life to share:
And here upon a thrifty beach,
That all the world may see,
I grave the cross, the faith to teach,
Beside the *fleur de lis*."

XIII.

The sun is sweeping down the sky,
His gorgeous robes behind him cast;
Like mem'ry, when the end is nigh,
That lingers on the fading past.
To view, the pipe of peace is thrown,
As loudly sounds the rustic horn;
To Jossakeed the sign is known;
And one and all await the morn.

TEUCHSA GRONDIE.

CANTO XII.

The Pestilence.

I dedicate this Twelfth Canto

To the Memory of

My late Friend and Relative,

DR. PLINY POWER:

Whose true and practical benevolence, professionally and otherwise, was uniformly exerted toward the poor, the needy and the suffering, wherever he found them, and whose good qualities of mind and heart will long be held in grateful recollection by his many surviving friends.

TEUCHSA GRONDIE.

CANTO XII.

THE PESTILENCE.

A. D. 1639.

PREFATORY NOTE. Mus-ko-da-sa signified the grouse. The pestilence was not uncommon among the Indian settlements of America. It was the result, mainly, of irregular diet and habits, and of privation and suffering, and was sometimes very destructive. When the pestilence raged it filled the savage mind, naturally superstitious, with the deepest terror and gloom.

I.

THE missionaries that were early sent,
To deep explore the western continent—
To place that boundless, rich inheritance
A jewel in the diadem of France;—
To make it bloom, in every forest home,
A prouder conquest to the faith of Rome;—
Were moulded men; well broken on the wheel
Of sternest discipline;—were hardened steel,
That fire and hammer, and the chilling flood,
In process long and all severe,

Had formed in one obedient brotherhood,
    The race of man to domineer.
By other process, with results the same,
The Indian race was one, in mental frame,
And body too. One dark, mysterious shade
Was ever set; nor variation made.
In war, in peace, in all-exciting chase,
Each one is found the type of all the race:
And when we see the child or chief or queen,
A lively portraiture of all is seen.
Expect not, then, in this our legend song,
    Distinctive characters arrayed;
One homogeneous, one commingled throng,
    Will move in undistinguished shade.

II.

The rising morn is on the wing;
The feathered tribe a welcome sing.
    The silver light of summer ray
    Is poured along the watery way:
And on the crystal mirror lies
The smiling azure of the skies.
    Nor slumbers Teuchsa Grondie fair;
    The chiefs are up—about the square:
The hook is cast with wonted zeal,
And flounders up the morning meal.
    The young and old are deep impressed,
    To well receive the stranger guest.
Two bark canoes are quickly man'd;
They lightly dance upon the strand.

The one proud Mus-ko-da-sa guides;
The other's name oblivion hides.
The bending oar the skiffs obey;
They rapid cut the glassy way.

III.

The stranger guests aboard the boats,
Again the little navy floats.
It trembles; but a steady sweep,
Will bear it safely o'er the deep.
The prows maintain an upward course,
To meet the current's downward force.
The bubbles, like the gathered tear,
A moment gleam, then disappear.
The curling eddies quiet roll,
Like perturbations of the soul:
The ripples from the dashing oar,
Are felt upon the distant shore.
To Duroc brave the charming view,
That once again before him lies,
Recalls the fading past anew,
And tears are trembling in his eyes.
And forth at once in fervid strain,
A song, impromptu, sweet he pours;
The village hears his voice again,
And glad respond the vocal shores.

SONG.

1.

We come not on the wild foray,
  Nor in the war-path roam;
We come as friends from far away,
  As to an ancient home.

2.

As these fair shores in glory shine,
  As constant flows this river;
So may our friendship n'er decline,
  So live and bloom forever.

3.

That lovely strand is drawing near,
  The village green we see;
And, standing yet, without compeer,
  That blooming maple tree.

4.

And in the crowd, if well we heed,
  Upon the sloping hill,
A form like aged Jossakeed,
  Beside the Whippoorwill.

IV.

The shallops touched the sandy shore;
Unladen was the little store;
  While chiefs were seen, and maidens fair,
  And urchins peeping on the square.
A hearty welcome was prepared;
A hearty feast was quickly shared;

For when was Teuchsa Grondie slow
To well receive a friend or foe?
'Twas eight and twenty flying years,
Since Duroc bid adieu, with tears,
And yet with swelling, parting lay,
To this dear village by the way.
Old Jossakeed was living still;
And three by name of Whippoorwill,
That still totemic line prolong,
Of her that sung the cabin song.
The fifth is in her maiden years:
Her mother on the scene appears,
With grandam that the warning threw
To worthy Vareau and his crew;—
The same that rising storm foresaw,
And sung beside the Equabaw.
And Duroc's voice she hears again;
Her soul responds in kindred strain:
And as they pass the maple tree,
She points him to the broken ross;
Where all as yet can plainly see
Le Vareau's sign of holy cross.

V.

Of all that fierce and bloody band,
Who swift destruction darkly plan'd,
Upon that dreadful night,
But two remained to tell the deed;
Two — Mus-ko-da-sa, Jossakeed,
The ghost had put to flight.

That night of terror and distress,
Had left its lasting — deep impress
Upon the savage mind;
Though fading years might rapid fly,
It lingered still — that gleaming eye,
The sprite had left behind.
And many yet remembered well
Le Vareau's cheerful morning bell,
And chants in open air;
But light impressions died away,
Like distant notes of roundelay,
And left no traces there.
Upon the village, time had crept;
And many with their fathers slept,
While others onward came;
And yet, as in a general plan,
The iron type of savage man
Was ev'rywhere the same.

VI.

While calmly, firmly, Jenocaire,
His altar raised upon the square,
The young were curious to behold
His flaming cross of burnished gold.
The mass, in solemn, lofty strain,
And swelling chant, were heard again;
While round about, in open space,
In wonder gazed the heathen race.
The aged, who before had seen
The like display upon the green,

In grim despair and smothered hate,
Could see, in all, approaching fate.
And yet the daily intercourse
Was dignified, as if per force;
And cautious, and respectful too,
Like foes that friendship would renew.
The mild, the prudent Jenocaire,
Would sow the seeds of conquest there;—
Would plant, as by a firm decree,
The sovereign cross and *fleur de lis.*

VII.

Familiar with the new belief,
Wa-bas-so and the Huron chief,
In careless mood, from day to day,
The listless moments passed away.
And yet their friendship to attest,
As branches of a kindred nation,
They met the sachems of the West
In deep and secret consultation.
"The French are friends," Wa-bas-so said;
"They come to help and not destroy;
United, naught on earth we dread,
Not onsets of the Iroquois."
"I fear the worst," says Jossakeed;
"When hated Iroquois shall fall,
We, victors, then in turn shall bleed,
And French dominion cover all."

VIII.

And worthy Duroc mingles free
Wher-e'er amusement lightly tends—
What-e'er the place or circumstance,
The same loquacious songster still;
His heart is pure simplicity;
He always finds a host of friends;
He often joins in rustic dance,
And gaily flirts with Whippoorwill.

IX.

But what can nature's charms bestow,
With all her boundless wealth,
If wanting choicest boon below—
The boon of simple health?
And what is life, with all its train,
If stung by secret, inward pain,
That prudence must suppress?
And what is all our earthly store,
If still there rankles at the core
A gnawing bitterness?
And what the empty pomp of pride,
That would a social canker hide,
With tinsel and with show;—
That shines and flaunts in borrowed plumes,
And what it has not, well assumes?—
A state of slavish woe.

X.

Dark signs are in the troubled firmament;
Portentous clouds bespeak a dire event.
Instead of crystal dew, translucent rain,
Upon the land and on the frighted main
Big drops of blood are seen, of purple hue—
Dread tokens from an angry Manitou.
Without apparent cause, the forest game
In languor walks, as if or sick or lame;
And shuns the haunts, which often did invite,
As loathing food, and even air and light.
And sometimes, too, upon the hunters' trails,
The strength of buck and lusty bruin fails:
And when the hunter, proud, his trophy wins,
Offensive putrefaction quick begins.
The rivers, too, and e'en the mighty lake,
Of pestilential odors all partake.
The fish in shoals, or dead or dying, float,
As if by sweeping plague already smote,
Nor food supply. And in the fields are seen,
The sickly corn, the withered squash and bean.
And meat, well dried and in the cabin hung,
By worms beset, to dying dogs, is flung.
No food, but roots and bark, for hungry man;
And these have felt the universal ban.
The air is drawn in heavy, stifled breath,
As if impregnate with the seeds of death.
The tainted breeze no cheerful odor brings,
But wider still the poisoned vapor flings.

The lurid sun shoots forth a languid ray,
Nor miasmatic fogs can draw away.
The blinking stars emit a feeble light;
The pallid moon affrights the shades of night.
The evening sky displays a livid hue,
To Land of Dreams a gloomy avenue.
On every hand — around, above, below,
All nature loud proclaims the coming woe.

XI.

At Teuchsa Grondie all is wild dismay;
The child, the youth, the old are swept away,
The brave, the matron and the chief;
The angry spirits roaming thro' the sky,
Unseen, the stoutest hearts can terrify,
And fill a stricken land with grief.
In every cabin home a fearful wail
Is heard, and sigh and moan the ear assail;
And sorrow reigns and black despair;
While calm, devoutly, in the trying hour,
The Jesuit invokes the heavenly Power,
Before the altar on the square.
And Duroc, too, and pious Jenocaire,
Relieve the sick and every danger share,
Devout, and bold in proper station;
And as the priest applies the cooling bowl,
He n'er forgets the safety of the soul;
He whispers words of consolation.

The Huron, too, his service kindly lends;
And care bestows, and vigils oft attends,
Inclining to the new belief;
But stern Wa-bas-so holds the stoic creed;
And sterner yet, and grim is Jossakeed,
Insensible to pain and grief.
The artful sorcerers — the "med'cine men,"
In league with goblin ghost, are busy then;
With mystic air and high pretense; —
With song, and beating drum, and hiss and yell,
With dance, contortion, and with magic spell,
To conjure down the pestilence.
Around the sick, the dying, and the dead,
A whirling, howling, shrieking train is led,
In unique, pantomimic show;
And terrible the fierce, satanic grin,
And stunning, too, the pandemonium din,
Of "painted devils" from below.

XII.

Nor this was all. To clearest reason blind,
A cloudy terror seized the savage mind.
Upon his present and his future doom,
Black superstition cast a dreadful gloom.
His fiery nature, on an impulse cast,
Might any moment hurl a thunder blast;
And priest and altar, and the solemn rite,
Might sink at once, detested, from his sight.
Instead of unrelenting Manitou,
In darkness clad, swift vengeance to pursue;

And sweep a race, in one consuming hate,
To land of shades or to a darker fate;
Was not the ever dreaded stranger guest,
The moving cause of man-destroying pest?
Wa-bas-so grim, and sombre Jossakeed,
Pervert his every look and word and deed.
His cassock dark, a crafty imp conceals;
His magic art, the evil sprite reveals.
Baptismal font, an equal terror lends;
And burning taper, future woe portends.
The genuflexions, signs upon the breast,
Are incantations of the hated priest.
In emblematic pictures, mystic charm;
In eucharistic host, a dread alarm.
The flaming cross is but the flashing eye
Of angry spirits roaming thro' the sky.
The solemn air of monk and neophyte,
To swift destruction gloomily invite.
The vesper chant, rings out a fearful doom;
The striking bell—a summons to the tomb.
In short, the presence of the stranger there,
Was rife with danger, terror and despair.

XIII.

Deep was the plot and dread the dark design,
That sprung, a gorgon, from a soul malign,
 And might angelic form invade;
The raging tempest of a troubled breast,
Might fall like lightning on the mountain crest,
 Or crushing shot of cannonade.

In forest gloom, in midnight's darkest hour,
A council met—a terror-stricken power,
As on the brink of dread unknown;
And there, in circle on the humid ground,
From man to man the whisper passed around,
With tear and sigh and smothered moan.
"Strike, boldly strike!" proud Mus-ko-da-sa said,
"Let both the French be numb'rd with the dead,
As mortal foes in deep disguise:"
"Strike!" said Wa-bas-so; "quickly let them bleed:"
"Strike, while we live and can!" said Jossakeed,
"To evil sprites a sacrifice."

XIV.

And thus the days of sorrow wear away,
In perils dark and dread, by night and day;
A fierce ungoverned race in wild dismay,
And wing-ed death upon the air:
On every hand is thickest, blackest gloom;
On every breeze is borne a coming doom,
That terror spreads, as from the gaping tomb,
To Duroc brave and Jenocaire.

TEUCHSA GRONDIE.

CANTO XIII.

The Land of Dreams.

TO THOSE,

THEY MUST BE FEW IN NUMBER,

Who cherish the belief that there is no future state for human intelligences, and especially no future state of rewards and punishments, the ideas and traditions of the Aborigines of America on the subject, which I have aimed herein faithfully to portray, and which could have sprung from no direct revelation, and from no missionary teachings, are most respectfully commended by

THE AUTHOR.

TEUCHSA GRONDIE.

CANTO XIII.

THE LAND OF DREAMS.

A. D. 1639.

PREFATORY NOTE. Pauguk signified a skeleton or a phantom of the imagination, called death; to see which indicated that death was near at hand. Po-ne-mah signified the future life or place of departed spirits in the distant Southwest. The Indians often declared to the missionaries that they wished to go, after death, to the place where their forefathers had gone, whether it were heaven, or hell, or po-ne-mah. The spirits of the departed were supposed to hover about the place where their bodies were buried till the great festival of the dead took place, as is described in the Fifteenth Canto.

I.

THE conscious—the undying soul,
Looks out beyond the present goal.
The lowest grade of human kind,
However dull, or weak, or blind,
Looks onward past the mortal hour;
Looks upward to a higher power.
The mortal, to immortal prone,
In search of sovereign Deity,

Explores the mighty, dread unknown,
And ranges through eternity.
Nor is the search an idle round;
Unnumbered deities confound;
From rudest pantheistic view,
To spirit of the Manitou;
From feticism's darksome way,
To glories of the god of day;
From idols wrought of wood and stone,
And mythologic heaven,
To God Eternal — One alone,
By revelation given.

II.

As pass the frightful hours away,
And terror reigns and sore dismay;
And any moment may declare
The horrid death of Jenocaire;
The pest inexorable calls,
And Jossakeed a victim falls.
His whitened hair disordered flies;
Dark gleam his sunken, haggard eyes;
And loosely hangs his withered skin,
Fit cover for his ghastly grin.
He prostrate lies upon his cot,
His schemes of vengeance all forgot;
For arm-ed phantom on the wing,
With arrow at the ready string —
The spectre Pauguk — grim as fate,

Is gazing from the troubled sky,
Proclaiming that the end is nigh;
Forbidding treachery and hate.

III.

A pensive, apprehensive band
Around the prophet mournful stand,
Beside his cabin near the green;
And all in anxious mood relate
Their thoughts upon the future state;
Socratic is the solemn scene.

JOSSAKEED.

My time is come. The Pauguk calls;
I feel his chill around the heart;
Like aged oak that withered falls,
I, too, must fall; I must depart.
And yet, in future blooming years,
I long shall live in distant West;
Where neither sorrow, pain nor tears
Are ever known among the blest.

JENOCAIRE.

Nay, set your thoughts on things above—
On dying Lamb, forgiving love;
Upon the cross uplifted high,
That points to home beyond the sky.
Your cherished future Land of Dreams,
Beyond the eve's resplendent beams,
Will vanish, as you silent tread
The gloomy regions of the dead.

From dust your body had its birth,
And soon it moulders back to earth;
    Your spirit mounts to upper air,
    Or sinks to darkness and despair.

TAI-GO-NE-GA.

Ah, why distract the parting hour?
    Of thorns the bed of death bestrew?
Leave him the choice of higher power —
    Of spirit, Christ or Manitou.

WA-BAS-SO.

Oh, vex him not with gods unknown,
    His faith the flying years have told;
He holds, he firmly holds his own;
    He faces Pauguk, ready, bold.

JOSSAKEED.

Yea, naught can shake my firm belief;
Nor pain acute, nor sorest grief.
    I wander fearless, though alone,
    To lands the fathers all have gone.
They lie in winding path, away,
Beyond the beams of setting day;
    They smile in regions distant far,
    Beneath, beyond the evening star.
Upon that wide extended plain,
Sweet love and peace forever reign.
    The fruitful seasons come and go,
    Unvexed by frost or driving snow.

Beside the bud and blossom fair,
The ripened fruit is ever there.
    The forests lend their cooling shade;
    There waves the grassy everglade,
Alternate with the broad savanna;
        No demons there appall;
There reigns alone the great So-wan-na,
        Great Spirit over all.

WHIPPOORWILL, *the younger.*

There buds and flowers of blooming spring
        In brightest robes abound,
And sweetest odors constant bring,
        In never ceasing round.
There birds of richest plumage shine,
        Of fairy form and fair;
And softest melodies combine,
        To charm the vocal air.

DUROC.

And yet nor song of bird or man,
    Can rival song of heavenly love,
That celebrates redemption's plan,
    Among angelic hosts above.
All glory be to God on high!
    Who fall-en, sinful man forgiveth;
There every pain and woe shall fly;
    I know that my Redeemer liveth!

MUS-KO-DA-SA.

Believe it not, proud Jossakeed;
Nor tale of crucifixion heed;

Go, join the long, the happy band,
Ancestral, in the spirit land.
There corn, tobacco, squash and bean,
Luxuriant to the view,
In one unbroken round are seen —
The gifts of Manitou.
There various fruits that charm the eye,
And melt upon the taste,
Successive bud, and bloom, and die —
A never-ending waste.
The spirit blest may there partake
Of choicest food his fill;
Nor him shall appetite forsake,
He feeds and hungers still.

TAI-GO-NE-GA.

What matter if we wander there,
Or to that home in upper air?
To me, the one — the other seems,
Alike a happy land of dreams.
To this, the monk—to that, the chief,
Would urge as in a firm belief:
Why may not faith adopt the two?
Believe them both, and both pursue?

WHIPPOORWILL, *the elder.*

Yea, more; are not the two the same;
The dif'rence only in the name?
In final rest of Jenocaire,
That draws us to the upper air;

In Po-ne-mah of Jossakeed,
Beyond the evening star, indeed;—
    One happy home I clearly trace,
    With slight mistake about the place.

JENOCAIRE.

Nay, nay; the broad, the winding way,
To Po-ne-mah is far astray;
    A place of demons, too, instead,
    And damn-ed spirits, dark and dread:
While up the strait, the narrow hight,
That leads to ever pure delight—
    That leads to God's eternal throne,
    Is by the cross and that alone.

JOSSAKEED.

The faith in countless ages cast—
The spirit of the mighty past,
    Can never err: The Land of Dreams,
    Is truth itself—is all it seems.
There, rivers glide along the plains;
There, dews and soft refreshing rains;
    And lakes are scattered here and there,
    Whose crystal vapors cool the air.
Rare fish abound: The angler's hook,
Among the tenants of the brook,
    And lake and river, teeming nigh,
    May richest food for man supply.
And charming valleys meet the eyes;
And gently sloping hills arise;

And sweetly undulating plain,
May well inspire a lofty strain.

DUROC.

It may indeed. If false or true,
The glowing picture charms the view.
A scene like this may well inspire,
The sweetest notes of tuneful lyre.

WA-BAS-SO.

Stay, stay; your eager praise withhold,
For more than half is yet untold.
The shades of bison, hart and bear,
Are ever seen abounding there,
With other game. Their spirits glide
Upon the plain in all their pride.
The souls of arrow, bow and knife,
Are ready, there, for sylvan strife.
And dreamy hunters, in the chase,
Pursue the game with rapid pace;
Nor yet, pursuer or pursued,
Is e'er oppressed with lassitude.

JENOCAIRE.

'Tis sensual all; and vile, at best;
'Tis not a pure, a heavenly rest.
The lofty spirit, while it springs,
To low — to earthly pleasure clings:
Bereft of flesh, and blood, and bone,
It clings to earth and earth alone; —

With all her sorrow, woe and pain,
Repeated o'er and o'er again.
The soul eternal there may roam,
And never reach a heavenly home.
There panting ghosts, a dreamy band,
Will still aspire to spirit land;
Will still aspire to realm untrod—
To bliss around the throne of God.

JOSSAKEED.

It matters not: My fathers, there,
Are calling me their bliss to share.
I seek the place where they are found,
In wide creation's utmost bound.
If they are not in realm above,
With all its never-dying love,
I wish it not. In other place,
I, too, would shun your hated race.
If in your pit of deepest woe
They dwell, where fiery torments glow,
I go, where they have gone before;
Their home is mine: I ask no more.
Give me the place, the place of all,
Where my forefathers loudly call:
Where their loved forms again I see,
Will be a heavenly home for me.
The sweetest pleasures there shall roll,
Unending round the human soul.
Oh, give! beyond the evening beams,
That happy home, the Land of Dreams.

IV.

The prophet heaved a parting sigh;
He saw the Pauguk drawing nigh.
He stretched himself upon his mat;
A palor on his features sat;
Yet pleasant smiles upon them play,
As sight and hearing pass away.
A gasp or two the sequel tell;
He gently waves a long farewell.

V.

Nor wife nor child the prophet left,
Around his grave to bend;
But Teuchsa Grondie was bereft
Of sachem, brother, friend.
And lamentations rend the air,
In field, in forest shade:
And tears of sorrow, black dispair,
The cabin home invade.
Nor does the pious Jenocaire,
His solemn mass forego;
He loudly chants upon the square,
His blessing to bestow.
Sweet flowers the Wa-won-ais-sa brings,
That on the corpse are spread;
And Whippoorwill — the younger — sings
A requiem for the dead.
In measure, to the soft refrain,
With sobs and sorrow deep,
A mournful, melancholy train
Around the body sweep.

VI.

For burial rite are preparations made:
In sitting posture, by the cabin shade,
As when he lived, the chief is set;
The girdle, rings and belts of warrior braves,
Are on him placed: His head in plumage waves:
He shines in paint of red and jet.
His tomahawk and lance are by his side,
His bow and knife his ready grasp abide,
For war prepared or for the chase;
The glow of life has fled, and yet he seems,
Imposing still, in war's resplendent beams,
A worthy type of all his race.
Amid the din of bell, and sob, and moan,
And bitter wail, and mingled groan with groan,
As if upon a mortal strife;—
Amid the whirling dance for honored dead,
That round the seated chief is fiercely led,
The corpse appears instinct with life.
Now all a silent, calm attention lend,
And Mus-ko-da-sa, of departed friend,
A glowing eulogy essays;
A life of sterling virtues is his theme,
That sheds upon the past a cheerful beam;
To future, its enlivening rays.

VII.

The dust, to dust; to ashes, ashes tend;
And all to narrow house at last descend.

And all, or nearly all, to future life
Aspire alike, as ends the earthly strife.
If brave or chief, if honored sachem dies,
The ample mound, a worthy tomb, must rise.
Beside the cornfield, in the rural shade,
And deep and wide is excavation made.
Within is placed the coffin wrought of bark,
To land of dreams a solitary ark.
In sitting posture there, the chief is placed,
With all his richest decorations graced.
To serve him on his way to spirit land,
His bowl and dish of meat beside him stand.
His weapons of the chase are with him sent,
Against the flitting, shadowy game intent;
That mimic war which here is but begun,
May be prolonged beyond the setting sun.
Reluctant to explore the distant way,
The lingering spirit hovers round its clay:
And constant women often here attend,
In sobs and moans before the shade to bend.
Secure against the sacrilegious hand,
Or fierce surviving foe, the tomb shall stand;
And long, in future ages, yet shall last,
A sacred relic of forgotten past.
Around it, mystic, legendary lore,
Its wizard tales shall in profusion pour:
While from its dearly cherished portal gleams,
A lively vision of the LAND OF DREAMS.

TEUCHSA GRONDIE.

CANTO XIV.

The Winter Hunt.

To the FARMERS of Michigan:

Who not unfrequently indulge in the sports of the fall and winter chase, yet whose extended improvements and productive culture have wholly changed some of the choice hunting grounds of former ages; and who may find in these pages entertainment and amusement for their long winter evenings, this Fourteenth Canto is respectfully inscribed by

THE AUTHOR.

TEUCHSA GRONDIE.

CANTO XIV.

THE WINTER HUNT.

A. D. 1639–40.

Prefatory Note. Wa-be-no-ka is a compound word and name which has no particular signification, although I derive the same in part from Wa-be-no, a prophet. Chi-ga-gou signified the place or meadow where leeks or wild onions were found. Kik-a-la-ma-zoo signified the mirage river, where the stones were often mistaken for otters. Sagamite signified a sort of compound stew of roots, plants and flesh, and was a common dish among the Indians. Was-bee was an ancient name for Grand River. The Indian mound at Kalamazoo has been a subject of much interest for many years.

I.

WHEN daily toils and cares perplex,
And sorely disappointments vex;
When weary burdens heavy bind,
And jaded is the active mind;
When slowly evening shades appear,
And sky and moon and stars are clear;
When nature's balmy reign is still,
Save cheerful notes of whippoorwill;—

'Tis sweet to leave the busy strife,
The plodding round of active life,
And to sequestered home retire,
To weave the mystic song—
To touch the soft, responding lyre,
And melody prolong.
But how, amid the rushing tide
Of business—surging far and wide,
Where wildest passions often swell,
Shall heavenly contemplation dwell?
Or how, along the troubled way,
Where brambles choke the ground,
Shall kindly muses deign to stay,
And poesy abound?

II.

'Tis simple, all. The sweetest rose,
Beside the thorn and thistle grows.
Upon the bent and crabbed shoot,
Is found the blossom and the fruit.
The pearls and corals of the deep,
Among the rocks their vigils keep.
The brightest gem that decks the fair,
Was found the rudest bed to share.
Beneath a livid, frowning sky,
The rainbow leaps to charm the eye.
The jagged alpine cliffs prolong,
The echoes of the mellow song.
Yea, true affection, as a guest—
A playful, kindly flame,

May nestle in a savage breast,
Within an iron frame.
And so along the troubled way,
Where toils beset from day to day;
Where active strife, in every form,
May rage like fiercely driving storm;
In purer fields of contemplation,
Above the murky plain—
A sweet relief and recreation
To lacerated brain—
The flowers of poesy may spring,
To entertain and please,
And fragrant odors freely fling,
To every passing breeze.

III.

Fair Teuchsa Grondie's people weep,
Despair on every side;
They call to spirits of the deep;
Their sovereign will abide.
The pestilence, on every hand,
Has bred a famine in the land.
The gardens wear a look forlorn,
And shrunken is the bean and corn.
The chase is desert far and wide;
Its winter stores are now denied.
The finny race are few and shy;
The angler toils without supply.
The blight has even left its mark
Upon the roots and forest bark.

The growing hunger to assuage,
As practiced oft in former age—
Legends are told, and told again,
In cabin home, but all in vain.
One sole escape from present grief—
The winter hunt must bring relief.

IV.

"Ho, for the chase!" Wa-bas-so said;
"The distant winter chase:"
The party Mus-ko-da-sa led,
The boldest of his race.
The younger Whippoorwill would go;
The hunt would Duroc share;
The Huron with his knife and bow;
And pious Jenocaire.
And many others, young and old,
Of now forgotten fame,
To brave the winter storm and cold,
Up rose with loud acclaim.
The child, the maid, the youth were there;
The aged, withered hag;
The mother would the hardship dare;
Nor did the prophet lag.
And e'en the dog and wolfish cur,
At once the object saw;
And with a whimper were astir,
Instinct with nature's law.

V.

A lad there was, of tender years—
 A son of Mus-ko-da-sa brave;
A chief among his little peers;
 His mother rested in her grave.
The age of ten he scarcely told;
 And yet, to hardy life allied,
And wild adventures manifold,
 The winter storm he bold defied.
He had his little bow and quiver,
 His little tomahawk and knife;
He could the prize-mark quickly shiver,
 And mimic fiercest battle strife.
The skiff obeyed his childish will,
 The line and hook were oft his care;
He played at ball with manly skill;
 In every hardship took a share.
The fox skin was his fancy dress,
 With gayest plumage on his head;
He pleased by playful sprightliness,
 And light amusements often led.
His mother was a Chippeway,
 His worthy father part the same:
The rising chief of future day,
 And Wa-be-no-ka was his name.

VI.

The usual Indian Summer past,
 The early snow upon the ground;

And coming on the winter's blast,
    And desolation spread around;
From hunger to obtain relief,
    Fair Teuchsa Grondie sallies forth,
Amid despondency and grief,
    To brave the icy, snowy north.
In clothing and in every need,
The poor supply is scant indeed:
    The skins and mats of former day,
    Must answer now as best they may.
The pappoose at the mother's back,
The kettle, head-belt and the pack;
    The hook and line, and knife and bow,
    Are all the freight the party know.
The breviary is the share,
With holy cross, of Jenocaire.
    Brave Duroc takes his cheerful spirit,
    In every place a signal merit.
To guard the huts from lurking foe,
And care upon the sick bestow;
    Some few remain, devoted still;
    Of these, the elder Whippoorwill.

VII.

As dim arose the lurid sun,
    Adieus were said without delay;
The toilsome journey was begun,
    To brave the winter far away.
Altho' the streams and oozy ground,
In icy chains were firmly bound,

The vines and fallen trees were met,
And brush the tangled way beset.
The naked ash and leafless oak,
Cold desolation wide bespoke;
Yet on the beech, the chicadee,
Blith, happy, held his jubilee.
Vast elms, without a parallel,
With arms athwart the sky,
Of distant ages darkly tell,
And sweeping blast defy.

VIII

The train the chiefs in silence lead,
And in the snow a pathway tread,
A path for weary band;
For miles they pass a level plain,
The former bed of rolling main;
Now, richest of the land.

IX.

A change appears. Upon the eyes,
From winding vale, the hills arise,
The scene to beautify;
No frowning rocks, the retinue
Of mountain range, obstruct the view —
Dark, towering to the sky;
But undulations far and wide,
Like heavy swells of ocean tide,
When slow abates the storm;

As if the earth of ancient date
Was hardened from a liquid state,
And in a troubled form.
The forest trees are thinly cast,
And freely drives the winter blast;
The hunter free may roam:
The oaks an ancient orchard seem—
Where fragrant blossoms early teem,
Around the rural home.
Extended plains, from Lake to Lake
This feature, in the main partake;
With river valleys wide,
Where deep and rich alluvions lie,
And darker forests hide the sky,
And damp and gloom abide.

X.

As far the party onward press,
And deep explore the wilderness,
By chance the turkey, partridge, deer,
Afford a scant, but welcome cheer.
To guard against inclement skies,
At night the huts of bark arise;—
A hasty, poor, protection cast
Against the winter's driving blast.
Upon a floor of brush and mat,
Around a central blaze,
The party hold their evening chat,
Of distant happy days.

And when the blazing brand is spent,
And deepest gloom enshrouds the tent;
    And wind and frost upon them creep,
    Tho' strange to tell, they soundly sleep.
Beneath the ice the streams are pent;
Of snow the evergreens are bent;
    Fierce winter, in his winding sheet,
    On every hand, the hunters meet.
The wind sends forth a surly howl;
Above, the clouds in anger scowl;
    Nor does the sun his cheer maintain,
    But leaves to frost unbounded reign.
The songs of Duroc now are still,
And warbling notes of Whippoorwill;
    But, on the frosty, bracing air,
    Loud swell the chants of Jenocaire.
And frequent on the stately tree,
He graves the cross and *fleur de lis;*
    A living sign to coming bands,
    Of conquest in these desert lands.

XI.

From Teuchsa Grondie — happy home,
Far, far away the party roam,
    Like restless, roaming pioneer;
A hundred frozen lakes they pass,
And frozen marsh and withered grass;
    No vengeful, skulking foe they fear.

The muskrat and the beaver lend,
Their winter robes, like kindly friend,
To those that sorely, sadly need;
At times, a gnawing hunger tries;
At times, abundant the supplies,
A famished, eager crew to feed.
Southwestern, now, from day to day,
The party slowly wend their way
Toward the leek fields, Chi-ga-gou;
They pass the prairie — cold and drear,
They pass the mirage Se-pee clear —
The river Kik-a-la-ma-zoo.

XII

Intent a season to abide,
The hunters, on the river side,
The cabin set; and soon, again,
The village rises on the plain.
The circling hills on every hand,
A wide and varied scene command.
Upon an open space of ground,
Is seen the ancient "Indian Mound;" —
A modest, unassuming pile;
But, like the structures of the Nile,
It speaks of distant ages past,
In deep and dark oblivion cast.

XIII.

Of poles and bark, and of a scanty size,
Upon the frozen ground the huts arise.

Around the central fire are always seen,
The mats, and skins, and boughs of evergreen.
Through holes and open spaces multiform,
The frost invades, and wind and driving storm.
And here, as in a kennel, den or sty,
The men and boys, and girls and women lie;—
And smoke, and cook and eat their sagamite,
With pappoose, dogs and vermin, day and night.
In filth and stench, in roasting heat or chill,
They sit, and coil, and twist, and lounge their fill.
The dense and stifling smoke, a pungent smell,
To eyes and lungs, of purgatory tell;
And penitential tears and groans are there,
For Duroc and the pious Jenocaire.
The tedious winter eve is whiled away,
By stories of the chase and battle fray;
And frightful tales of legendary lore,
The necromancer always has in store.
And vulgar jest and ribaldry abound,
While roars of laughter make the hut resound.
The Jesuit will oft the den forsake,
And on the snow, devout position take;
And solemn, there, beneath a frosty sky,
And flashing milky-way, lift up on high
His ringing chant, with elevated Host,
To God — the Father, Son and Holy Ghost.

XIV.

By day the hunt its wild excitement lends,
And oft a surfeit to the cabin sends;

While Wa-be-no-ka, with his little bow,
The turkey chases on the crusty snow.
In turn, fierce hunger, famine, sore assail,
When game, and fish, and roots together fail;
And then, with tears, and cries, and much ado,
A wail is sent to guardian Manitou.
And sickness, too, is there, and death and woe;
And friends are laid beneath the cruel snow;
But when the solid frost shall leave the ground,
The burial rite shall swell the "Indian Mound."
And joy is there. Amid the winter's chill,
A stranger guest—an infant Whippoorwill.
Most cruel lot! Yet heaven will guard and bless
The unclad offspring of the wilderness.
Young Wa-be-no-ka, thus in early life,
Beholds his love, his future happy wife.
And in his joy, melodious, Duroc sings,
And little presents to the stranger flings.
And tho' the juggler fiercely sends a frown,
And even threats to strike intruder down,
Yet calmly Jenocaire, the cross on high,
Invokes a kindly blessing from the sky.

XV.

The melting, gushing, laughing spring,
From genial South, is on the wing:
    Before his budding, blooming sway,
    The snow and frost shall flee away.
" And now," says pious Jenocaire,
" Away, for Teuchsa Grondie fair."

"Ah yes, I go!" says Whippoorwill;
"And yet I go in sorrow still:
The whispering birds the tidings bear,
That my dear mother is not there:
Ere long she'll rest in land afar —
In home beyond the evening star."
Brave Mus-ko-da-sa gives the word,
And all assent with one accord.
The huts are struck; the packs are made,
And on the head-belts firmly laid.
The infant child, in tidy rack,
Is placed upon the mother's back;
And Wa-be-no-ka in his pride,
Will walk beside his little bride.
By lake and river, hill and vale,
They thread the ancient "Indian trail."
Amid a rough a "rolling land,"
They pass the Was-bee, River Grand.
They onward press, and soon they see
The River Huron — Qua-to-gie.
In single file — extended train,
They strike across the woody plain.

XVI.

And now behold the curling smoke arise,
That cheers returning hunters' longing eyes.
With one long yell the expedition ends,
And Teuchsa Grondie hearty welcome lends.

TEUCHSA GRONDIE.

CANTO XV.

The Festival of the Dead.

I inscribe this Fifteenth Canto,

TO

THE MEMORY

OF THE

SCATTERED REMNANT

OF THE

ALGONQUIN RACE:

WHICH WILL DOUBTLESS, ERE LONG, DISAPPEAR
ENTIRELY, TO BE KNOWN AND
REMEMBERED ONLY

IN HISTORY, IN TRADITION,
AND IN SONG.

TEUCHSA GRONDIE.

CANTO XV.

THE FESTIVAL OF THE DEAD.

A. D. 1644.

PREFATORY NOTE. The festival of the dead, as it was called, was of frequent occurrence among the American Indians. It took place about once in fifteen or twenty years, and it is represented as having been one of the most repulsive sights that could be presented to the eyes or the imaginations of civilized men. The spirits of the dead were supposed to linger about their former homes till this great festival took place. There was a large Indian mound still remaining within two or three miles of Detroit as late as the forepart of the nineteenth century. It may have been constructed at some festival as described in this Canto.

I.

IN every clime and every age,
As rolling years their course have led,
The saint, the savage and the sage,
Have felt a reverence for the dead.
The pyramids of ancient Nile,
The Gothic Abbey of the Thames,
Mount Vernon, with its modest pile,
In this assert their rival claims.

Nor here, alone, does greatness tend;
    In humble life, the stricken heart,
Towards the dear departed friend,
    Sincerest homage will impart.
Yea, in the rudest wigwam cot,
    That sweet refinement never blest,
Affection lingers round the spot,
    Where loved remains are now at rest.
And farther still affection beams;
    Nor present life its vision bounds;
It stretches to the land of dreams,
    As well attest the ancient mounds.

II.

Five years have calmly rolled away,
Since Teuchsa Grondie prostrate lay,
    In grief and humble penitence,
    Beneath a frightful pestilence.
And deepest sorrow, floods of tears,
Have marked the sad and gloomy years.
    Departed spirits linger still;
    Their vacant place in cabin fill;—
Awaiting for the festal day,
To speed them on the destined way—
    To final home—to land afar—
    To land beyond the evening star.

III.

The ceremony to prepare,
    In all the pomp of savage grief,

The council met upon the square —
    The prophet, sachem and the chief.
In circle, seated on the ground,
    The pipe its inspiration gave;
Each look was thoughtful and profound,
    Each exhortation calm and grave.
Nor friendly clans are now forgot:
    The Tat-e-rat, the Qua-to-gie;
The Chippeway, the Wyandot,
    Miami, Pottawattamie;
The Kickapoo, the Es-ta-kick,
    The Sac, the Adironidack;
The Ottawa, the Chic-ta-ghick,
    The Fox, the Michimackinack: —
They freely come, from hill and vale,
    Light rowing in the bark canoe;
Or, by the distant winding trail,
    As at the call of Manitou.
And wild the scene of disarray,
    At Teuchsa Grondie — ever fair;
Shouts usher in the festal day,
    Around the maple, on the square.

IV.

From river bank, and field, and lowly mound,
And far sequestered — consecrated ground;
From hut and hamlet of the friendly clan,
The solemn exhumation now began.
In every state they come. The recent dead
Are lifted from their temporary bed;

The relics — shapeless forms, in swift decay;
The moldy bones, without their lifeless clay;
Of both the sexes, and of young and old;
The child, the lover, sachem, chieftain bold —
A frightful throng! A melancholy train,
Come forth their final burial place to gain.
Within the council-house upon the green,
This dread array in hideous plight is seen,
Clad in the richest furs; as if the sprites
Yet sighed and lingered for the final rites.
Amid a horrid feast, the deepest wail
Of woe, and doleful chant, the ear assail;
And loved remains are held in fond caress,
While cries invoke great Michabou to bless.
Affection for the dear departed friend,
And faith obscure, with superstition blend;
And he that should a relic form deface,
Would feel the signal vengeance of his race.
Brave Duroc and the pious Jenocaire,
Are both invited in the rites to share:
They pass a night in that infernal den —
A sight and stench beyond all human ken.

V.

The morn awakes. The rising day
Beholds a pompous, rich display
Of choicest fur and skin;
With gayest plumage of the chase,
And gleaming paint on limb and face,
Amid a frightful din.

The vast assembly, on the square,
For long procession now prepare,
Around their honored shrine;
And Jenocaire, in pious love,
Is there the lesson to improve,
Beside the cross divine.
The bodies — melancholy load,
Are lifted from their brief abode,
Still wrapt in costly skins;
The moldy bones, in fagots strung,
On kindred shoulders light are flung:
The solemn march begins.
Loud lamentations, doleful cries,
That swell in cadence to the skies,
Their mournful story tell —
Of strong affection surging deep,
Like rolling tempest's mighty sweep,
Or ocean's heaving swell.
The feathered tribe, upon the wing,
In sympathy, forget to sing;
The passing breeze is still;
No one, this day, can joy impart,
Not Duroc with his lightsome heart,
Or even Whippoorwill.
To rising ground they now repair,
In sight of Teuchsa Grondie fair,
But in the forest gloom;
Obedient to their chief's command,
Around the future mound they stand,
The relics to entomb.

VI.

Two fathoms deep, the burial pit,
    And twice two ample fathoms wide;
A circle that might well admit
    A thousand bodies side by side.
Around it high a scaffold rose,
    Of post, and pole, and bark, and brace;
From which the relics to expose,
    And cast into their resting place.
In wider circle, still away,
    Beneath the heavy forest shade,
The fires their glowing lights display;
    The solar beams before them fade.
And now the youth at public games,
    For prize engage; the leap, or flight,
Or shooting match, their zeal inflames,
    Until approach the hours of night.
The prizes, by the mourners paid,
    Who thus the wild excitement spread,
Are on behalf of kindred shade—
    The present spirits of the dead.

VII.

And next, within a spacious ring,
The funeral gifts the bearers bring;
    A varied and a bright array—
    A vast—a fabulous display:
The beads, the costly wampum string,
That binds the peace of chief and king;

The calumet of sacred sway,
That every foeman must obey;
The gayest plumage of the chase,
That would the proudest chieftain grace;
The braided mat, the moccasin;
The tasty frock of otter skin;
Of porcupine the bristling quill;
The eagle's claw, the vulture's bill:
The wing of jay, and stately drake;
The spotted skin of rattlesnake:
The grinning fox in mimic art;
The noble antlers of the hart;
The fur of muskrat, wolf and bear,
And mink and beaver:—all are there.
Nor only this is brought to view:
The paddle and the bark canoe;
The *racket* for the drifted snow;
The arrow and the polished bow:
The war club and the scalping knife,
That grimly tell of deadly strife
Upon the battle plain;
The tomahawk and woven shield,
With pendant scalp from bloody field,
Proud trophies of the slain.

VIII.

The voice of Mus-ko-da-sa, clear,
Rings out above the swelling din:
"To cherished relics ever dear,
The last sad office now begin."

Behold, anew, the warm caress,
  While sob and moan the ear assail;
The forest rings of wild excess,
  On high resounds the mournful wail.
At lifted hand, up rise the throng,
  And each a gift or relic bears;
The chieftains chant the funeral song;
  To mount the scaffold each prepares.
Another signal: Up they fly
  The sloping ladders; yells resound:
With care upon the scaffold high,
  Are gifts and relics spread around.

IX.

Now Mus-ko-da-sa mounts a lofty stand,
And silence craves, by gentle wave of hand;
  The troubled, surging waves are still:
The cross above the Jesuit is seen;
Old Duroc gazes with a solemn mien,
  Beside the thoughtful Whippoorwill.
"The rite," thus Mus-ko-da-sa calm begun,
"The rite we owe, this day is nobly done,
  To those we bid a long farewell;
Thanks to you all, for this your pious zeal;
Yours are the pangs the stricken mourners feel;
  May peace within your cabins dwell.
These many gifts affection well attest,
Towards the friends ere long to be at rest,
  In distant spirit land of dreams;

They linger still about their former home,
But ere the dawn, to evening star they roam —
    Beneath the star that yonder gleams.
Ye happy souls! that round us hover now!
Accept these gifts; these solemn rites allow!
    Oh, pardon what is done amiss!
Your signal virtues, while with us you dwelt,
Your deeds of valor that the foeman felt,
    Will smooth your path to land of bliss."

X.

He ceases with the closing day:
    More brilliant now the fires arise;
The sparks in gleaming circles play,
    The curling smoke invades the skies.
The stakes are set; the kettles hung;
    And in the boiling sagamite,
Dry scraps of human flesh are flung,
    The wildest frenzy to excite.
And all, the horrid feast, partake,
    While shouts rebellow thro' the gloom;
The echoes of the night awake,
    Like mournful echoes of the tomb.
The funeral honors to enhance,
Prepare the midnight whirling dance:
    In glowing paint and plumage gay,
    Among the fires, a bright display,
With one consent, and to and fro,
Away the vast assembly go;

And fierce arises, long and dread,
A yell that might awake the dead.
To calm beholder of the sight,
That fiery scene at dead of night—
The whirl, contortion, demon yell—
Is like a scene from nether hell.
The brute creation, too, are there;
The hawk and eagle wildly stare.
The wolf sends up a dismal howl,
And loud responds the frighted owl.

XI.

The night advances. Jenocaire,
And Duroc, still the wonder share.
Wa-bas-so's voice now loudly swells,
Above the deafening savage yells:
"Let silence reign; let all be still,
For funeral song of Whippoorwill."
At once the mighty ocean roar,
Like battle storm, is heard no more;
And thro' the glare, all eyes intent,
Are on the charming songstress bent.
At first her voice, in solemn tone,
And mellow strain, is heard alone:
Anon it gathers wild excess,
And echoes through the wilderness,
In one voluptuous swell;
And then the stirring choral song,
Brave Duroc and the host prolong—
A frightful funeral knell.

FUNERAL SONG.

1.

Farewell, dear friends, a long farewell!
Ye soon shall wander far,
With happy spirits there to dwell —
Beyond the evening star.

CHORUS.

Farewell, farewell: ye wander far,
To home beyond the evening star.

2.

Take bow and arrow, meat and drink,
The weary way is long;
And boldly pass, oh, never shrink,
To that dear land of song.

CHORUS.

Oh, shrink not, tho' the way be long,
From that dear land, the land of song.

3.

The sparks that from these flames arise,
And in the darkness spread;
The stars that gleam along the skies,
Are spirits of the dead.

CHORUS.

Yea, spirits of the mighty dead,
To land of dreams in triumph led.

4.

Their spirits — are the northern light,
Their souls — the milky-way;
In glory, there, they take their flight,
To one eternal day.

CHORUS.

Along the shining milky-way,
They march to that eternal day.

5.

Nor we, to lot of man, are blind;
    We soon the end shall see;
We shall not linger far behind,
    From that eternity.

CHORUS.

Ah, long we cannot stay behind,
From that long home — eternity.

XII.

The echoes linger: Mournful spell,
Is broken by redoubled yell;
    And to the scaffold all repair,
    The last sad funeral rite to share.
And first, within the pit, a bed
Of robes of richest fur, is spread.
    The kettles then are careful set,
    With bow and food, and calumet;—
To serve the spirits, on their way,
To land beyond the setting day.
    Pell-mell the relics then are thrown,
    With horrid yell, and frightful groan;
And when in order all are laid,
A winding sheet of robes is made:
    The whole with earth is covered o'er,
    To rest till time shall be no more.

XIII.

Throughout the west, may often still be found,
From long forgotten past, the "Indian Mound":

And doubtless many more, in swift decay,
By frost, and flood, and time, were swept away.
What frightful scenes around them once befell,
No echoes from the past shall ever tell.
Thus fated, too, the race of human kind
That formed them, shall a swift oblivion find.

TEUCHSA GRONDIE.

CANTO XVI.

To FATHER P. J. DE SMET,

OF THE ORDER OF JESUITS:

Who has been, for over a quarter of a century, a missionary among the Indians of the distant West, and whose ability, energy and devotion, and probable sufferings and privations, render him not an unworthy successor and representative of the early Jesuit missionaries on this continent, this Sixteenth Canto is most respectfully inscribed by

THE AUTHOR.

TEUCHSA GRONDIE.

CANTO XVI.

THE MISSIONARY.

A. D. 1645.

PREFATORY NOTE. The word Okie was a general name for ghost, demon or guardian spirit. The new chapel is supposed to have stood on or near the site of the present French Church, on Larned street, Detroit. The *Demon Feast* was a horrid midnight revel, which took place in times of great danger and terror, and in which brutal obscenity, human sacrifices and cannibalism were practiced.

I.

FROM all the sweets of social life,
And charms of all-endearing home,
To brave the torch and scalping knife,
The Jesuit would distant roam.
The world might hold him in derision,
But crowns of glory led him on;
Clear was his faith, like raptured vision,
In view of final victory won.
His mother Church he n'er forgot;
Her rule of faith he questioned not;

His action, too, with firm belief,
Was guided by his ruler chief.
And when his mission was begun,
The cloistered life he well might shun;
In every land of every zone,
The active life was all his own.
The cross to western world he bears,
With an intense, unflaging zeal;
And every danger freely shares,
His work by martyrdom to seal.
Go where you may, the Jesuit declares
His presence still. The princely court he shares:
The school he guides. In hood, or in disguise,
With tact and skill, his arts he ever plies.
At the confession, conscience firm he gains;
And in the social circle calmly reigns:
His constant aim—to sway the human mind,
And, in united faith, the world to bind.
And yet with all his faults, from pole to pole,
He spreads the truth, and feeds the human soul.
In Ethiope; on Chillian Mount sublime;
In Paraguay; in Congo's sunny clime;
In Bactriana, and in China far;
In Japan's thousand isles; in Caffrara;
In California; on the Amazon;
In Australasia; by the Oregon:
In *Nouvelle France;* in Aztec Mexico;
In Iceland chill; and—where soe'er we go—
To Earth's remotest bounds, we find him there;
Yea, here he dwelt, at Teuchsa Grondie fair.

II.

For Duroc and for Jenocaire,
A hut was raised beside the square.
    The stake and pole sustained the roof,
    Against the storm, a slender proof.
From open top, the daily light;
    The winter thro' the crevice broke;
A central fire illumed the night,
    Intense with suffocating smoke.
Beneath a rustic tripod slung,
Above the fire, the kettle hung:
    Nor did the dainty Frenchman scorn,
    The sagamite and roasted corn.
To form at night the lowly bed,
The mat and skin are neatly spread.
    Upon the walls of bark around,
    Rude pictures of the faith are found.
The red-men gather in to see,
A *house* in pure simplicity.
    Here, oft, his home the savage makes,
    And oft the food and couch partakes.
And here the monk, in cloak and hood,
Proclaims the Christian brotherhood;
    He shares in turn the cabin shades,
    Nor soup of wolf or dog evades.

III.

The faithful priest arose at early dawn,
And walked abroad upon the sloping lawn,
    To gaze upon the opening East;

Perhaps thro' cornfield, to the forest nigh,
He bent his steps; and there, beneath the sky,
Devout his many sins confessed.
And then, from hut to hut, and on the square,
In social converse, would he calm declare,
The Christian faith, the final ban;
Of science, too, and arts he often spoke;
And free discussion would he oft invoke,
Upon the destiny of man.
Did sickness rage, distress and pain assail,
And cabin home resound with mournful wail,
With terror and despairing cries;
At once the priest would care and skill impart,
Nor fail to point the mind and heavy heart
To happy home beyond the skies.
The child and youth—the hope of every age—
An often soiled but yet unwritten page—
Susceptible of deep impress,
Were gathered to the house of Jenocaire,
And taught the Avé, Pater, Crédo, there,
And sign of cross and holy *Messe.*
The priest and Duroc, too, the burden share
Of daily toil—provide their humble fare;
The water bring, the garden till;
The game pursue, the eager angler play;
Prepare their meat and mush, from day to day;
And calls of charity fulfill

IV.

That little bower of evergreen,
Upon the square — attractive scene;
    And where beholder still might see
    Le Vareau's cross upon the tree;
Where wonted prayer was often made,
At morn, and noon, and evening shade;
    Where solemn chant was often sung,
    In swelling strain of Latin tongue;
And where the savage often went,
To gaze in mute astonishment —
    At scenes that pointed to the goal,
    And deeply stirred the human soul;
That little altar, on the square —
Devotion in the open air; —
    That altar of the pioneers,
    Of fondest hopes and darkest fears; —
That temple, in the common view,
The first that Teuchsa Grondie knew;
    Its high estate was now to yield,
    For chapel in the open field.

V.

The poles were cut and neatly set;
Above, in bended form, they met.
    Upon the sides and overhead,
    The flakes of bark were neatly spread.
The little door, in Gothic form,
Protected from the driving storm.

Upon the top, arose the spire,
And cross, for savage to admire.
Within, the simple altar shines,
And taste and poverty combines.
No golden glitter there is found,
But flowers and evergreens abound.
Of boughs a crucifix is made;
A torch dispels the gloomy shade.
Of leaves and mats the ground is spread,
With richest plumage overhead.
A fairy scene the whole appears;
It deep abounds with hopes and fears:
The faith may here its fruit display,
Or fury sweep the whole away.
And will Jehovah well consent,
To dwell in such a tenement?
He will, He will! The hut His home,
As well as Lateran at Rome.
In Gallic and Algonquin tongue,
His name shall here be loudly sung,
And wild devotion deep engage;
Nor shall the echoes then decay,
When Indian race shall melt away,
But onward swell from age to age.

VI.

Here chants the monk his solemn prayers;
The loud response brave Duroc bears.
The sacred vestments for the priest,
Are braid of bark or skin of beast;

Nor does the humble monk disclaim,
The plumage of the forest game.
    The aromatic plant distills
    The incense that the chapel fills.
From simple bread of pounded maize,
The Host arises to the gaze,
    As lowly bows the neophyte;
From luscious fruit of forest vine
Is drawn the sacramental wine:
    Imposing is the solemn rite.
The rolling chant of *Notre Dame*
May pure devotion high inflame,
    As vaulted arches loud reply;
But service in the sylvan grove
Bespeaks angelic strains above,
    That swell the praises of the sky.

VII.

The daily toils of pious Jenocaire,
In dens of sickness and of deep despair,
    Are constant thro' the weary year;
Wher-e'er his care can minister relief,
Or where a kindly word can soften grief,
    There is he found to help and cheer.
To dying children, artful — by disguise —
The priest baptismal waters oft applies,
    To save them from an endless night;
And as the precious jewels pass away,
From life of sorrow to eternal day,
    Rejoices with a pure delight.

And often sympathetic love is felt;
The youthful mind and heart will often melt,
Nor grace and living faith disown;
But savage mind mature, is like the rock,
That firm resists the ocean's mighty shock;
To faith ancestral ever prone.
His clinging, stubborn faith, in every ill,
Hangs on his Okie — spirit — demon, still,
As hangs the vine upon the oak;
To break or bend it, is to break the man,
And shake the independence of his clan,
And force it to a slavish yoke.
His sensual nature, too, his lofty pride,
His listless indolence, would still abide,
In dreamy, gloomy superstition;
From rigid morals of the monk he turns;
The virtues of the faith severe, he spurns,
Preferring rather dark perdition.
To cure the sick, and sore diseases heal,
The song and dance, and overheated zeal,
The virtues of the cross excel;
And feasts and incantations constant feed,
A universal — pantheistic creed,
And faith, and truth, and hope repel.
Nor this is all: The solemn council sits,
And grave and dreadful *Feast of Dreams* permits,
For earthly ills a sovereign power;
Disorders fierce assail the frighted night,
A frantic spirit rages with delight,
And madness rules the midnight hour.

VIII.

The necromancer, in his dreams,
A wild supernal demon seems;
His incantations, day and night,
Inspire a gloomy, dread affright.
Dark tales of woe obscurely told,
Still darker scenes of woe unfold;
And dread suspicion everywhere,
Alarms the pious Jenocaire.
Says Duroc: "Like to like applied,
Shall turn the strongly setting tide;
Play back the role, with good intent;
Let art supply the argument.
Our cause demands a like condition —
The ruse applied to superstition:
Dispel by art these dismal scenes;
The end shall justify the means."
In secret thought the pious man,
With eager wishes for success,
Revolves the shrewd, unhallowed plan —
The crooked road to righteousness.
"Can vile deceit and fraud impair,
The sacred bond of righteous laws,
When thus purveyed and forced to share,
The triumphs of a holy cause?
I come to save from darkest woes,
And here a hostile weapon find;
Why turn it not to crush the foes,
Against the truth of God combined?

The magic art, satanic dream,
The human mind in fetters hold;
Why practice not a kindred scheme,
The truth of God to here unfold?"
Thus calmly, pious Jenocaire,
His object and the means combined;
Nor was it meet the world should share
The councils of the godly mind.
Yet worthy Duroc read, in brief,
As reads the man of ready wit,
The inclinations of his chief:
He seconds well the Jesuit.

IX.

With solemn and majestic mien,
The friar walks upon the green:
He gazes at the upper air;
He speaks to wing-ed spirits there.
He vents a deep sepulchral moan;
The chapel echoes back the groan.
The altar, at the dead of night,
Emits, unbid, mysterious light.
The cross, as from an inward throe,
Moves up and down and to and fro.
The rude Madonna on the wall,
Responsive bows to friar's call.
The demons, from beneath the ground,
Send forth a dread, unearthly sound.
Above, the spirits, on the wing,
In sweetest notes angelic sing.

At night is seen the lightning's flash,
And loud is heard the thunder crash.
    The crafty monk with anger shakes,
    The chapel with the altar quakes:
    He loudly calls on demon world,
    To come with banners high unfurled.
"Enough!" says Mus-ko-da-sa brave,
    In terror and in deep contrition;
"From these affrights the village save;
    Thou art the true, the great magician."

X.

A sudden change was thus affected
    Upon the heathen, young and old;
And Jenocaire they all respected,
    While he in turn was firm and bold.
The falsity of dreams he taught,
So oft with deep distresses fraught:
    The law of social virtue lent,
    Unnumbered vices to prevent.
He preached against the *demon feast*—
Its crimes, that sink below the beast:
    He bold condemned the festival,
    That marked the hungry cannibal.
He firm denounced, with earnest breath,
The cruel torture, fire and death.
    The savage race he fain would cherish,
    And lift above the beasts that perish;
    He fain a standard high would raise,
    Of Christian faith, and hope, and praise.

XI.

Nor were these labors spent in vain;
They modified the savage cain;
They shed a light upon the blind;
And though the brute was brutal still,
He felt the genial dew distill
Within his dreamy, troubled mind.
The will, the feeling, sentiment,
However set and firmly bent,
Are subject to the moving power,
That springs from deeper, wider scope
Of mental range, and higher hope,
In life, and in the mortal hour.
The plastic mind of eager youth,
Would listen to the word of truth,
As taught or sung by Jenocaire;
They often to the chapel went,
And oft their choral voices lent,
And knelt, devout, in worship there.
And those of still maturer years,
Or led by hopes or gloomy fears,
Would oft approach and often falter;
In doubt to grasp the living faith —
To walk the strait and narrow path,
And bow before the sacred altar.
The youthful Wa-be-no-ka, too,
Would oft the flaming chancel view,
With charming little Whippoorwill;

Would gaze upon the solemn rite,
And hear the earnest monk invite,
    And yet resist persuasion still.

XII.

The powers of darkness took alarm—
    The minions of satanic beast,
And bared a mighty, vengeful arm;
    So thought the pious, zealous priest.
A council Mus-ko-da-sa held;
With anger every chieftain swelled:
    "If sure destruction we delay,
    Our cherished faith has had its day;
And with our faith our every clan,
Shall quickly feel the fatal ban:
    Then strike the monk, his creed efface;
    Then strike and save our ancient race."

XIII.

The holy father, calmly, saw it all,
For no rude terrors could his soul appall.
His former friends their face averted now,
And met his kindness with a frowning brow.
The children, too, the youthful neophyte,
His presence shunned, as if a dreaded sight.
They poured upon him taunts and ribald jeers,
And called on Pauguk to excite his fears.
And yet, nor threat, or jeer, or dire menace,
Could dim the smile on his benignant face:

He stood erect, alone, sublime in form,
Like tower of strength exposed to thunder storm.
His calmness, boldness, in the trying hour,
Imposed an awe, as if from magic power.
Undaunted air, amid the fearful strife,
Subdued his foes and saved his forfeit life.
And thus shall lofty virtue — truly grand,
In firm integrity, forever stand;
Resist the wild — the overwhelming flood,
Secure in faith and in the strength of God.

TEUCHSA GRONDIE.

CANTO XVII.

To Right Reverend

S. A. McCOSKRY, D. D., LL. D.,

The first Bishop of Michigan:

Who, in a successful pastorate of over thirty years, from a time when the Peninsular of Michigan was little less than an unbroken wilderness, has had abundant opportunities to observe much of the scenery, a description of which is herein attempted, and the rapid changes that have taken place in the course of his episcopate, this Seventeenth Canto is, as an expression of regard and esteem, most respectfully dedicated by

THE AUTHOR.

TEUCHSA GRONDIE.

CANTO XVII.

THE SUMMER HUNT.

A. D. 1646.

PREFATORY NOTE. Fadladeen will be remembered as the crusty old critic of Lalla Rookh. The Indians had no mode of computing time except by the phenomena of nature. Wa-we-aw-to-nong was another ancient name for Teuchsa Grondie. Mich-i-saw-gye-gan, from which it is presumed the State of Michigan derives its name, was an ancient name for Lake Michigan. The word Se-pee, standing alone, signified a river. Mos-ke-go Se-pee signified Marsh River, and was the same as the present Muskegon. Wash-bee-you was another ancient name for Grand River. Serpents were objects of superstitious worship among the Indians. It will be remembered that the little Whippoorwill, who accompanied the expedition described in this Canto, was born at Kalamazoo, in the winter hunt of 1640, as related in the fourteenth Canto.

I.

IS this a legend, history, or what?
   An epic, or a narrative in rhyme?
The hero where, and where th' evolving plot?
   The unity — of action, place and time?
To run a poem, in a general plan,
   Thro' many ages! Actions come and go,

And flitting man succeeds to flitting man!
  Ah, what is this but trifling puppet show!
Gruff Fadladeen your criticism stay:
  May not a nation play the epopee?—
That rises, worthy rules, and melts away;
  That perishes in struggling to be free?
The tenant of the forest, in his lair,
  Is roused by footsteps of advancing foe;
He springs to arms, for home the worst to dare,
  And yet his fate is sure however slow.
A nation, wronged by diplomatic art,
  That binds, unseen, where all was free before,
May act the hero, play the noble part,
  May worthy strike, and fall to rise no more.
Brave Poland, conquered, tells a bitter story;
  And Hungary, in battle storms begot;
And Erin, on a thousand fields of glory:
  The red men of the forest share their lot.
Yea, worse by far. Those, live and vegetate,
  In irksome fetters, dreaming of their nation:
While these rush onward to a darker fate,
  To sure, and swift, and dread annihilation.
Then ye who ask, if epic, narrative,
  Historic, legend, or descriptive, call
The muse to sing; we prompt the answer give,
  Nor this or that alone, but one and all.

II.

And now vague rumors darkly told
Of preparations manifold,

Among the vengeful Iroquois,
For distant and revengeful war.
The singing birds the story tell,
Of tomahawk and dreadful knell.
The Huron and the Ottawa—
Wa-bas-so and Tai-go-ne-ga,
The danger snuff, upon the wind,
And Teuchsa Grondie leave behind.
Each had his Mohawk foeman slain,
Beside the Thames; at Thunder Bay;
And guilty conscience told again,
Of war-path and of battle fray.
The forest wild they swiftly thread;
They reach the rapid Matchedash,
They give the warning, dark and dread,
Of rising cloud for thunder crash.

III.

No savage home however rare,
If told in legend or in song,
Could with that charming spot compare—
The lovely Wa-we-aw-to-nong.
And yet, again, when summer smiled,
And richly bloomed the forest wild,
The hunter would the chase proclaim;
Would cabin home and village scorn,
And, with his bow and pouch of corn,
Would sally forth in quest of game.

IV.

"Ho, for the distant summer chase!"
    The worthy Mus-ko-da-sa cries;—
"The bow, the snare, the eager race:
    But first attend the sacrifice."
The Indian corn, that luscious grain,
    That may a thousand fold bestow;—
That might a famished world sustain,
    To aborigines we owe.
To them we owe another plant,
    Which habit makes a pleasant yoke;
A constant—welcome visitant,
    That cheers awhile and "ends in smoke."
But, to propitious Manitou,
    May well arise the acrid flame
Of wild tobacco; tribute due
    For large supply of forest game.
The chieftain raises lofty pyre
    For sacrifice, upon the square;
And then, devout, applies the fire,
    Despite the frowns of Jenocaire.

V.

"Ho, for the chase," the chief repeats:
    At once arise on every hand,
For bold emprise and daring feats,
    Of men and youth a worthy band.
Brave Wa-be-no-ka, first we see,
And next, his friend, young Ta-to-kee;
    And Whippoorwill to dress the game;

The mother and her child will go,
For none expect the skulking foe,
And others now unknown to fame.
Old Duroc, too, the bow would take,
When Mus-ko-da-sa proudly led;
And even Jenocaire forsake:
The Father calmly shook his head.
A yell is heard at rising sun;
The brief adieus are quickly told;
The summer hunt is now begun,
For wild adventures manifold.

VI.

In forest shade they disappear;
The village still prolongs the cheer.
In lowland wet, in heavy swale,
They wind along the ancient trail.
The foliage bars the sun by day,
And soft displays the sylvan scene;
At night the weary party stay,
And rest beneath the evergreen.
They note the flying sands of time,
By rays that thro' the branches creep;
The buds and blossoms — measured chime,
Their monthly records faithful keep.
Across the river, round the lake,
Their devious way the party take.
In vale and marsh, and over hill,
The game invites them onward still.

The tangled path they often see
Beset by limb and fall-en tree;
    And then they pass the rolling plain,
    And then the prairie smiles again.
No mountain range the course impedes;
    No frowning ledge debars the way;
But fertile plain on plain succeeds,
    To feed the world in future day.

VII.

The hoary elm and stately oak,
    With bannered arms against the sky,
Invite the crashing thunder stroke,
    The sweeping wind and storm defy.
The ash sustains the pendant vine,
    As frailty ever clings to power;
The walnut and the somber pine
    Above the birch majestic tower.
Like orchards of forgotten times,
Like pleasure parks of eastern climes,
    The "Openings" of the west appear—
    The paradise of fallow deer.
And then behold that flowery gem—
    The prairie in the forest set;
Of western world the diadem,
    That hunter band can n'er forget.
The rivers in their gentle flow,
    To shady banks the coquet play;
On lonely vale a charm bestow,
    And yet forever haste away.

The whole—a mighty hunting ground,
  That long possession sanctifies—
    Extended Mich-i-saw-gye-gan;
Where game and richest furs abound,
  And wild adventures oft arise;
    The happy home of savage man.

VIII.

And oft is seen the Indian village—
The huts of bark and scanty tillage;
    Where, far sequestered and alone,
    The woes of life are rarely known.
And then, again, in sylvan shade,
    The single cabin home is met;
The lodge, perhaps, of renegade,
    Or surly, gloomy anchoret.
Perhaps the hut a shelter gives,
    To wife and child in sorry plight;—
A band of lawless fugitives,
    With roots and fish for sagamite.

IX.

And Flora shines in native bloom,
    In every nook and sunny station—
The handmaid of the forest gloom,
    In this fair field of vegetation.
Viola smiles in purple hue,
    The primrose from the winter peeps;
The crocus laughs in deepest blue,
    The myrtle on the prairie creeps.

The snowdrops, early spring, awake;
    The daisy opes at morning ray;
The lily skirts the wizard lake;
    The buttercups their gold display.
The amaranth eternal springs,
    Of love the honeysuckle tells;
The cowslip bold its blossom flings,
    The foxglove by the streamlet dwells.
Though sickly, oft, the forest queen,
    And Flora seems as if astray;
She yet adorns the sylvan scene,
    And roses crown the bright array.

X.

In such a paradise, the game,
Of every species, every name,
    Was quickly found, on every hand,
    To rich reward the hunter band.
The speckled trout, the streamlet lends,
    The perch and pike, the river yields;
The muskrat on his hut depends,
    Artistic dam the beaver shields.
The lazy badger oft is seen;
    The hare, beneath the shady leaf;
The artful, cautious wolverine;
    The crafty fox, a very thief.
The porcupine the prairie shares,
    The wolf presents a surly face;
In majesty the bear appears,
    The antlered buck in lofty grace.

The panther glares upon the tree,
Behind the log the weasel peeps;
The squirrel chatters in his glee,
The noble elk in grandeur leaps.
The partridge drums upon the log,
The duck upon the lake is seen;
The heron struts beside the bog,
The quail beneath the evergreen.
With crest erect the turkey glides;
The vulture flaps his heavy wings;
The fisher guards the river sides;
The mockingbird derisive sings.
The owl, by night, the better sees;
The robin early morning greets;
The pigeon darts among the trees,
The bees extract their flowery sweets.
The eagle, high, a monarch soars,
The hawks their airy circles fill;
The nightingale his music pours;
And, nightly, charms the whippoorwill.

XI.

In such a wilderness of game,
In such a floral temple wild,
The chase was sought with loud acclaim,
And flying weeks and months beguiled.
The little Whippoorwill could spring
The artful net, deceitful snare;
And Ta-to-kee the elk would try;

And Wa-be-no-ka from the string,
Would arrow send to surly bear;
And bring the eagle from the sky.
While stratagem and cunning art
Would oft the richest fruits bestow;
The wily game could play its part,
At times, as well as hunter foe.
Old Mus-ko-da-sa took his ease,
But well enjoyed the daring feat;
And while success would always please,
He shrugged his shoulders at defeat.
The party scoured the distant plain,
And many trophies could they boast—
The proudest of the wide domain;
While many noble ones were lost.
And Wa-won-ais-sa, as of yore,
Her weary guests to entertain,
Prepared the daily sagamite;
She dried the meat for winter store,
And packed it; then, in thrilling strain,
She played the nightingale at night.
And Wa-be-no-ka, day by day,
A kindly office to fulfill,
The choicest piece would often lay
Before his little Whippoorwill.

XII.

Nor, in the hunter's happy lot,
Were myths and jeebi train forgot.

In beast, and bird, and lake and tree,
The savage could a spirit see;
And in the bow and arrow true,
Auspicious okie sprung to view.
In universal plan, unfurled,
He saw a pantheistic world.
To serpent race was always due,
The worship of the Manitou.
Did watersnake beside the bog,
Appear to wait the silly frog;
Did massasauga, 'neath the brake,
His forky tongue in anger shake;
Did king of serpents terror sing —
A warning to the stranger fling,
With arching neck, and flashing eye,
The rash intruder fierce defy —
And quick for deadly spring prepare;
The savage would arrest his way,
His deep devotion there would pay,
And every injury forbear.

XIII.

And thus the roving hunter band,
Prolong the chase thro'-out the land;
Till autumn, in its golden sear,
Bespeaks the desert winter near.
They pass the Mos-ke-go Se-pee,
They camp upon the Wash-bee-you;
The mirage stream they often see —
The limpid Kik-a-la-ma-zoo.

Nor do they miss the lovely spot
    Where mound is seen. The winter chill,
In scanty hut, is n'er forgot—
    The birth-place of the Whippoorwill.
They gather flowers upon the plain,
    That on the lofty mound they spread;
And sorrow gushes forth again,
    In recollection of the dead.

XIV.

"For home," brave Wa-be-no-ka cries,
    "To place the meat in winter store;
Inclement are the angry skies,
    The pleasant summer hunt is o'er."
For home they start with one consent,
  Before the winter storms assail;
    Ere comes the biting, frosty air;
      Before the snow is on the plain:
In single file their course is bent,
  Upon the well trod Indian trail;
    And soon will Teuchsa Grondie fair,
      Receive her hunter band again.

TEUCHSA GRONDIE.

CANTO XVIII.

To Hon. WILLIAM H. SEWARD:

The Scholar, Orator and Statesman;

Who, as Secretary of State, during one of the most complicated and difficult periods of our foreign relations, conducted the diplomatic affairs of the country, with the skill, tact and judgment that enabled the government to turn its whole strength against a domestic enemy, and thus to maintain the unity and power of the nation unimpaired, this Eighteenth Canto is, as an acknowledgment of public services, respectfully inscribed by

THE AUTHOR.

TEUCHSA GRONDIE.

CANTO XVIII.

THE EMBASSY.

A. D. 1649.

PREFATORY NOTE. In the war of the Iroquois against the Hurons in 1649, a tribe dwelling near Niagara was induced by the former to remain neutral, and hence, was afterwards called the Neutral Nation.

Ish-ko-dah signified fiery. Kah-gah-gee, black. Sub-be-kah, the spider. Pez-he-kee, the bison. Ko-ko-ko-ho, the owl. Che-to-waik, the plover. Shau-go-dah, a boasting coward. Ken-na-beck, the serpent. Keneú, the great war eagle.

Ho-dé-no-sau-nee was the confederate name of the Iroquois.

Detroit sunsets, in clear weather, are celebrated for their beauty and splendor.

I.

IN social life, the secret foe,
By every act and look is read;
His presence, whereso-e'er we go,
Inspires at once the secret dread.
Though gracious be his every word,
With lowly bow and smiling air,

We yet instinctively record
 The crafty serpent lurking there.
And though his mien be free and bold,
 Without a sign of false pretense,
We yet instinctively withhold
 The thing he seeks—our confidence.
And so with nations. Intercourse
 May courtly phrases interlace,
And blandishments bestow, per force,
 With smiling, condescending grace:
And to the inattentive eye,
 A calm the surface may bespeak;
And yet a hurricane be nigh,
 That soon upon the world shall break.
The wise detects deceitful snare;
 He looks beneath the courtly form;
He snuffs the lightning in the air,—
 Prepares to meet the rising storm.

II.

To wide amalgamation due,
 Among the distant Huron nation,
Was soon displayed the Celtic hue,
 In blood and faith and social station.
In spite of endless, bitter strife,
 For daily comfort simply told,
 In every hut and every place;
The freedom of the forest life,
 With hunger, want and piercing cold,
 Had charms for the Caucasian race.

The kindly, social, cheerful French,
Who would the savage life retrench,
    And deep remold the savage man;
Themselves were molded to the cast
Of savage type, for ages past,
    As seen in roving forest clan.
And now, as distant echoes came,
Of Mohawk spirit in a flame,
    For vengeance of the Iroquois;
And skulking warfare was begun;
The Huron and the French were one,
    With ever friendly Ottawa.

III.

The singing birds the tidings bring,
Of threatened war, upon the wing;
    Nor do the summer hunters fail
    To trace the foeman on the trail.
Behind the dusky forest green,
The skulking foe is often seen:
    The cuckoo sounds the fierce alarm;
    The pappoose dreads the coming storm.
"A council!" cries Tai-go-ne-ga;
    "For danger sure is drawing nigh;"
"Yea," says Wa-bas-so — Ottawa,
    "The tints of blood are in the sky."
The messenger is light and fleet;
    The scattered towns obey the call;
The chiefs and aged sachems meet,
    To calm advise, in council hall.

Each one proclaims approaching war,
From terror-dealing Iroquois;
  Nor will the vengeful foeman wait:
The embassy at once to send,
For worthy allies, all commend,
  To Teuchsa Grondie on the strait.
The suffrage names the Ottawa;
And with him brave Tai-go-ne-ga;
  A third — ambitious Kan-ne-tow:
The Jesuits their office play,
And name the father Bourdelais,
  Who shall the danger undergo.
The sack of corn, the scrap of meat,
The quiver and the bow, complete
  The luggage for the land afar;
But tomahawks in crimson dye,
And purple war-belts lifted high,
  Shall challenge to the bloody war.

IV.

A southern course at first they take,
Towards the Ca-da-ra-qui lake;
  And then towards that plunging flood,
  The dreadful Hé-no's dark abode.
The maple, beach, and stately elm,
And ash, compose the forest realm.
  The deep, unbounded twilight shade,
  Might well afford an ambuscade.
Extended circuit thus they try,
To seek a friendly, firm ally:

A kindred clan of Huron race,
Perhaps would Huron cause embrace.
But, long before, had Iroquois
Denounced exterminating war,
Against whoever should maintain
The Huron, or his belt retain.
This kindred clan could favor either,
From its commanding, central station;
It firm resolved to favor neither,
And hence, was called the Neutral Nation.

V.

In sorrow, but without delay,
The Huron party haste away,
Still hoping for the best:
They loud exclaim, "Be peaceful still;
We go to those that can and will;
And cowards they detest."
Upon the ancient trail they press,
Through an unbroken wilderness;
Lake Erie's waves they hear:
They reach a river of renown;
Beyond, that celebrated town—
Fair Teuchsa Grondie near.
To evening sky the sun is fled;
He pours his beams of fiery red,
That one celestial glory shed,
Above, and far and wide:

The forest green — a living mass,
The clouds, that richest gold surpass,
The river, like that "Sea of glass,"
            The glory may divide.
The central ball is lost to view;
The clouds are turned to purple hue;
Conflagrant skies are bathed anew,
            As in an ocean flood:
Who can behold this bright array —
This gorgeous scene of setting day,
And not his deep devotions pay
            To Majesty of God?

VI.

As early morning beams arise,
The skiff across the river flies:
      The town receives the embassy
      With open hospitality.
The Jesuit, in any sphere,
Well knows his brother pioneer;
      And Bourdelais and Jenocaire,
      At once the closest friendship share.
      Old Duroc sings and dances bold,
      Another Frenchman to behold.
And Mus-ko-da-sa freely sends
   His greeting to Wa-bas-so brave;
      And Wa-be-no-ka kindly speaks —
         Tai-go-ne-ga, the worthy still:

And every host an effort lends,
To free access, the way to pave;
And each the stranger's comfort seeks;
Above the rest the Whippoorwill.

VII.

Says Mus-ko-da-sa, "Let the call
Go forth to sachems, one and all,
To meet upon the public square,
To hold a solemn council there:
This worthy embassy from far,
Would speak to us of coming war;
They would a question advocate,
Of deepest moment to the state."
Throughout the town the heralds go;
The sign, a bloody hatchet, show:
The chiefs and sachems understand,
And soon obey the high command.
The fiery warrior Ish-ko-dah
Is coming with black Kah-gah-gee;
The spider chieftain—Sub-be-kah,
With lordly bison—Pez-he-kee.
Sage Ko-ko-ko-ho rolls his eyes,
And comes with quiet Che-to-waik;
Loud Shau-go-dah the foe defies,
And comes with serpent Ken-na-beck.
And Wa-be-no-ka proudly meets
With seignior chiefs of mighty name;
These, stately Mus-ko-da-sa greets,
With others now unknown to fame.

VIII.

Around the maple, on the square,
The council meet in open air.
The embassy the center hold;
Concentric circles these infold,
And all are seated on the grass;
The oldest form the inner class:
Each sachem gravely smokes his pipe;
In prudence and in wisdom ripe.
And round about a motley crew,
Of boys and girls, and dandies too;
In paint and plumage — bright array,
As if adorned for festal day.
And Wa-won-ais-sa, too, is there,
Of every movement anxious still;
For she the griefs of war must share,
With charming little Whippoorwill.
The embassy their friends address,
Each speaker rising in his place,
In loud and wild — vehement strain;
The common danger they impress,
On ever proud Algonquin race;
United action they maintain.

TAI-GO-NE-GA.

A common foe, my brethren, calls us here;
A cause, to us — to you — to freedom dear.
Confederate foes provoke a groundless war;
Ye know them well, ambitious Iroquois.

With sway and vast dominion not content,
They would subdue and rule the continent.
If in a manly struggle we shall fall,
Triumphant foes will soon envelop all.
Your far-famed Teuchsa Grondie, in its turn,
Her people slaughtered, will in fury burn;
  A desolation wide be made:
For mother's, children's, people's, freedom's sake,
This purple belt, this bloody hatchet take:
  The gallant French will give us aid.

WA-BAS-SO.

My brothers; hated Iroquois
Would every cabin home destroy:
  His deep, revengeful, fiery hate,
  Towards our race, can n'er abate;
And I return, with firmest will,
Whatever hatred can distill.
  I hate him whereso-e'er I go;
  I long to deal the deadly blow.
The prisoner, too, shall suffer death,
  By fiercest tortures we can wage;
Oh, could we lengthen out his breath,
  And make him groan a dying age!
But this, with you, is not our end;
No hatred can a race defend:
  A firm alliance we bespeak;
  Strong arms and numbers here we seek.
  Take up the hatchet, let it tell;
  A foe shall die with every yell.

KAN-NE-TOW.

Yea, brothers, fathers! every throw
    Of tomahawk, in bloody strife,
Shall bring detested foemen low;
    We then will ply the scalping knife.
And when the victory is won,
    When beaten foe at last retires;
Upon the war-path we will run,
    And wrap his home in vengeful fires.

BOURDELAIS.

My friends and brothers dear; I would maintain
The peace of God throughout His wide domain.
Our calling this: To reconcile the world
To Him our sacred banner is unfurled;
But when shall come the fearful war-whoop yell,
As now dark rumors — indications tell,
We must declare for God and sacred right,
And them alone; yea, we must nobly fight.
The Briton is behind the Iroquois; —
The skeptic faith, in his relentless war; —
The foes, to Huron race and holy cross,
That should be purged away as useless dross.
Our cause is just. Nor can we fear alarm,
If once sustained by your avenging arm.
Take then the hatchet; let the war-whoop ring;
Your safety calls, and war is on the wing.

IX.

They cease: The hatchet, crimson red,
Is hurled upon the ground;
And smothered murmurs, deep and dread,
Would every foe confound.
But tho' each soul for vengeance cries,
Each face is calmly set;
And graceful clouds of smoke arise
From every calumet.
"Adjourn the council," loud proclaims
The fiery Ish-ko-dah;
"To-morrow each his answer frames,
For peace or furious war."
The great war eagle, bold keneú,
Is circling high in common view;
And Wa-won-ais-sa wild displays
A deep alarm in every gaze.

X.

Again the solemn council meet;
Again the embassy they greet.
Response is made in short addresses.
Each chief, in turn, his mind expresses.

MUS-KO-DA-SA.

Speak freely, but with calm debate;
Let prudence guide this act of state.
If cause exists we take the gage,
A fierce, relentless war to wage.

To me, no cause the hatchet craves,
Against Ho-dé-no-sau-nee braves;
Should war arise from mere dislike?
If we assail, they will return;
Perhaps our ancient village burn:
'Tis not at us they boldly strike.

KAH-GAH-GEE.

To help a friend is always well;
Nor should alliance be forgot,
Against the future — trying hour;
I bravely go if you compel,
But clearly think we better not
Upon us bring a dreaded power.

PEZ-HE-KEE.

Suppose the Huron nation fall,
And thus our war-path briefly end;
Who then shall here, among us all,
Our homes and families defend?

SHAU-GO-DAH.

I, I will do it; show me where
The foeman skulks, of any land;
And I his scalp will quickly tear,
Yea, dozens, with a single hand.

KO-KO-KO-HO.

Ko-ho! — before the war's begun,
The loudest, fiercest to exclaim,

Are oft the very first to run—
    Are often lost to every shame.

CHE-TO-WAIK.

We oft have heard of Iroquois;
    They n'er respect the sacred right;
The war-path bold they push afar;
    The flames and torture their delight.
Their rumored foray, far and wide,
    That soon will make the forest ring,
We too, alas, may here abide,
    Unless defiance now we fling.

KEN-NA-BECK.

Defiance, yes; nor longer stay;
Let every gallant Chippeway
    Assist the Huron, Ottawa,
    Against the grasping Iroquois.
Come, worthy braves of Wyandot;
Come fierce Miami; cast your lot,
    In this defensive preparation,
    To guard the kindred Huron nation.

SUB-BE-KAH.

Nor guard alone; if now awake,
We may a signal vengeance take
    Upon hereditary foe;
Suppose we have not felt his arm,
He now excites a just alarm;
    Strike, friends, or dread a deeper woe.

ISH-KO-DAH.

Like hungry wolves, to fierce devour,
I see that proud confederate power
Around our homes and nation lower;
A bold, a brave, but murd'rous band·
Then seize the hatchet, lying there;
Let war songs rend the frighted air;
Eternal friendship let us swear,
Against whoever dare withstand.

WA-BE-NO-KA.

Too young am I to raise my voice;
Too young opinions now to hold;
And yet I have a lively choice;
Impending danger I behold.
I long the war song loud to sing;
I long to yell the whoop of war;
I long the tomahawk to fling;
I long to scalp an Iroquois.

XI.

The sitting council, deeply stirred,
Is yet as calm as summer day;
Nor yet the firm response is heard,
Although each look forbids delay.
The belt old Mus-ko-da-sa takes;
He hangs it on the maple tree;
Suppressed applause the silence breaks;
The bond of friendship all can see.

He takes the hatchet, calm, severe;
    He hurls it in the upper air;
Auspicious omens quickly cheer,
    Keneú, observant, circles there.
The war-whoop rings in wildest yell;
    The village hears the deafening roar;
The forest echoes back the swell;
    Responsive sounds the distant shore.
The war-path shall its terror lend;
    The chiefs will soon obey the call;
But who shall cabin homes defend,
    When Iroquois upon them fall?

TEUCHSA GRONDIE.

CANTO XIX.

To Prof. JAMES R. BOISE, LL. D.,

Of the University of Chicago,

This Nineteenth Canto is respectfully inscribed, as a testimonial of the high esteem in which his many virtues as a man, his uprightness and earnestness of character, his varied and profound learning. and his devotion to his profession, are held by many, and, among others, by

HIS SINCERE FRIEND.

TEUCHSA GRONDIE.

CANTO XIX.

THE ILLINOIS.

A. D. 1649.

PREFATORY NOTE Ithacus, see book twenty-first of the Odyssey. Saw-saw-quan, a fierce and stirring war cry. O-nun-da-no-ga or O-nun-da-ga-o-no-ga, now Onondaga. The Se-pee Qua-to-gie, the river Huron. Chi-ga-gou, now Chicago, a meadow of leeks and wild onions. Ca-ne-ra-ghick, another name for the same place. Mis-chi-go-nong, another Indian name for Lake Michigan. Ill-i-nou-ack, another name for the same lake. Chic-ta-ghick was an Indian name for the Illinois nation, which was very powerful before and at the date of this Canto.

I.

DARK rumors of a coming war
Are rife in anxious cabin shades;
In frightful dreams, the Iroquois
Spring, yelling from their ambuscades.
How frail, as a protecting shield,
The hut a breath may sweep away,
Against the foes that terror wield —
That glory in the night foray!

How shall the mother, wife, pappoose,
Be guarded from the tomahawk,
When fiends their vengeance shall unloose,
And midnight horrors grimly walk?
Fear not; let wildest foe beset—
Inspire his every dread alarm,
A demon purpose to fulfill;
His every onset shall be met
By Wa-be-no-ka's manly arm,
When guided by his Whippoorwill.

II.

The friendly, firm alliance made,
Tai-go-ne-ga, in forest shade,
Is quickly lost to view;
He goes to meet the thunder crash,
That glooms above the Matchedash
Like angry Manitou.
The pressing danger still demands
The help of other warrior bands.
Far west, towards the evening beams,
Towards the happy land of dreams,
The Chic-ta-ghick—the Illinois,
Have felt the wrath of Iroquois.
The Mohawk, on the western plain,
His worthy foe has often slain;
And chieftains of the prairie wait,
In vengeance to retaliate.

The hunters of the buffalo,
In dangers manifold,
Can bend the strong, unerring bow,
Like Ithacus of old.
"The allied forces to augment,
Let embassy at once be sent,"
Wa-bas-so firm declares;
"Then in the fiery battle fray,
The four-fold cord shall win the day;
Then meet us he who dares."
"No time to lose," says Kan-ne-tow;
"I with Wa-bas-so freely go;
Come, worthy Che-to-waik:"
The three are soon upon the way;
And Jenocaire, without dismay,
The trip will undertake.

III.

The ancient path they rapid trace;
They thread the Se-pee Qua-to-gie:
The Kik-a-la-ma-zoo they pass,
The broad Mis-chi-go-nong they see.
They push along the sandy shore;
The crystal waves are at their feet,
With gentle, but a constant roar;
The water fowl their coming greet.
To left is an unbounded plain;
A waste of waters at the right;
Each, like the mighty ocean main:
The true sublime they both excite.

A meadow springs upon the view;
　　A sluggish stream the eye bespeaks;—
The place of onions—Chi-ga-gou,—
　　The Ca-ne-ra-ghick—place of leeks.
A bed of grass they soon prepare;
　　The sun displays his setting beams;
And soon, to drowsy Jenocaire,
　　The future springs in pleasant dreams.

CHI-GA-GOU.

DREAM OF JENOCAIRE.

1.

Beside the Ill-i-nou-ack main —
　　The river's gentle swell,
From lonely cabin on the plain,
The magic city springs amain,
　　Without a parallel.

2.

Within the space of fifty years—
　　The story seems a jest,
As growing greatness onward steers,
She proudly stands without compeers
　　In all the mighty West.

3.

Although in marshy prairie set,
　　Her dwellings firmly stand;
And lofty spire and minaret
Arise—a gorgeous coronet,
　　And blaze on every hand.

4.

The riches of the mighty West
Flow through her golden gate;
The East returns the rich bequest;
While spacious magazines attest,
That she is truly great.

5.

Her active people never tire,
They seem upon the run;
They risk, and lose, and then acquire;
Their swelling babel they admire;
They think it just begun.

6.

The Ill-i-nou-ack flood they draw,
Sweet fountains to create;—
The dreamer hears a whistling car;
He wakes—amid a gusty flaw:
The place is desolate.

IV.

The party leave the Chi-ga-gou;
Again their onward way pursue.
A narrow portage soon they pass,
Amid the wild and tangled grass.
The Illinois is at their feet,
Its gentle banks they rapid thread;
The gull and duck their coming greet;
No skulking foe is there to dread.
They note the vast—unbounded plain,
Fit emblem of the ocean main.

Itself an ocean; firmly set,
Before upheaved the mountains yet;—
Before, to sovereign fiat due,
The waters from the land withdrew.
And still its restless waves appear,
In rolling swell, to persevere;
As loth to leave chaotic state,
And reign of darkness abdicate.
The distant shores, to dazzled eye,
Beneath the rising sun,
Are mingled with the azure sky,
As if the two were one.
The glories of the setting day,
As on the ocean swell,
Upon enraptured vision play;
Enchanting is the spell.
Here bison, elk, and stag are found,
The hunter to inflame;
And birds of richest plumes abound;—
A paradise for game.
From soil, to swelling bounty wed,
Spontaneous verdure teems;
Wild flowers the richest fragrance shed,
As in the land of dreams.
The cabins on the grassy plain,
In graceful form arise;
A proof to frost and driving rain,
And of an ample size.
"Great God!" says pious Jenocaire,
"Oh, lend a listening ear!

Let this fair land thy blessing share;
Oh, plant thy standard here!"

V.

The manly, stately Chic-ta-ghick,
Magnanimous as nobly brave,
Despising forms of rhetoric,
A welcome to the stranger gave.
The embassy at once appear
Before the council of the state;
The chiefs and sachems calmly hear
The strong appeal, the fierce debate.
Brave Che-to-waik in one address,
The stern Wa-bas-so in another,
Maintain, with lofty manliness,
The sacred claims of friend and brother.
"The fierce, ambitious Iroquois —
The common foe of all our race,
Proclaim a war of deadly hate,
Assail the friends we dearly cherish;
Come, ever fearless Illinois,
A common cause let all embrace;
Come, join the chieftains of the strait,
Or one and all must quickly perish."

VI.

The Chic-ta-ghicks at once reply,
By worthy chief Ni-kan-no-kee;
The bloody hatchet flames on high,
As fiercely speaks Ki-san-ko-see.

NI-KAN-NO-KEE.

We hate him, for we know him well;
His war-path, here, has often led;
Here oft has rung his war-whoop yell;
And for the future still we dread.
Shall we his high permission ask,
To hunt the bison on the plain?
Na, na! at once throw off the mask;
Revenge the chieftains he has slain.

KI-SAN-KO-KEE.

Our brothers;—Huron, Ottawa;
And ye of Teuchsa Grondie fair;
We here defy the Iroquois;
We hurl the hatchet in the air.
He strikes at the Algonquin race;
He would usurp the mighty West;
The firm alliance we embrace;
His boasted empire we contest.
The gage of battle here we fling,
Against the proud confederate;
Of war-whoop shall the forest ring;
The torture glut our deepest hate.
To conquest, too, we shall aspire;
We stop not on the Matchedash;
O-nun-da-no-ga council fire
Shall hear the mighty thunder crash.

THE CALUMET DANCE.

The war declared, the wampum belt
An ever worthy present makes;
War's vengeful spirit wide is felt,
Earth with the yell of battle quakes.
And now, alliance to attest,
And compliment the stranger guest,
The dance, beneath the forest shade,
Shall lend its solemn masquerade.
Each chieftain bears a calumet:
To this, is hung the eagle's crest;
Of that, dark bruin's claws partake;
Here, pends the horn of buffalo:
To that, the jaw of wolf is set;
Here, graceful swings the hornet's nest;
There, gleams the skin of rattlesnake;
And here, the scalp of slaughtered foe.
Upon the central mat is placed
An image of the Manitou;
The calumet, with weapons graced,
Beside it stands in public view.
The singers mount the lofty stand;
The people, seated, all are mute;
Each chieftain takes the pipe in hand,
And all, the Manitou salute.
Now each, in turn, as music swells,
Fantastic whirls the giddy round;
In wild contortions each excels,
And wildest echoes fierce resound.

Ki-san-ko-see, in solemn mood,
Presents the trophy to the sun;—
The pledge of common brotherhood,
Then passes it to every one.
With hatchet now, Ni-kan-no-kee
The sacred calumet assails;
And yet, before Ki-san-ko-see
With calumet, the hatchet quails.
On high, the chief, the trophy raises;
Defiance hurls to every foe;
In loudest strain the victor praises,
Then hands the pipe to Kan-ne-tow.

THE BUFFALO HUNT.

The sun is set. The evening star,
Above, a blazing sapphire seems;
It smiles upon that land afar —
That happy home, the land of dreams.
'Tis morn: The sun is all aglow;
And far is heard, by wakeful men,
The bellow of the buffalo,
The cackle of the prairie hen.
A drove of bison on the plain
Is quickly seen by one and all;
And who can now the chase refrain?
Or who resist the leader's call?
To right, leads forth, Ni-kan-no-kee,
His file a lengthened circuit goes;
The like, to left, Ki-san-ko-see;
The herd of bison they inclose.

The sparks are flung to withered grass,
And soon in blazing circle flame;
One only space is left to pass,
And there the hunter waits the game.
Fierce yells around the circle rise,
And then begins the rapid race;
The buffalo in terror flies,
And wildly seeks the open space.
His bellow echoes through the air,
He tosses high his shaggy main;
Let none his savage fury dare;
He madly plunges o'er the plain.
They swiftly flee the burning grass;
They rush along the narrow pass;
And there, from cautious ambuscade,
A frightful havoc soon is made.
The arrow and the flying lance,
The glories of the chase enhance;
The tomahawk and scalping knife,
Are reeking from the bloody strife.

VII.

The prairie hunt its danger brings;
Despair may then avail;
The wounded bison terror flings,
To those who dare assail.
An arrow stings a tender part;
The brute, with rolling eyes,
And reckless from the fiery smart,
At hunter chieftain flies.

Fly, fly, for life! Ni-kan-no-kee;
Nor for a moment turn to see
The fury on thy track;
The hunter flies with lightning speed;
He quickly turns; ah, feat indeed;
He springs to bison's back.
The monster, reckless of his course,
In rage exhausts his mighty force;
The rider fiercely yells;
One hand is anchored in the hair,
The other swings the knife in air;
The deadly weapon tells.
In such exhaustive, rapid race,
When life is rushing out apace,
No contest can be long;
The bison sinks upon the plain,
Triumphant yells resound again:
The two shall live in song.

THE PRAIRIE DANCE.

The beeves a royal feast afford,
And all partake with one accord.
Around the luscious sagamite,
The chiefs their tales of war recite.
And while the necromancers joke,
And sachems gravely, wisely smoke,
And all is life and happy glee;
"Ho, for the dance, the prairie dance,
The great occasion to enhance:"
Aloud exclaims Ki-san-ko-see.

The valiant chiefs the movement lead;
The call unnumbered thousands heed.
They march upon the level plain;
Aloud resounds the wild refrain.
The evening sun pours back his fires;
And Saw-saw-quan, the step inspires.
With one consent, and to and fro,
Away the vast assembly go.
And up and down, and here and there,
With yell and shriek, they wildly tear.
The paint and plumage, blazing high,
Throw back the glories of the sky.
The echoes of the deafening roar,
Like billows on the distant shore,
Are heavy, solemn, dread;
Or like the mighty thunder crash,
When volleyed lightnings rend the ash,
And desolation spread.
To pious, thoughtful Jenocaire,
As fierce the action grew,
Legions of devils reveled there,
And hell had sprung to view.

VIII.

Again, the morning sun displays,
Renewal of his setting rays;
And loud declares brave Kan-ne-tow,
"Our country calls, and we must go."
"Adieu," exclaims Ki-san-ko-see;
"We follow," says Ni-kan-no-kee.

Of cheerful mien and lightsome heart,
The embassy at once depart.
They quick repass the mighty plain;
The Ill-i-nou-ack smiles again.
They pass the meadow, Chi-ga-gou;
The river Kik-a-la-ma-zoo.
They stop to spend a chilly night,
Where oaks and evergreens invite.
Without a fire, upon the ground,
They lonely sit; the shades around.

IX.

From first to last, in all the weary way,
Had Jenocaire endured contempt and jeer;
He now withdrew, in quiet shade to pray,
Where none but God could lend a list'ning ear.
As fervent spirit rose to throne of grace,
Insensibly the flying moments passed;
And deeper still the shadows grew apace,
Till one dark veil upon the land was cast.
He seeks the way, again, for safe return;
To walk he dare not and he tries to creep;
If loud he calls, the chiefs the call will spurn;
And yet he calls: The chiefs are fast asleep.
He wanders on; he wanders far astray;
No hope is left upon the desert plain;
He falls asleep; the spirit wings its way;
The worthy priest is never seen again.

Farewell, old friend: We leave thee with a sigh;
Thy faithful order shall thy fame prolong;
By thee, no place was shunned, in which to die;
Thy many signal virtues live in song.

TEUCHSA GRONDIE.

CANTO XX.

We-koon-de-win.

TO THE

TEACHERS

OF THE

PUBLIC SCHOOLS OF DETROIT:

This Twentieth Canto is respectfully inscribed, as a recognition and acknowledgment of most important public services, in building up and perfecting a system of free schools, which, with reference to its general organization, its many details and its economy, is believed not to be surpassed in excellence by the school system of any city on the continent.

TEUCHSA GRONDIE.

CANTO XX.

WE-KOON-DE-WIN.

A. D. 1649.

PREFATORY NOTE. The Indian word We-koon-de-win signified a fast, which lasted from five to ten days, and to which the young men subjected themselves, in search of their guardian genius for after life, before assuming the character and the duties of manhood. A portrayal is here attempted of some of the hallucinations and frightful visions of that terrible ordeal. Young Ta-to-kee seems to have had therein a presentiment of his early death, which took place soon after, as related in the twenty-second Canto.

I.

WITHOUT the pious Jenocaire,
The homeward way the party hold;
And soon, at Teuchsa Grondie fair,
The grand result is quickly told.
"How could the priest be led astray?"
Enquires the doubting Bourdelais,
Suspicious of a secret foe;

But fiercely rings the saw-saw-quan,
And loudly swells, from man to man —
  "Brave hunters of the buffalo!"
And Mus-ko-da-sa, Che-to-waik,
A solemn festival would make,
  To polish bright the friendly chain;
But brave Wa-bas-so, Kan-ne-tow,
To Matchedash at once must go,
  The first rude onset to sustain.
"Ho, follow soon," they loud exclaim;
"Ere long shall war-fires boldly flame
  Against the threatening Iroquois;
And with you bring that doughty foe,
That lays the mighty bison low —
  The prairie roaming Illinois."
Away, away: In bark canoe,
  They shoot across the sweeping tide;
They wave the hand — a kind adieu;
  The deadly issue they abide.

II.

In future years, behind the veil,
  That slow recedes as we advance,
What unknown sorrows may assail!
  What unknown destiny bechance!
The present time alone is ours;
  No future moment we command;
And yet the mind to hid-den powers
  Will fondly stretch imploring hand.

How oft, in life's uncertain way,
The merest luck or accident
Will turn our footsteps far astray,
Or lead them to a high ascent.
Upon a few, or good or vile,
A guardian angel seems to smile;
On others, demon spirits frown,
And dark misfortune drags them down.

III.

Young Wa-be-no-ka now aspires
To worthy manhood; to begin
Heroic life. Ambition fires
His soul to hold We-koon-de-win.
Nor would his friend, young Ta-to-kee,
That solemn rite — the fast evade;
Each would his guardian spirit see —
Invoke his talismanic aid.
Beside an ancient burial mound,
Within the sombre forest shade,
Where ghosts and flitting sprites abound,
Two little huts of bark are made.
And there, in torture, day and night,
The tenant, with his blackened face
Must firm deny his appetite,
And frightful visions calm embrace.
His flagging spirits to maintain,
The father, mother, often cheers,
Until the final point he gain —
Till happy augury appears.

To shrink unmanly from the rite —
    To falter in the trying hour,
Is burning — deep disgrace to slight,
    And bold defy the guardian power.

IV.

Eight days of hunger, firmly told,
To famished Ta-to-kee unfold
        His fetich token true;
And Wa-be-no-ka nine essays,
Before his vision clear displays
        The guardian Manitou.
The trial o'er, the food is lent,
To fevered, reeling abstinent;
        At first in slow degree;
Least quick reaction's rising swell,
In overwhelming madness tell
        Upon the devotee.
From day to day the strength returns,
While new-born fervor hotly burns;
        Escaped from youthful ban;
The many friends congratulate;
The boy is now the chieftain's mate;
        He feels himself a man.
Now stirring war-song he may sing;
Defiance to the foeman fling;
        In council hold the sway;
He now may challenge fiercest war;
Yea, now may fight the Iroquois,
        In battle's dread array.

V.

As calm descending summer sun
Behind the western main was lost;
And lovely evening shades begun —
Fair Teuchsa Grondie's constant boast;
The manly Wa-be-no-ka sat
With brother chieftain Ta-to-kee,
To have a pleasant social chat,
Beneath the charming maple tree.
The gentle river swept along;
Refreshing was the evening breeze;
Dame nature breathed in purest song:
A paradise must always please.
As often told by Jossakeed,
Above that river, fairy train
Had danced in airy, whirling speed,
With Michabou and chieftain slain.
And soon the conversation turns
Upon the dread We-koon-de-win;
When fancy, heated, fiercely burns,
And okies gibber, demons grin.

TA-TO-KEE.

The second day, the gnawing pain
Of hunger would a breach constrain;
And yet in silence, on the mat,
With firm resolve, I calmly sat.
In dreamy mood I lightly slept;
I saw a stone that slowly crept:

Nor genius that; nor would it stay;
Like stupid frog it crawled away.

WA-BE-NO-KA.

Beneath the third revolving sun,
My horrid visions thus begun:
A shell — a circle, green in hue,
Approached and passed my troubled view.
Was that my okie, patron, friend,
To guide and guard me to the end?
Na, na indeed! not for a feast
Would I accept the filthy beast.

TA-TO-KEE.

As grimly still I held the fast,
From stately elm that near me stood,
A leaf was torn by sweeping blast:
Was that the spirit I had wooed?
Believe it not: Although the leaf
In circles fluttered, in its grief;
And seemed to ask my leave to stay;
And oft aspired to win the sky,
As loth at last to fall and die;
It soon in silence passed away.

WA-BE-NO-KA.

I firmly sat, with fevered brain,
When thro' a narrow, shaded lane,
Appeared a walking beaver skin;

It lingered long within my view,
As if a conscious Manitou—
    As if my favor it would win.
In this might eager hunter trace
A lively image of the chase—
    The image of the art of war;
But I the tomahawk would fling,
Of war-whoop make the forest ring;
    Assail the hated Iroquois.

TA-TO-KEE.

As still my tutelary guide
    I eager sought, with many sighs,
Sir bruin, leaping in his pride,
    Before my troubled vision flies.
Of conscious might, he neither seeks
    The quarrel, or will quarrel shun;
"Let me alone," he calmly speaks,
    "I nor assail nor will I run."
Ah, is not this the guide I need?
    My guardian spirit do I see?
Na, na; the active life I lead;
    The war-path has a charm for me.

WA-BE-NO-KA.

Five lonely days their course had run,
    And biting hunger still inflamed;
The buffalo, with setting sun,
    A glorious augury proclaimed.

That fearful horn, that rolling eye,
 That shaggy mane, that monster breast;
That bellow, swelling to the sky;
 The guardian Manitou attest.
But shall I for my genius take
 The brute, so easy conquered, ever?
I would the mighty foeman break:
 Take such a guide! No, never, never.

TA-TO-KEE.

As thirst and hunger sore beset,
 And weary was the very life,
My heavy eyes in languor met
 The gleaming of a scalping knife.
It seemed to float upon the air,
And lightly, playful, circle there.
 Of blood it seemed to bear the stain;
 Yea, drops of blood it seemed to rain.
As I would strike the mortal blow,
And strip the scalp from mortal foe,
 Proud trophy of the battle fray;
I eager clutch the flaming brand;
It pierces deep my shrinking hand:
 Away, bad sprite, away, away!

WA-BE-NO-KA.

As sinks the day beneath the west,
 And wakeful eyes to darkness yield,
And jeebi train the gloom infest,
 My vision marks an ample shield.

A target of the bison's hide,
Its frowning locks a terror fling;
The tomahawk it turns aside,
Resists the war club's mighty swing.
A shield! An omen I behold:
Suppose a warrior party bold,
Assail our Teuchsa Grondie here;
Suppose relentless Iroquois
Surround us with the storm of war;
What then shall be my proper sphere?
Shall I a fierce defiance send?
The dear old cabin home defend?
And our loved village — famed and fair?
Defend the mothers? Whippoorwill?
And be to all a buckler still?
I will, I will; or perish there.

TA-TO-KEE.

The night is dark. The threatening sky
Bespeaks the gathering tempest nigh.
The sweeping blast — the whistling wind,
Awakes the phantoms of the mind.
The cuckoo tells of coming rain;
The ko-ko-ko-ho hoots again.
The howl of wolf, as from the tomb,
Is echoed through the forest gloom.
I gaze intent. A horrid sprite,
Springs, grinning, on my troubled sight.
It lightly skips from place to place;
It stops and chatters in my face.

It heaves a deep, sepulchral sound;
It dances on the burial mound.
    It is not Pauguk, yet it seems
    To beckon to the land of dreams.
    It nestles in my very cell:
    Avaunt! I cry; and break the spell.

WA-BE-NO-KA.

I, too, recall that fearful night,
The terrors of disordered sight;—
    A goblin world broke loose again,
    Grim spectres of a fevered brain;
The lightning's vivid, blinding flash;
That awful bolt the thunder crash!
    Such dreadful elemental war
    Is like the raid of Iroquois.
As downward drove the surging rain,
And rattling thunder pealed again,
    As if the final end were come;
Up sprung, upon my troubled view,
A demon host, a horrid crew;
    My every sense and power was dumb.
The withered arm, the stretching claw,
The bony chest, the haggard jaw;
    The glassy eye, the grinning teeth,
    Bespoke the messenger of death.
Beneath the dripping forest shade,
They dance a ghostly masquerade.
    Alternate flashes quick reveal
    The train that darkness would conceal.

They form like fiery squadron bold,
To dash upon my cabin hold —
Upon We-koon-de-win alone;
They come! They leave the storm behind;
I dash the cabin to the wind;
They vanish to a world unknown.

TA-TO-KEE.

The morning comes. The air is clear,
The forest smiles in brightest hue;
Oh, must I longer persevere!
When shall I see my Manitou!
I peer among the forest trees;
I catch the guardian spirit there;
I hear a voice upon the breeze —
A voice of grief and deep despair.
I see approach a shady form,
A muffled human form it seems;
It drips as from the drenching storm,
It sighs as from the land of dreams.
It quiet stops before my face;
It gazes on my humble bed;
Its darksome colors change apace,
To purple, then to brilliant red.
An upward course it now assumes;
The highest limb it seems to dare;
It now displays its gorgeous plumes;
The robin-redbreast warbles there.
Its ringing notes are loud and long;
They charm the cheerful morning hour;

The forest echoes back the song,
    In token of resistless power.

WA-BE-NO-KA.

That morning I remember well:
    The storm has cleared the murky air;
The rising beams in grandeur tell,
    And shed a flood of glory there.
Oh, would the genius now appear!
    This dismal fast and torture end!
Oh, spirit, lend a listening ear! —
    My guardian Manitou and friend!
I gaze into the azure sky;
    An airy figure slow descends;
It calmly, smiling, hovers nigh;
    A helping hand it gently lends.
We rise above the forest shade;
    No heavy weights to earth enchain;
Cerulean arch we soon invade;
    We walk upon a flowery plain.
There, sparkling waters ever flow;
    There, vale and forest charm the eye;
There, elk and bison tempt the bow;
    There, birds attune the vocal sky.
Below, we see the mighty lakes,
    The wigwam and the village fair;
Above, the sun his circuit makes;
    The constellations glitter there.
A lovely form beside me stands;
    She speaks — I feel a waking thrill;

My guardian angel soft commands;
I hear the voice of Whippoorwill.

VI.

While thus the lively conversation led
To scenes that held communion with the dead;
And dark unfolded human destiny,
And linked the life with long eternity;
The sun had sunk below the western plain:
The rising moon, with all her starry train,
Is glowing from the East. The silver stream
Reflects the glories of the heavenly beam.
The youthful chiefs betake themselves to rest
Upon the ground; no foemen now molest.
Each feels a guardian power, of special grace,
That time nor darkest woe can e'er efface:
Or in the chase or in the fiercest war,
It gleams in view, an ever radiant star.
Each feels the glow of patriotic flame;
But of his genius each conceals the name.

TEUCHSA GRONDIE.

CANTO XXI.

The War Party.

TO THE

RANK AND FILE

OF THE

VOLUNTEER SOLDIERY OF MICHIGAN;

AS WELL TO THOSE THAT SURVIVED,
AS TO THE MEMORY OF THOSE
THAT PERISHED:

Who, at the recent call to arms, rallied around the standard of the Union and of a common country; and who bravely and gallantly sustained the honor of the State and the glory of American arms in that great struggle, this Twenty-first Canto is respectfully inscribed by

THE AUTHOR.

TEUCHSA GRONDIE.

CANTO XXI.

THE WAR PARTY.

A. D. 1649.

CRITIQUE. Perhaps the reader has failed to notice the identity of the rhyming sylables in the following instances: procession — succession; repartee — felicity; along — prolong; hood — brotherhood; feat — defeat; still — distill; maintain — retain; hold — behold; preserve — deserve; main — amain; and perhaps other cases.

If the reader has not noticed these *quasi* rhymes, we may infer that they are less open to criticism than they might otherwise be regarded.

This species of rhyme is of frequent use in French poetry, and, while it is rare, it is indulged by the old masters in English composition. I should say that good taste required it to be seldom used, and it may be regarded as admissible when, and when only, the words that contain the rhyming sylables are not the same. Dryden makes done rhyme with undone, and abstinence with incontinence; and Pope makes ease rhyme with disease, and divide with provide. Other instances may be found. See, also, the second stanza of the twenty-seventh psalm, and the third and fourth stanzas of the one hundred and seventy-seventh hymn of the Book of Common Prayer.

I.

FROM love of power and thirst for gain,
In high contempt of righteous laws,
A nation, on its own domain,
May be assailed without a cause.

Again, a nation may assail,
    Against the wisest admonition;
Vengeance, in council, may prevail,
    And pride, and malice, and ambition.
But who unrighteous war shall wage—
    The mighty moral balance break,
Shall reap a fiery heritage,
    Shall dregs of bitter cup partake.
The stern despoiler may prolong
    Oppressive sway and haughty tongue
For generations; yet the wrong
    Shall leap again to whence it sprung.
The moral laws that bind the man,
    The nations hold; for human kind
Are ruled by universal plan,
    And nations are but men combined.

II.

In solemn council, on the green,
Beneath the tree, as we have seen,
    Old Mus-ko-da-sa, firm and bold,
    His honest mind had freely told.
In words of weighty argument,
His voice for peace was calmly lent;
    To him no cause was adequate;
But when the suffrage told for war,
He fierce denounced the Iroquois;
    A worthy pillar of the State.

At home or in the distant land,
As one would Teuchsa Grondie stand;
As one, respond to honor's call:
In council, every tongue was free;
In action, confraternity
Would triumph or with honor fall.

THE WAR FEAST.

The worthy Mus-ko-da-sa sends
His herald thro' the waiting town;
Each leader brave the call attends,
As of a chief of high renown.
And Ken-na-beck, and Ta-to-kee,
And Che-to-waik, and Kah-gah-gee,
And Wa-be-no-ka, all are there;
And Ko-ko-ko-ho, Sub-be-kah,
And loudly boasting Shau-go-dah,
And many more, the feast to share.
In war paint bright the cabin gleams,
And richest plumes the party grace;
With sagamite the kettle teems —
Of flesh of dogs — an honored race.
The guests are seated on the ground,
The central wigwam fire around;
And each the entertainment shares;
And each, with calumet in hand,
Resolves to march and bravely stand,
Wherever Mus-ko-da-sa dares.
They form the circle, man to man;
From mouth to mouth the pipe is passed;

Wild, fiercely, rings the saw-saw-quan;
For weal or woe the die is cast.

THE WAR DANCE.

As genial summer morn awakes,
For coming dance the chiefs prepare;
The war post, firm, a centre makes,
Beneath the maple on the square.
As gather round the shades of night,
The bonfire blazes on the green;
The cabin homes are seen afar:
The placid stream reflects the light;
The woods fling back a gorgeous scene;
The sparks bedim the evening star.
The night advances. Round the post
An ample ring the people form;
A mingled mass — a mighty host,
Dread tokens of a thunder storm.
Both sexes, every age, are there,
In gayest plumage of the chase;
In hideous paint, beyond compare,
A demon gleams in every face.
Aloud is heard the rustic drum,
And vocal music hoarse and deep;
The crowd respond in buzzing hum,
While feet and hands a cadence keep.
Excitement rises: Warlike yell,
Awakes the midnight's dreamy spell;
The heavy masses deeply tell
Of ocean swelling from afar:

A chieftain leaps within the ring;
'Tis Mus-ko-da-sa, leader, king;
He fiercely yells at every spring;
He chants the song of coming war.
Successive chiefs the dance supply;
The heavy war club swings on high;
The war knife flashes to the sky;
The tomahawk its terror lends:
Each brave recites his worthy deeds,
And long ancestral honors heeds;
In every whoop a foeman bleeds;
Around the post the war impends.
In every attitude of fight,
Each actor springs with all his might;
The yells alarm the wakeful night;
The painted chieftain frightful gleams:
Applauses echo far and wide;
Excitement swells from side to side;
Each vows the war-path to abide,
Tho' worthy blood a torrent streams.
They mingle now. They whirl and leap;
Mad voices wildest cadence keep;
Deep calls to loud responding deep;
Around the victim post they sweep;
And each a victory obtains:
Upon the square the thunders dwell,
And fiercer battle storm foretell;
The distant shore hurls back the swell;
The forest roars a funeral knell:
A universal frenzy reigns.

III.

While sinks the bonfire in decay,
Above, appears the milky-way:
The wakeful moon displays her horn;
And Teuchsa Grondie waits the morn.
Meanwhile the pensive Bourdelais,
Approaching contest to survey,
Retires to hut of Jenocaire,
To calm revolve the subject there.
Old Duroc sinks to heavy sleep;
The monk will still his vigil keep.
A torch affords a fitful light,
The chill, oppressive gloom despite.
The cross upon the rustic walls,
Bright visions of the faith recalls.
Deep slumber heathen world enchains,
The night in awful silence reigns.
"The one against the other play,"
Says calm reflecting Bourdelais;
"Perfidious Albion — heretic,
In wanting balance, soon will kick
The beam above. The Iroquois,
Is but a creature in the war;
And France, in brave Algonquin host,
Shall vindicate her lofty boast, —
That England and her buccaneer
Should fly the gallic chanticleer,
As wicked flee the wrath to come; —

That *fleur de lis* and holy cross,
Should purge the West of every dross,
  And firmly plant the faith of Rome."

IV.

The morning dawns. Upon the square
The smoking brands obscure the air;
  The war post tells a fearful strife;
Upon its front, and back, and head,
Are signs of raging battle dread,
  From tomahawk and scalping knife.
Above the curling watery-way
Light fogs their airy wings display;
  They bathe the morning's rising beams:
But as the heats of day arise,
They vanish to the upper skies,
  Or hie away to land of dreams.
Fair Teuchsa Grondie now awakes:
A hatchet Mus-ko-da-sa takes,
  Of bloody hue—the warrior's boast;—
Adorned with plumage—black and red,
It gleams around the chieftain's head;
  He strikes it fiercely in the post.
The sign that war is now begun,
  Is thus displayed to every eye;
And who its glory now will shun?
  Who fail the foeman to defy?
The chief in panoply of war—
  In paint and plumage, yells the call:

"Ho! for the hated Iroquois!
To bravely win or nobly fall."
The busy women food prepare,
Directed by the Whippoorwill—
The meat of elk, and wolf, and bear,
And roasted corn the pouch to fill.
And Mus-ko-da-sa loudly sings;
His war song rings upon the air;
Above, on wide expanded wings—
The great War Eagle circles there.
From chief to chief the fervor spreads,
And many, too, of lesser note;
The dance, in turn, each bravo leads;
The war-whoop bursts from every throat.
Again the yelling masses leap,
As on the fearful night before;
The rolling echoes hoarsely sweep
From forest to the distant shore.
"March, quickly march!" the chief exclaims,
And still he wildly, fiercely sings;—
"But hold—a guest the wood proclaims;
The war-whoop yell of stranger rings."

V.

All eyes are turned upon the west,
To ascertain the stranger guest;
And there is brave Ni-kan-no-kee;
With bison hunters on the trail,
Whose pealing yells the ear assail;
To rear, behold, Ki-san-ko-see.

A worthy host from distant plain,
The solemn treaty to maintain,
Come pouring forth the Illinois;
They draw the mighty western bow,
The tomahawk they distant throw,
They firm detest the Iroquois.
A long procession wend their way,
To meet the guests without delay,
And lead them to the public square;
The loud war-song again to sing,
And make surrounding forest ring,
At far-famed Teuchsa Grondie fair.
Nor were the Chic-to-ghicks alone:
In paint and plumage lofty shone
A worthy chieftain — Ni-ni-vay;
A fierce war party round him stand,
A wild, a crafty, vengeful band,
From brave Miamis, far away.
As western allies rapid strode,
Apast their river side abode,
The prairie song they loudly sung;
The listeners caught the genial flame,
As when the hunter snuffs the game;
The bloody hatchet fierce they flung.
" A welcome, all," says Che-to-waik;
" Come, and the war feast all partake;
And then we hurl the thunder crash;
The whispering birds already tell,
Of far resounding war-whoop yell,
Upon the distant Matchedash.

By Whippoorwill the feast is spread,
And soon the warrior guests are fed,
In gleaming paint a bright array;
Around the square the chieftains walk,
With bow, and knife, and tomahawk,
And all the pomp of war display.
Nor is the mighty western chief
Unmindful of the new belief,
And chapel built by Jenocaire;
They enter by the narrow way;
The chants are sung by Bourdelais;
Untutored red-men wildly stare.

VI.

"Ho! for the war-path!" loudly cries
Bold Mus-ko-da-sa, leader brave;
Responses echo to the skies,
And roll along the distant wave.
But first, auspicious Muse, declare,
What allied nations proudly share
The dangers of this gallant war,
Against the hated Iroquois.
In front appear the Chippeway,
Who chase and war-path oft essay,
From snowy clime of polar sea,
To southern land of Cherokee.
And next the roving Ottawa,
As fearless, as devoid of law —
A fragment of a mighty clan,
That oft has felt the heavy ban

Of Mohawk vengeance. From afar,
His kin shall join the mighty war;
To share its glory and its grief,
With leader brave, Wa-bas-so chief.
And in the dance, beneath the maple tree,
Is seen the crafty Pot-ta-wat-ta-mie.
One common danger he would bravely dare;
One common fate he too would nobly share.
Nor to the threatening danger now is blind,
The brave Mo-nom-o-nee. He's not behind.
Each worthy chieftain, in himself a host,
Bold strikes the hatchet in the warrior post.
To kindred, clan and nation ever true,
In horrid paint appears the Kickapoo.
The plain is his beside the Illinois;
A common foe, he hates the Iroquois.
Nor in the worthy list must be forgot
A Huron branch, the fearless Wyandot.
When anxious brother on the brother calls,
He flies and conquers, or he nobly falls.
Miami clan, in league confederate,
Already fill the ranks of stern debate.
O-nun-da-no-ga braves they loud defy,
For they have felt the stern oppressor nigh.
They fondly, too, a vast ambition cherish,
And every foe must die or they must perish.
Nor can defensive war their wrath control;
They mark the Mohawk Valley as the goal.
And last, the bison hunters of the plain,
Shall all the fiery storm of war maintain:

His mighty arm shall draw the stubborn bow;
With crushing weight the bloody hatchet throw.

VII.

Old Teuchsa Grondie by the river side,
Beholds the swelling pomp with honest pride.
Her cabin homes were built by kindred clans;
She ever spreads the mat for kindred bands.
Her worthy sons will join the stern array;
Will sweep in vengeance to the distant fray:
And she, in turn, may feel consuming war;
May reek, perhaps, with blood of Iroquois.

VIII.

The armor speaks of savage life:
The tomahawk, the scalping knife,
    The pebble with the ready sling;
Elastic spear of slender ash,
The war club of the stunning crash,
    The arrow with the feathered wing.
Defensive armor, too, is there:
The braided greave, the limb to spare;
    And breastplate, wove, the chief assumes;—
The horny shield from bison hide,
The helm that turns the blow aside;
    The panoply of shading plumes.

IX.

"Ho, for the war-path!" loud exclaims
    Brave Mus-ko-da-sa on the strand;

Responding saw-saw-quan inflames
    The ready — eager warrior band.
Of bark canoes, the little fleet,
    Is lightly dancing on the tide;
They all embark, nor dread defeat;
    The mighty onset they abide.
Away they move. The oars they ply;
    They gently cut the watery way:
Nor silent go: Exultant cry,
    The farewell sends till future day.
Nor this is all; for, clear and strong,
Now rings on high the parting song,
    As pass the fleet the river o'er;
Old Duroc's voice is heard again,
And Whippoorwill, in lofty strain;
    The chorus peals from shore to shore.

THE PARTING WAR SONG.

1.

Away, ye brave! To land afar,
    Ye boldly march — to wild foray;
Against the hated Iroquois,
Ye bear the storm of fiery war:
    Then boldly strike; away, away!

CHORUS.

Ye boldly march — to wild foray;
Strike, boldly strike; away, away!

2.

The war-path through the forest lies,
    And ever watchful is the foe;

Beware the crafty, skulking guise:
A prowling wolf — entrap the prize;
    And hurl the unexpected blow.

CHORUS.

Tho' ever watchful be the foe;
Yet hurl the unexpected blow.

3.

Let deadly arrows eager sing,
    Let war-whoop thunder on the plain;
The bloody hatchet bravely fling;
Let shrieks of slaughter fiercely ring;
    Tear reeking scalp from warrior slain.

CHORUS.

Let war-whoop thunder on the plain;
Tear reeking scalp from warrior slain.

4.

And if upon the bloody field,
    Where Pauguk in his terror gleams,
The foe shall to your prowess yield;
The fiery tortures grimly wield,
    And send him to the land of dreams.

CHORUS.

Where Pauguk in his terror gleams,
There send them to the land of dreams.

5.

And when from sweeping hurricane,
    Ye soon repass this noble river,
Full welcome from the battle plain;
The war song shall resound again:
    Hail, Teuchsa Grondie, now and ever!

CHORUS.

Ye soon repass this noble river;
Hail, Teuchsa Grondie! Hail forever!

X.

As disappears from view the proud display,
The neophytes, with thankful Bourdelais,
In long procession to the chapel wend,
Before the holy altar there to bend.
They chant, in solemn tone, the Te Deum,
And swell the lofty strain with Christendom.
And Teuchsa Grondie waits with ear intent,
For whispering birds to tell the great event.

TEUCHSA GRONDIE.

CANTO XXII.

Battle of the Wilderness.

To U. S. GRANT,

PRESIDENT OF THE UNITED STATES:

Under whose direction, as Lieutenant-General of the Union Armies, those vast and comprehensive military plans for the overthrow of the Southern Confederacy were matured, and by whose skill, vigor and good fortune their success was realized, and the union of the States was fully restored, this Twenty-second Canto, the title of which recalls the celebrated Battle of the Wilderness in 1864, is respectfully inscribed by

THE AUTHOR.

TEUCHSA GRONDIE.

CANTO XXII.

BATTLE OF THE WILDERNESS.

A. D. 1649.

PREFATORY NOTE. The Long House signified the country or general territory of the Iroquois; of which the Mohawks guarded the eastern and the Senecas the western end. Among the Indians, prisoners of war, if such they might be called, were often adopted into the nation and families of the victors, upon abjuring their own name, kindred and nation. Firearms are supposed to have been first used against the Indians of the West by the Iroquois, in the war with the Hurons, in 1649.

I.

BENEATH the summer's rising sun,
The march of war is now begun.
Young Wa-be-no-ka, gallant still,
Throws back a kiss to Whippoorwill.
The march is up the river side,
In view of gently sweeping tide.

To left, the Mah-nah-be-zee smiles —
The naiad queen of western isles:
To right, a heavy forest shade,
That well might screen an ambuscade.
The single files, with rapid pace,
The narrow way in silence trace.
That silence of itself foretells,
By speech in most impressive form,
The near approach of maddening yells —
The dread impending thunder storm.
They onward press. The grassy plain,
Along the Ot-si Ke-ta strand,
To bison hunter tells again,
Of happy home in prairie land.
They pass the Nah-ma, honored stream;
The spot where young Tai-go-ne-ga
The Mohawk slew in vengeful chase;
And where the dark prophetic dream,
Like gloomy shadow from afar,
Revealed the future of his race.
Now deeper in the forest shade,
The ancient winding trail is made.
No voice the dismal silence breaks;
No trumpet clang the echo wakes.
No pioneer explores the way;
No watch is set by night or day,
Of stealthy foe to give alarm;
The savage, on his high emprise,
Upon his Manitou relies,
Unworthy foeman to disarm.

II.

As vagrant rays of morning beam
Thro' shady foliage dimly gleam,
Afar is heard a savage yell;
The forest echoes with the swell.
And soon athwart a bushy screen,
A chief in paint and blood is seen:
He swiftly comes, like bounding roe;
Thrice welcome noble Kan-ne-tow!
In hurried breath he soon relates
The work of all involving fates.
"The Iroquois, with mighty crash,
Have burst upon the Matchedash.
The flames — the slaughter, far and wide,
Have swept — an overwhelming tide.
The allied party soon will meet,
The victor foe in full retreat; —
With trophy scalps and spoils of war,
And prisoner chief — Tai-go-ne-ga; —
Wa-bas-so, too, and aged sires,
For grim O-nun-da-no-ga fires."
"We gladly meet him, now and here,"
Says Mus-ko-da-sa with a cheer;
"The victor shall his trophies yield;
His path we cross in firm array,
We strike in fiercest battle fray;
We perish or we win the field."

III.

The braves and chieftains on the spot,
Resolve to share the leader's lot.

At once is preparation made,
To form the crafty ambuscade.
Behind the tree, the rolling ground,
The log, the bush, is shelter found.
In front, no sign of stealthy lair;
To rear — the war is crouching there.
A silence now pervades the gloom,
Like awful stillness of the tomb.
Each throbbing breast, without control,
Betrays the palpitating soul.
Each eye is peering for the foe;
Each hand is on the ready bow;
Each throat awaits, the yell to ring;
Each nerve is ready for the spring.
The ear is bent, as if afar,
To catch a tread of wary scout;
Or murmur of approaching war,
Or victor foeman's pealing shout.
Like waves upon the rocky shore,
Like O-ni-ag-raah's dreadful roar,
Like alpine swell of distant horn;
Like rolling thunder of the lakes,
The storm of coming war awakes
The frighted echoes of the morn.
And nearer still the frantic yell,
And gathering clamor, loudly swell;
The forest lends a vocal strain;
While Teuchsa Grondie crouching lies,
To sudden leap, in dread surprise,
And spring upon the foe amain.

IV.

A torrent down a narrow way;
An ocean sweeping to the Bay;
So thro' the heavy, gloomy wood,
Comes pouring on the mighty flood.
The trophy scalps upon the bow,
The reeking plunder of the slain,
Of war-path tell; and grimly show,
The harvest of the hurricane.
The stricken warrior, bleeding, too, is there,
The sorrows of the weary march to share;
His ghastly eye in fury gleams;
Perhaps the Pauguk seals his earthly fate,
While yet he lingers at the narrow gate,
That leads to future land of dreams.
Nor are the dead abandoned to the foe;
The savage brave would sepulture bestow;
The bloody corse he carries far;
For kindred spirits wait the funeral rite,
Before they go, on that eternal flight,
To home beneath the evening star.
The captive warrior chief, in triumph led,
Sad victim for the sacrifice;
With horrid cut and bruise from victor dread,
Allows no sigh or moan to rise.
Ah, how the brave Wa-bas-so proudly leads!
As conscious of a life of worthy deeds!
He sees the worst, he braves the goal:

And how the firm, erect, Tai-go-ne-ga,
Sustains the adverse fortunes of the war,
    While deepest anguish wrings the soul!
Shall they the cruel gauntlet undergo?
The blows and gashes of exultant foe?
    O-nun-da-no-ga vengeance feel?
Shall they the fiery torture soon endure,
Or nation, kindred, name—their all, abjure?
    Never; burst forth the thunder peal!

V.

The yell of Mus-ko-da-sa loudly rings;
On high the shady plume he boldly flings;
To mortal strife each ready chieftain springs,
    From lowly crouching ambuscade:
Ho-dé-no-sau-nee whoop for instant war;
For when or where did haughty Iroquois,
A battle shun with e'en the Illinois?
    What danger did he e'er evade?
At once, on every hand, the forest teems
With war's magnificence. The battle seems
A demon world let loose. With frantic screams,
    Each foe upon his foeman bounds:
The whizzing arrow from the bow is sent;
The tomahawk is hurled with dire event;
The scalping knives triumphal woes augment;
    The swinging war-club loud resounds.
And while by Chic-ta-ghick the heavy bow,
That lays the monarch of the prairie low,

Is twanged incessant at undaunted foe;
And noble warriors rapid fall;
A flash is seen; a thunder dread, awakes;
The singing bullet frightful havoc makes;
The sturdy western brave in terror quakes;
Such power unknown may well appall.

VI.

Auspicious Muse! On that eventful day,
When race met race, in sternest battle fray;
Whose bloody story fame shall widely tell—
Say, who survived; who nobly fought and fell?
Ah! first and foremost of Algonquin band,
Was doomed to perish by a friendly hand.
The brave Wa-bas-so, captive, while we see,
He falls by random shot from Ta-to-kee.
We now have told his story, from afar,
Since first he traced the rapid Ottawa,
And trod, alone, the winding, dangerous way,
To strike, and save a friend, at Thunder Bay.
We bid you, worthy chief, a kind farewell;
A hardy race ye now have run;
If song can swell it, your renown shall swell,
From rising to the setting sun.

VII.

As adverse battle storm in fury blends,
Tai-go-ne-ga springs joyful to his friends;
And back he hurls his ever mighty blows,
With shout on shout, to late exultant foes.

But, ah! again; how shall the pen relate,
The woes on woes of unrelenting fate!
As Mus-ko-da-sa, terror in his eyes,
In panoply of war to slaughter flies;
And scatters far and wide the hostile bands,
They quick surround; he falls into their hands.
A worthy partner, too, Ni-kan-no-kee;
O-nun-da-no-ga tortures both shall see.
In turn, five warrior braves, a fate the same,
On Teuchsa Grondie square shall feed the flame.
To hide the sight — let kindly curtain fall;
The bare recitals — deep the soul appall.
To calmly tell — recoils the frighted pen;
Dread scenes, that blot the very name of men!
In future years, in vengeance shall be told,
The fierce retaliations manifold;
Till then, in order due, we onward press,
And still recount a day of wretchedness.

VIII.

No rest or slack the eager furies know:
A brave Oneida springs for Kan-ne-tow,
As tiger springs. They grapple. On the ground
They fall, and yell and strike and fiercely wound:
Yet both, exhausted, yield the fearful strife;
Nor this nor that can boast except his life.
A nimble Seneca, from tree to tree,
Deals fatal blows to youthful Ta-to-kee.
The brave Cayuga makes the forest ring,
And carries death upon a rapid wing.

Wher-e'er he goes he clears a dreadful way;
Beneath him falls the lofty Ni-ni-vay.
Nor falters now the boaster Shau-go-dah;
His blows resound, with those of Sub-be-kah.
As from the Mohawk's thunder many flee,
The fatal bullet reaches Kah-gah-gee.
Nor idle looker on is Che-to-waik;
His ringing war-cry makes the battle quake:
And here and there from death to death he goes,
While Ko-ko-ko-ho seconds well his blows.
Oh chant, ye Chic-ta-ghicks, your jubilee!
For wide the havoc of Ki-san-ko-see.
His mighty bow like singing bullet tells,
And brave on brave the death-cry loudly yells.
Ah, where each warrior is himself a host,
A thousand braves can make the field a boast.
And while the battle stern the West maintains,
Immortal fame O-nun-da-no-ga gains.

IX.

Yet high above the rest in terror gleamed
Young Wa-be-no-ka. Wildest fury beamed
From every feature. Others nobly fought
For power and glory: He for vengeance sought.
As blow and clang and shout the battle fill,
He n'er forgets his little Whippoorwill.
"Perhaps," he says, "beneath the maple tree,
She waiting sits, her worthy chief to see:
And soon the singing birds to her shall tell,
That I was victor, or I nobly fell.

Nor I for love alone the war maintain;
My brother chief, dear Ta-to-kee is slain.
How were our lives in equal tenor cast!
Ah, how we long endured the horrid fast!
But oh, my father! Taken, led away,
To swell the horrors of a festal day!
The gauntlet, torture, fierce consuming fire!
Great Michabou! My soul to blood inspire."
He thus, in fury, to the battle springs;
And louder still the mighty war-whoop rings.
Tho' bullets, hatchets, arrows round him fly;
He is not fated now and here to die.
Fair Teuchsa Grondie shall his arm demand
In future day, and he a bulwark stand.
His swinging war-club every foe appalls,
And who but meets him, on the instant falls.
O-nun-da-no-ga feels the trying hour;
Ho-dé-no-sau-nee trembles for her power.
The bravest chiefs, with terror-stricken cry,
To face him shrink, and quickly turn and fly.
And still he strides, among the heaps of slain,
Like fierce Achilles on the Trojan plain.

X.

But which, in all this galaxy of fame —
This war of races, might the vict'ry claim?
A havoc of the two was made:
The fight was worthy; from the Illinois,
Thro' every clan, to dreaded Iroquois:
Success was in the ambuscade.

Retreating victor band, in all their might,
Are cut in pieces, routed, put to flight;
    Their Huron spoils and trophies lost:
And yet the homes of all the mighty West
Shall deeply mourn, and everywhere attest
    The victory an empty boast.

XI.

And now, upon the field the shades of night
Are gathering fast; the sun abhors the sight;
    The distant war-whoop dies away:
The victor sleeps upon the battle plain,
And many there shall n'er awake again:
    The flapping vulture snuffs the prey.

XII.

The morning dawns. The distant yell
Disturbs the solemn, mournful spell;
    And yet the foe is well content,
    To rest the fearful argument.
His routed forces gather far,
    And each for home in sorrow tends;
They pass the O-ni-ag-a-raah;
    The Long House now a welcome lends.

XIII.

"For home, for home!" says Che-to-waik;
"The honored slain, the wounded take.
    The dead shall rest in hallowed ground,
    Beneath the lofty burial mound.

Upon the mighty festal day,
    Their acts may furnish worthy themes;
Their spirits rise from battle fray,
    And wander to the land of dreams."
With rising of the morning sun,
The silent march is now begun.
    The bearers of the dead precede;
    The wounded, then, the party lead.
The captives, next, the march sustain—
A bounden, melancholy train:
    To fiery sacrifice they go—
    To torture and the deepest woe.

XIV.

The march is weary. Day by day,
The long procession wend their way.
    At length the Ot-si Ke-ta gleams,
    Beneath the sun's retiring beams.
They pass extended grassy plain;
The Mah-nah-be-zee smiles again.
    The village home is full in view;
    Fair Teuchsa Grondie charms anew.

XV.

The singing birds, on joyful, swiftest wing,
Have told the story—warbled everything;
And eager crowds, upon the village strand,
In wildest shout receive the victor band.
The pious Bourdelais to chapel goes,
And there devoutest thankfulness bestows.

"Proud Albion, with the haughty Iroquois,
Are routed," he exclaims, "in holy war:
We next will sweep them from the continent;
To swift destruction may they all be sent."
The trophy scalps, beside the braided corn
And venison dried, the cabin home adorn.
Old Duroc, Whippoorwill, exulting sing,
And make the square and vocal forest ring.
And yet for kindred slain, in deepest tone,
Is heard from stricken hearts the heavy moan.
In thunder shouts the allies bid adieu;
And Teuchsa Grondie trusts her Manitou.

TEUCHSA GRONDIE.

CANTO XXIII.

To JANETTE M. MILLARD,

MY COMPANION AND BELOVED WIFE:

Whose anxious solicitude, in the progress of this work, with reference to its character and success, has been equaled only by my own; to whose kindness, affection, constancy and many other virtues, I wish to bear testimony; and to whose name and character I desire to present a memorial, which shall remain as long as a recollection of my own labors may survive, this Twenty-third Canto is affectionately inscribed by

LEVI BISHOP.

TEUCHSA GRONDIE.

CANTO XXIII.

WHIPPOORWILL.

A. D. 1655.

PREFATORY NOTE. Manitoulin is a large Island in the northern part of Lake Huron. Monedo, a nymph; (see Canto VI). Mish-e-mo-ka, or Mish-e-mok-wa, the Great Bear. O-pe-chee, the robin. Ga-ne-e-ar-teh-go-wa, the totemic clan of the Turtle. Os-we-ga-da-ga-ha, the totemic clan of the Hawk. By the totemic order or system of descent, names, honors and property went through the female line instead of the male.

It will be noticed that there is some confusion in recounting the totemic relations of Wa-be-no-ka and Whippoorwill; and the paternal ancestors of the latter are nearly all omitted. This is designed as an intimation of the irregularities of that system among the Algonquin tribes.

Courtship and marriage are intended to be presented in this Canto, as the customs of the Indians may be supposed to have been already modified, in this respect, by the teachings of the French missionaries.

The martyr Lallamant, when he was suffering the tortures of death, exclaimed to Brébeuf, who was passing through the like tortures: ' We are this day made a witness to the world, to angels and to men."

I.

THE bloody harvest of the brave,
The pangs that wring the desolate,
The flashes of malignant star;
The wealth that sinks beneath the wave;
Are but a partial estimate
Of evils of consuming war.
The cannon's roar may die away,
The wounded may forget their pains,
The widows, orphans, dry their tears;
And yet a frightful disarray,
In moral — social life remains,
A blot upon succeeding years.
The wastefulness of public store,
The recklessness of human life,
The rule that right is only might;
Like waves, prolonged, upon the shore,
When calm succeeds the raging strife,
Will still display a fearful blight.
Nor this is all: A giddy throng,
That prey upon the public need,
That flaunt the wages of their shame;—
The gangrene of the war prolong;
A vulgar taste for glitter feed;
A thirst for empty show inflame.
'Tis all the same in savage life:
When war has spent its light'ning flash,
And sacrifices mad the brain;

The youth are oft in bloody strife;
In paint and plumage maidens dash;
The loosest morals deeply stain.
Nor could the village of the strait
Escape the scourge. The hut and square
Were rife with rollic and display;
And leer and smile to captivate;
For months the social curse was there,
Till settled life resumed the sway.

II.

Now Wa-be-no-ka was a man,
The ruling genius of the town;
A leader sachem of his clan,
A victor chief of high renown.
With earnest heart he sought a wife,
To soothe, sustain, in every ill;
And in the bloom of maiden life,
Was now the younger Whippoorwill.
Of graceful medium was her size,
And long and dark her floating hair;
And deep and thoughtful were her eyes;
A noble spirit harbored there.
Her braided frock is light and neat,
The raven's plumes her head adorn;
Bright moccasins inclose her feet;
Her look, her mien — the smiling morn.
As forth she walks upon the square,
With dignity, sedate and slow;

A throng the admiration share,
    And say, "Behold the Monedo."
And like her long ancestral race,
    She too, in richest notes can sing;
Her thrilling strains the cabin grace,
    And make the vocal forest ring.

III.

And Wa-be-no-ka loved the maid,
    And Whippoorwill his love returned;
Nor she a vain coquetry played,
    Nor he the artless lover spurned.
Since first, a Kik-a-la-ma-zoo,
    She saw the day, is winter life,
He kept the blooming child in view,
    At last to take her as his wife.
As love is wont, the lovers oft,
    Beneath the maple on the square,
The evening spent; and language soft
    Was breathed in pure affection there.
Her hand he places in his own;
    Upon her brow he plants a kiss;
They read from nature's book alone,
    And neither act nor think amiss.
Of course the moon is smiling then,
    With laughter-loving, starry train;
They joyful see, to mortal men,
    Another Eden come again.

IV.

The mother, from the cabin shade,
Discreet, her observations made;
She calm beholds the scenes of love,
And she and sachems all approve.
For nuptial feast, upon the square,
The joyful lovers now prepare;
And young and old with lightsome heart,
In preparations take a part.
And soon upon the lawn is seen
The graceful bower of evergreen,
And arching limbs of oak and ash:
The feast is ample; game and fish,
And herb and fruit; and dainty dish
Of Indian lineage — succotash.
No form, as one, the couple makes;
Each one the other simply takes;
Free as the will the nuptial bonds:
Yet Bourdelais cannot refrain,
To solemn bless the happy twain;
"Amen," old Duroc calm responds.

V.

The guests are seated; appetite
Is satisfied; amid acclaim,
The bridegroom rises to recite
Ancestral line and deeds of fame.
Imposing, stately, is his form,
His placid smiles the timid gain;

And yet, like raging thunder storm,
He rages, on the battle plain.

WA-BE-NO-KA.

I boast a long, illustrious line;—
Ah! Mus-ko-da-sa was my sire;—
Where highest honors well combine
A lofty spirit to inspire.
My mother was the O-pe-chee,
To Po-ne-mah she early flew;
My grandam—stately O-me-nee;
My grandsire Mish-e-mo-ka slew.
His father brave, was Un-ta-go,
Of Ga-ne-e-ar-teh-go-wa;
He dashed the bison at a blow,
He slew a lurking Iroquois.
His wife—we trace the totem still,
And tho' obscure, the line prolong—
Was mother of the Whippoorwill,
Who sung at night the "Cabin Song."
And this my proud ancestral fame,
That I, in time, will vindicate;
And venge a father's honored name,
And soothe a never-dying hate.

VI.

The chief is silent. Shouts resound,
From forest o'er the gentle tide;
He takes his seat upon the ground,
Beside the blushing, charming bride.

The mother — Wa-won-ais-sa, too,
In cheerful musing seemed to say; —
The worthy should the worthy woo,
And triumph in the nuptial day.
But who shall speak for Whippoorwill,
And to the chief an answer make?
The anxious mother, silent still,
Inviting, nods to Che-to-waik.

CHE-TO-WAIK.

Of clan — the Os-we-ga-da-ga,
The mother and the bride from far
Their lineage hold — the race prolong,
Of her that sung the "Cabin Song."
The second, was the modest wife
Of Kit-ta-coin-si, who, for life,
Sir Bruin fought, upon the tree,
In games of autumn jubilee.
The third, revealed, in time of need,
The bloody scheme of Jossakeed;
When hardy monk, in ghostly plight,
The band of chieftains put to flight.
The fourth, the friendly warning gave,
Le Vareau and his crew to save; —
The Mohawk's treachery foresaw,
Upon the stormy Equabaw.
The fifth, the stirring chorus led,
In funeral dirge, of worthy themes,
At festival of honored dead,
To waft their souls to land of dreams.

The last — the present lovely maid,
    Her birth, and early hardship knew.
In winter hut, in snowy glade,
    Beside the Kik-a-la-ma-zoo.
The virtues of a lengthened line,
In this fair maiden all combine:
    And such a charming girl, in brief,
    Is worthy bride for such a chief.

VII.

The speaker sits, in lofty pride;
The shouts re-echo far and wide;
    And all, in merry-making still,
    Demand the song of Whippoorwill.
The maiden rises at the call,
To grace the happy festival.
    The mother joins the sweet refrain,
    And Duroc tunes his voice again.

THE BRIDAL SONG.

1.

How charming is the bridal day!
    What more can mortal crave?
Then golden visions round us play;
And mind and heart are borne away,
    Upon the swelling wave.

2.

The many friends around us press,
    With mingled hopes and fears;
Their wishes tell of happiness;
And sympathizing natures bless
    The mother's kindly tears.

3.

But who shall draw the veil aside
That hides the future life?
What happiness may there abide:
What blasted hopes may swell the tide;
What never-ending strife!

4.

Enough, enough! the thought refrain:
Far better not to know:
For who could present life sustain,
If pregnant future hurled amain,
Anticipated woe!

5.

Oh, then, improve the passing hour,
Forgetting care and sorrow;
The future leave to heavenly power;
Nor mar the happy bridal hour,
With evils of the morrow.

VIII.

She sits again — the charming bride,
Her Wa-be-no-ka by her side;
Each with the other well content;
The host a deep emotion share,
And shouts, redoubled, rend the air,
To celebrate the great event.
And Duroc feels his youth return,
A pure affection calmly burn;
His pet had been the Whippoorwill:
He fondly knew her tender years;
Inspired her hopes and dried her tears,
And like a father loved her still.

IX.

And now arises Che-to-waik,
As if by inspiration;
A speech of courtesy to make,
Towards a ruined nation.
The worthy chieftain Kan-ne-tow,
From Manitoulin far,
Is present, due respect to show,
With brave Tai-go-ne-ga.
The two a friendship strong attest,
No time nor place can sever;
For this dear village, ever blest,
Beside the noble river.
Says Che-to-waik: "My brothers dear,
That wander far and wide,
Thrice welcome to our festal cheer;
As honored guests abide.
And now we pray you to relate,
The mighty thunder crash,
That sealed the Huron Nation's fate,
Upon the Matchedash.
We met retreating victor foe,
And rung his dreadful knell;
But tell us of the crushing blow,
That on the Huron fell.
The story, fame has often told,
Like echoes on the air;
But ye can all the truth unfold,
For ye were bravely there."

X.

And now, amid enthusiastic cries,
The honored guests with modesty arise:
They calm proceed the wild foray to tell;
The eager throng upon the story dwell.

KAN-NE-TOW.

The day is clear: The priest his mass recites,
Before his altar, with his neophytes.
The loosely set, unguarded palisade,
Is nothing worth; no preparation made.
And while the crafty foe we know so well;
His onset know; have often heard his yell;
Upon the trail, are many chiefs away,
Or on the war-path, skulking for the prey.

TAI-GO-NE-GA.

Unconscious of the tiger in his lair,
The women, children, feeble age, are there;
When lo! a demon legion, from the shade
Of frighted forest, gleam in masquerade!
In plume, and horrid paint, and pomp of war,
On rush the vengeance-seeking Iroquois.
The war-whoop yells in pealing thunder ring;
Swift doom awaits, and death is on the wing.

KAN-NE-TOW.

The palisades are forced. The mighty flood
Upon us rushes. Cabins float in blood.

Incarnate devils o'er the fall-en stalk,
With scalping knife and reeking tomahawk.

TAI-GO-NE-GA.

Think ye that we without a struggle yield?
Ah, when did Huron brave disgrace a field?
We boldly hurl redoubled blow for blow;
For each that falls, there falls a worthy foe.
Yea, two or three for one our prowess feel;
We grapple hand to hand with hooks of steel.
The foe, for conquest fights — for lofty fame;
But we, for home — for nation — very name;
And he that strikes for home, against alarm,
Shall feel a thousand forces nerve his arm.
But, ah! the sickening scenes that deep appall,
When children, feeble age, and women fall.
When these lie gasping 'neath the scalping knife,
What virtues can redeem the horrid strife!

KAN-NE-TOW.

The torch applied, devouring flames arise;
The shrieks of burning victims rend the skies.
The foeman shout is swelled to deafening roar,
As happy cabin sinks to rise no more.
The mother flees with helpless infant form
To forest shade, for shelter from the storm;
And yet the infant's cry, in plaintive air,
Attracts the bloody tiger quickly there:
Upon the spot the hapless two must perish;
No melting hearts Ho-dé-no-sau-nee cherish.

The missionaries — Daniel, Lallemand,
Brébeuf and Garnier — all, heroic stand:
The crown of glory lends its heavenly cheer;
The martyr's horrid death they never fear.
Beneath the knife, the torture and the fire,
The cross is theirs. Triumphant they expire!
Ah! what a spectacle is there and then
Displayed, "to world, to angels and to men."

BOURDELAIS.

In every land, by every Christian tongue,
From sea to sea, from shore to shore,
Their martyr deaths heroic, shall be sung,
Till time itself shall be no more.

KAN-NE-TOW.

The worst is ours. We suffer a defeat;
And yet the bloody foe must fain retreat.
Ye met him, on the way, in ambuscade,
And of the victor soon the vanquished made.

TAI-GO-NE-GA.

Our case is pitiful. The Huron Nation,
Once proud and strong is now a desolation.
And yet, amid our overwhelming woes,
To Iroquois we rest eternal foes.
The forest often rings with Huron yells,
As on the war-path swiftest vengeance tells.
We hapless wander, exiles, far and near;
And, wand'ring thus, we find a welcome here.

XI.

As thus the chieftains told their story,
Of sorrow, but of forest glory;
　　A sympathetic current strong,
　　The earnest listeners bore along.
And now, involuntary tear,
Upon the cheek would domineer;
　　And then again the wildest yell,
　　Is heard in long resounding swell.

XII.

The sun has sunk beneath the West ;
　　The mat and cabin call away;
And Teuchsa Grondie takes to rest,
　　To dream upon the festal day.

TEUCHSA GRONDIE.

CANTO XXIV.

To Hon. LEWIS H. MORGAN,

The Learned Historian of the Iroquois:

To whose suggestions and friendly criticisms I have been much indebted in the course of this work, and from whose historical writings I have drawn much valuable knowledge, and much graphic portraiture of Indian life and character, this Twenty-fourth Canto is very respectfully dedicated by

THE AUTHOR.

TEUCHSA GRONDIE.

CANTO XXIV.

THE SPY.

A. D. 1660.

PREFATORY NOTE. Wa-we-aw-to-nong, was another ancient name for Teuchsa Grondie. Ga-wa-no-wa-neh, signified the great Island River — the Susquehanna. Ga-ha-to, or Ga-ha-to-geh, signified a log in the water — the Chemung River. Skwe-do-wa, a great plain — Elmira. Ka-na-ta-go-dah, Onondaga Castle, the great central point of the Iroquois. The hospitality of all the Indian nations was proverbial. The gauntlet was run between two lines of Indians, each one of whom inflicted what blows he could upon the prisoner as he passed.

The word Teuchsa Grondie was an exclamation of surprise and delight at beholding, perhaps for the first time, the beautiful scenes of the Detroit River. As much as to say: Teuchsa Grondie !— What a charming spot ! What a lovely scene !

I.

FIVE years have swiftly passed away
Since Wa-be-no-ka, in his pride,
Upon the public — festal day,
Made Whippoorwill his happy bride.
She 's happy still. No idle freak,
Or wayward passion, was his love;
Nor hers — a liking of the weak:
Such union time may well approve.

They feel no disappointment sore,
That ill-wed strangers oft deplore;
    For each the other long has known;
    As youthful mates the two have grown.
And Wa-be-no-ka's cabin shade,
A genial home indeed is made;
    For where presides the Whippoorwill,
    There seems an Eden blooming still.

II.

A worthy statesman penetrates
The policy of foreign states,
    To guard against the secret foe;
That no disaster may arise,
From sudden onset or surprise;
    Or unexpected — fatal blow.
Though quiet seem the Iroquois,
They love the path of distant war;
    They love to yell the battle song:
And any moment may display,
The vengeful foe — the wild foray,
    At lovely Wa-we-aw-to-nong.
And Wa-be-no-ka shrewdly knows,
That naught but heavy — crushing blows,
    Can e'er atone the ambuscade; —
That overthrew the victor band,
In proud retreat from Huron land,
    And there a bloody havoc made.

The chief the subject calm revolves;
And then, in secret, firm resolves,
    The "Long House" deep to penetrate;
To learn if vengeance now aspires,
Around O-nun-da-no-ga fires,
    Against the village of the strait.
He calls his pappoose to his side;
Invokes, his future life to guide,
    The guardian spirit of the brave;
"And if," he says, "away, I perish,
Your father's name forever cherish;
    Avenge, avenge his early grave!"
He bids adieu to Whippoorwill;
Untold his secret mission still,
    To die with him if he should fall;
And yet the prudent, thoughtful wife,
No question put, no gossip rife,
    In woman's shrewdness read it all.

III.

With sack of corn and faithful bow,
And ready knife for game or foe;
    Like deer upon the everglade,
    He plunges in the forest shade.
At first a southern trail he takes:
The deep "Miami of the Lakes,"
    He boldly swims. The "dismal swamp"—
    His daily shelter, nightly camp.
No mat or hut the rover craves,
    Or cheerful brand of cabin hearth;

The wet and chilly night he braves,
    In leafy bed upon the earth.
The sun and stars — his trusty guides;
    He flies along the hill and plain;
Thro' sombre vale he boldly strides,
    Nor tangled brushwood can detain.
To enter by the eastern side,
    The foe to lull from watchful care,
He wisely makes the circuit wide,
    For lands of kindred Delaware.
He mounts the Alleghany chain,
    Its lofty peak sublimely treads;
Descends its dark ravines again;
    The rapid Juniata threads.
He stems the Ga-wa-no-wa-neh;
    Admires the level Skwe-do-wa;
He winds the calm Ga-ha-to-geh,
    Towards proud Ka-na-ta-go-dah.

IV.

As if of common brotherhood,
Upon the confines of the wood,
    He yells, to gain a friendly pass;
    Then seats himself upon the grass.
The sachems hear the loud behest,
And walk to meet the stranger guest.
    The chieftain to the town is led;
    No formal salutation said.
The cabin shade a welcome lends,
And forest luxury attends.

To satisfy the appetite,
Is brought a dish of sagamite.
"Take, freely take," the matrons cry,
"Ye dweller 'neath another sky;
Whate'er ye see ye may command,
Ye stranger from a distant land."
The daily intercourse was free,
In boundless hospitality:
And still a foeman might beset,
Beneath the forms of etiquette;
But while the host might shrewdly guess,
The earnest question none could press.

V.

And Wa-be-no-ka now may scan,
The warriors of a mighty clan:—
The brawny arm, the stately tread;
The graceful plumage of the head;
The calm and yet expressive face,
That would a painter's easel grace;
A will, to firmest purpose lent,
That terrifies a continent.
"Ah, how shall my unguarded town,
My happy home, of high renown,
Withstand, in hour of deepest woes,
O-nun-da-no-ga's mighty blows?
Fear not, my soul, that awful day,
If come it does, as come it may;
This arm shall worthy triumph still,
For my dear boy and Whippoorwill."

VI.

His nation and his clan perplex
The Iroquois of either sex.
They all can see the Chippeway;
And yet, upon a fatal day,
The captive chief, to torture led,
Might rise again as from the dead,
And victor nation's glory share—
A worthy brave of Delaware.
And one there was, of piercing eye,
Who thought he dimly could descry
The terror-dealing—mighty form,
That swept the field, a raging storm,
And changed a triumph to defeat
Upon that terrible retreat,
When Iroquois, with thunder crash,
In ruin laid the Matchedash.
And yet no certain feature tells,
Of him whose leap and horrid yells,
And heavy blows and flashing eye,
Could make the bravest turn and fly:
For then, of paint and reeking blood,
In deep disguise, the hero strode;
But now, his every look and mien,
Though bold and firm, is all serene.

VII.

When Wa-be-no-ka first beheld
This capitol of mighty foe,

His heart, in joy, a moment swelled,
　　Then sunk, in turn, to deepest woe.
Surprised, he saw an ancient friend,
　　A western chief of former years;
But oh, ye guardian hosts defend!
　　No Mus-ko-da-sa there appears.
The friend—Ni-kan-no-kee the brave,
　　The hunter of the buffalo;
But neither recognition gave,
　　For neither could the other know.
Upon the worthy Illinois
　　Were scars and cruel mutilation;
Inflicted by the Iroquois,
　　To deep insult a distant nation.
The two a cold reserve maintain,
　　Whene'er observing eyes attend:
And yet, in secret, feel again,
　　Their genial spirits freely blend.

VIII.

Upon a pleasant summer day,
　　In sign of recognition still,
The two, adversely, glide away,
　　And meet upon a distant hill.
At once the worthy chiefs embrace;
　　A sympathetic power is felt;
Tears trickle down each manly face:
　　True friendship stoutest hearts will melt.
They sit beneath a sturdy elm;
　　Huge limbs are interlaced above;

And here, amid the forest realm,
They mingle sentiments of love.

WA-BE-NO-KA.

Ah tell, my noble brother, quickly tell,
What to my father, to yourself befell;
As western chiefs the mighty onset made,
Upon the victors, from the ambuscade.
The scars, I see, of unrelenting ire;
Ah, how did you escape the vengeful fire?
Before me Mus-ko-da-sa's spirit gleams;
Oh, is my father in the land of dreams?

NI-KAN-NO-KEE.

On that retreat the heavy packs we bore;
Malignant foes our limbs and bodies tore.
Behold the scars! The mutilated hands!
That tell of tortures of the victor bands.
And then the gauntlet; frightful scene to tell!
When blows on blows a horrid tempest fell.
I reeled and fainted, in the dreadful hour:
Ah, who can paint the insolence of power!

WA-BE-NO-KA.

And how did Mus-ko-da-sa bear the ban?
Why do I ask? I know he played the man!

NI-KAN-NO-KEE.

He did, he did! As blows upon him rained,
And long before the distant goal he gained;

With fiercest anger rolling in his breast,
He yells the war-whoop of the mighty West;
A war-club seizes from a hostile arm,
And wields it right and left with dread alarm.
The whole assistant crew affrighted cry;
And all for life upon the instant fly.
How my proud heart of western glory swells,
To see him chase them with redoubled yells!

WA-BE-NO-KA.

The gallant chief! I dread to know his fate:
I pray you, first, your tortures to relate.
Your pangs alone my vengeful soul will fire,
Tho' all unknown the sorrows of my sire.

NI-KAN-NO-KEE.

The fire and torture were for both, it seems;
Both had they destined to the land of dreams.
We both prepared to brave the awful test;—
In death, the heroes of the mighty West.
But worthy matron of the Iroquois,
Had lost her husband in the Huron war:
It was her pleasure that I might survive:
She is my wife. Behold me here alive!
The lot severe; but hardest lot of all,
Myself Ho-dé-no-sau-nee chief to call.
Myself to abnegate, like anchoret!
My nation, name and kindred to forget!
I did it all; and oft in bloody war,
I rang the war-whoop of the Iroquois.

Yet who can stifle his regard for home?
To your loved strait my spirits often roam.
Yea, farther still: In thought, I oft regain,
The cherished cabins of my native plain.

WA-BE-NO-KA.

My father; oh! I tremble to recall,
The gloomy story of his dreadful fall.
His counsel was for peace, upon the square,
When we of Huron league debated there.
But when for war the common suffrage cries,
His war-song echoes to the vaulted skies;
And frighted foemen quickly turn and flee,
When his stern voice commands the victory.

NI-KAN-NO-KEE.

Then listen; calmly listen, if you can:
He perished, but he perished like a man.
In yonder council house, the live-long night,
They plied their tortures—frightful to the sight.
He cheerful sung, and dared them to the worst;
They filled the air with jeers and yells accurs'd.
The morning came; and at the rising day,
In public view, his mangled carcass lay.

WA-BE-NO-KA.

But tell me, did they not extort the sigh,
Or stifled groan, as Pauguk lingered nigh?

NI-KAN-NO-KEE.

Not one escaped him. Lend a full belief:
In death I gloried in my worthy chief.
At every blow he smiled as at a jest;
And closed his eyes at last as if to rest.

WA-BE-NO-KA.

Great Michabou! Thy name be ever rung!
My father, too! Thy fame be ever sung!
But tell me, does no relic yet remain
Of Mus-ko-da-sa, thus untimely slain;
That I in cabin home may long preserve,
As such heroic honors well deserve?

NI-KAN-NO-KEE.

Not one that you can touch. And yet there are,
In council house, memorials of the war.
Wa-bas-so's club; the knife of Ta-to-kee;
The bows of Ni-ni-vay and Kah-gah-gee;
And Mus-ko-da-sa's belt and plumy crest;—
Are there display'd—proud trophies of the West.

WA-BE-NO-KA.

I take them or I die! I blot the shame;
Or house and trophies perish in the flame!
But further speak; give me the worst to know;
Ah, who can brook a father's overthrow!

NI-KAN-NO-KEE.

With patience hear. The scalp of Ta-to-kee,
Adorns the pipe of warlike Do-ka-tee.

The scalp of Mus-ko-da-sa, shameful lot,
Is flaunted on the head of O-to-quot;
And from your father's arm, the leathered skin,
Is proud tobacco pouch of Tang-gu-shin.

WA-BE-NO-KA.

My arms, my arms! I tear them all away,
Tho' twenty chieftains should my fury stay!

NI-KAN-NO-KEE.

Your patience hold; your fiery vengeance bound,
O-nun-da-no-ga warriors thee surround;—
A race of men that hurl the dreadful blow—
That never quail before a mortal foe.
Ye soon may strike at those ye deep detest;
For rumors tell of war against the West:
Ere long, at home, beside that noble river,
Ye every stain may wash, and wash forever.

WA-BE-NO-KA.

Roll on the day! Come blackest storm of war;
I long for vengeance on the Iroquois!
I'll risk my own dear village of the plain,
For one fell swoop at hellish clan again.
But what the rumor? Tell me how and when,
Shall bloodhounds issue from this horrid den?
And what the cause? The allies, leaders, chief?
I want the worst. To know — affords relief.

NI-KAN-NO-KEE.

The cause attend. At distant Thunder Bay,
A Mohawk died, ignobly, by the way.
And then again, the pregnant cause to swell,
An Iroquois at Nah-ma Se-pee fell.
Yet more; your village — Teuchsa Grondie fair,
Allows detested French the hut to share.
But more than all: In bloody Huron war,
    Retreating from the Matchedash,
The ever proud, triumphant Iroquois,
    Sustained a dreadful thunder crash.

WA-BE-NO-KA.

Well, let them come. Our huts, around the square
To guard, a thousand braves shall rally there.
No puny arms shall there contend for fame;
The foe shall fall, or fly to whence he came.

XI.

The setting sun, beneath the west,
Invites the chieftains home to rest.
    The night bestows a quiet sleep;
    No sentinels their vigils keep.
No thought is there of lurking foe,
Of strategy or murd'rous blow;
    And yet in deepest hour of night,
    Is heard a yell of sudden fright.
Each warrior springs in wild amaze;
The council house is all ablaze;

And trophies, there, of western fame,
Are wrapt in one consuming flame.

XII.

At length the morning beams arise;
But where the scalps and pouch so dear?
The three, a point of much surprise,
With stranger chieftain disappear.

TEUCHSA GRONDIE.

CANTO XXV.

To Mrs. RICHMOND JONES,

Elmira, N. Y.:

As a testimonial of high regard for her personal character and her many virtues; and as a recognition of the valuable, highly benevolent and devoted personal services rendered by her, in the military hospitals at Elmira during the war, in relieving the wants of the sick, the wounded and the distressed, and in kind ministrations around the dying bed; this Twenty-fifth Canto is affectionately inscribed by

HER SINCERE FRIEND

TEUCHSA GRONDIE.

CANTO XXV.

THE WAR CLOUD

A. D. 1665.

PREFATORY NOTE. Ka-na-ta-go, Onondaga Castle. Do-na-ta-gwe-no-da, an opening — Bath, N. Y. Yon-do-ti-ga, a great village — another ancient name for Teuchsa Grondie. Wa-wa-tay-see, the fire-fly — the little son of Wa-be-no-ka and Whippoorwill, who will be a great hero if this history shall hold out long enough.

The original Ottawas occupied the valley of the great river of that name in Canada. The Neutral Nation occupied both sides of the Niagara River. The Eries, or E-ri-gas, and the Andastes occupied the south side of Lake Erie. The Hurons occupied the territory on the Matchedash River, and the Matchedash Bay, now a part of the Georgian Bay in Upper Canada. All these nations were destroyed by the Iroquois between 1648 and 1672, thus leaving our village completely exposed to that terrible enemy.

Under the totemic system a nation, or a confederacy of nations, usually contained eight clans or orders, which were closely interwoven and bound together by marriage and by the rules of descent.

On occasions of great danger the Indian prophets sometimes consulted the oracles, in a small bark hut constructed for the purpose.

I.

FIVE happy years have told their flight,
Since that heroic, vengeful night,
When Wa-be-no-ka, stranger guest,
In one exultant — victor flame,
Destroyed the hall of proudest fame,
With prouder trophies of the West.
And while the hero loves to roam,
He dearly loves his cabin home; —
Secure from every threatened ill;
To Wa-wa-tay-see, sprightly boy,
He tells his tales of Iroquois,
And chats with charming Whippoorwill.
The son, a shoot of worthy race,
Respectful to indulgent sire,
To doting mother ever kind,
And yet with soul of sterner stuff;
The future age shall worthy grace,
A proud, unrivaled fame acquire,
If this our history, unconfined,
Shall be extended long enough.

II.

And Wa-be-no-ka makes a feast:
The friend and far invited guest,
In circle 'round the central fire,
Are shining in their gay attire.
And Whippoorwill, in social rite,
Distributes richest sagamite;

And Wa-wa-tay-see, succotash,
Of native corn and bean and squash.
The story and the ready joke,
A roar of laughter oft provoke;
The moments fly in happy cheer,
For all is friendly and sincere.

III.

Behold a stranger guest arise;
And silence reigns; and eager eyes
Are on him bent. His words are free —
The kindred Pottawattamie.

NO-NE-YAH.

My brothers of this ancient town,
That fills the land with high renown;
The singing birds have often told,
The feat of Wa-be-no-ka bold;
By which O-nun-da-no-ga hall,
With trophies, perished, one and all;
And of his long and weary flight,
Upon that vengeance-dealing night.
And yet the story seems obscure;
The famous tale we would assure; —
We, strangers of the West afar;
Speak, Wa-be-no-ka, freely tell,
What in that noble race befell;
How you escaped the Iroquois.

WA-BE-NO-KA.

The night I chose, to daring feat perform,
Was dark and troubled: Raged a thunder storm.
The sleeping chiefs themselves were in my power;
My arm I held, for prudence ruled the hour.
The torch applied, the war-whoop yell I ring:
With pouch and scalps I soon am on the wing.
An hour the start is well, before the day
The trophy loss and havoc shall display.
The foe to draw from this my native home,
With fiery speed, a southern course I roam.
Thro' vine and brush and bramble is the flight,
A frightful path to traverse in the night.
The morning dawns. I hear the ringing yell
Of vengeance, thro' the distant forest tell.
I backward look: I see the smoke arise
From council hall, and mingle with the skies.
And Do-ka-tee on every pathway flings
Pursuing scout, as on the eagle's wings.
Think ye their nimble hunters on me gain?
Na, na; the chief that roams the western plain,
From pride alone, outstrips the rushing wind,
And leaves the foe and danger far behind.
I sport with my pursuers. Speed I slack;
And frequent cross the stream to hide my track.
I stop upon the hill to mock their rage;
And when they heave in sight, I disengage
Myself from all their toils. My wife and boy,
Alone, would bring me from the Iroquois.

I reach Ga-ha-to; plain of Skwe-do-wa;
I rapid pass Do-na-ta-gwe-no-da;
And as nor day nor night my feet I stay,
The foemen yield; their echoes die away.
I rest a day among the Erie clan;
A fatal visit: Thus I bring the ban
On that devoted nation. Iroquois
Renew their fierce, exterminating war;
In full belief that they have sent the spy,
O-nun-da-no-ga prowess to defy.
I hasten home, secure from every ill,
To Wa-wa-tay-see and to Whippoorwill.
Ah, see! above our heads! in pious phrase,
The household gods to nerve my future days!
Those sad memorials of my kindred dear,
Shall constant draw the sympathizing tear.
The trophy scalps, my father's withered arm,
Shall fire my soul in every dread alarm;
In storm of war, shall every action string,
And Iroquois shall fall at every spring.
And thus my story have I briefly told:
Ah! me, a stricken chief, you here behold!
Be ready, braves, the warrior bow to bend;
To hurl the hatchet; cabin home defend.

IV.

The chief is silent. Long and loud applause
Is quick succeeded by an earnest pause,
As upturned eyes the relics meet:

And love and admiration quickly turn
To thirst for vengeance; chieftains eager burn,
In arms the bloody foe to greet.
The hour is late. The owl aloud proclaims
The morning star — the rising east in flames;
The heavy air of night is chill:
The guests their many vows of friendship make,
And all, adieus of Wa-be-no-ka take,
And Wa-wa-tay-see, Whippoorwill.

V.

The mighty drama opens: Iroquois,
By universal, desolating war,
The continent would domineer;
Their eight-fold cord — totemic order band,
Can hurl a force against a foreign land,
That few can stem and all may fear.
The Hurons have already felt the wrath,
Of those that carry terror in the path
Of fiery onset. Also, distant far,
The common foe have crushed the Ottawa,
And sent them to the West, to cherish hate,
And signal vengeance there to meditate.
The E-ri-gas, the onset wild sustain;
They quickly fall; their efforts all are vain:
They swell the ranks of mighty victor foes,
To deal, in distant lands, their common blows.
The Neutral Nation, on the thund'ring shore
Of O-ni-ag-raah, soon are seen no more:

The Hurons, in distress, upon them call;
The call they slight, and now in turn they fall.
They beg for mercy, yet no mercy gain;
Ho-dé-no-sau-nee spurns divided reign.
In sweep of conquest, brave Andastes last,
Are 'neath the power of haughty victors cast.
France, in her new possessions, trembling stands,
Before the fierce assaults of Mohawk bands.
The common foe a proud defiance flings,
And just alarm thro' western forest rings.
Ah, lovely village, by the lovely strait!
Who shall protect thee from the common fate.

VI.

And Teuchsa Grondie feels the rising storm;
Alarm is on the wing in every form:
The eagle's yell, the hoot of frighted owl;
Of dog the snarl, of wolf the dismal howl;—
A bow and arrow painted in the sky;
A scalp upon the moon, that all descry;—
A jeebi train along the milky-way;
The blazing comet shooting far astray:—
The northern light that upward faintly streams;
The blinking stars above the land of dreams:—
The glimpses of the moon behind the cloud;
The setting sun within a purple shroud:—
The deeper shadows of the forest gloom;
The river, darkened, as for coming doom:—
A sulph'rous odor in the summer rain;
Big inky drops from raging hurricane:—

In short, a sense of danger in the air,
That mutely tells of coming foe —
A dread, a terror, breathing everywhere,
Of deep calamity and woe.

VII.

"My brothers, come," says Che-to-waik;
"Assemble on the public square;
Of Michabou wise counsel take;
The Manitou will meet us there."
A frame of poles is quickly made —
A circle, is its petty size;
The bark and skins are on it laid:
From this the oracles advise.
With plumage now, the others deck
The wise, prophetic Ken-na-beck.
Into the hut he slowly creeps:
Awhile the spirit quiet sleeps.
The priest his supplication makes,
In deep and melancholy tone;
And then the hut in fury shakes,
And soft is heard prophetic moan.
The eager circle wait devout,
Beneath the maple's cheerful shade;
And soon the prophet sallies out,
And then is explanation made.

CHE-TO-WAIK.

And are the signs for coming war?
Oh, tell us, brother, tell us true!

Are we to meet the Iroquois?
    How speaks the guardian Manitou?

KEN-NA-BECK.

The storm arises. Mighty council hall,
That sunk to ashes, rises at the call,
Of sternest purpose. There the war-whoop rings;
O-nun-da-no-ga chief to vengeance springs.
The spy that wrapt Ka-na-ta-go in flame,
To proud Yon-do-ti-ga, of noble fame,
He skulking traces; vows the town shall fall;—
That fire and fury shall envelop all.

WA-BE-NO-KA.

And let him come. His ever burning lust
For wide domain, shall lay him in the dust.
The precious relics that I bore away,
Shall nerve this arm to stem the wild foray.

KO-KO-KO-HO.

But will the spirits, in the trying hour,
Our blows direct with superhuman power?
Forbid the conquest of the ancient town,
And grant our chiefs to win a high renown?

KEN-NA-BECK.

Who bravely fights, the Manitou will aid;
The Pauguk grim, will seize the renegade:
Then boldly strike; and fearless, worthy stand;
For wife, and child, and home, and native land.

BOURDELAIS.

As dire events are in the troubled wind,
Permit the humble monk to speak his mind.
Your mode of warfare best to you is known;
But we, of other land, suggest our own.
We bow, at first, before the throne of grace,
And there invoke a blessing on our race;
Our many sins, for which the scourge is sent,
In word and deed, we there sincere repent:
The God of battles call, our blows to guide,
And for our country and the right decide:
And when triumphant we at last return,
The Te Deum we chant; the incense burn.
And still, the means we use, to proper end;
With line and moat and guard the town defend.
Strong arms, brave hearts, may win the doubtful day,
But ramparts will insure the battle fray.
Dame nature, this, a fortress n'er intended;
And yet the town is easily defended.
To southward is the ample river tide;
The moat shall rise upon the triple side.
From thence we safe may hurl the deadly blow,
And firm resist the onsets of the foe.

VIII.

In Condé's ranks the monk had learned,
To some extent, the art of war;
And this to good account he turned,
Against the threatening Iroquois.

The good advice the chiefs attend;
Adopt it with reluctant praise;
And working parties quickly lend
A willing hand the moat to raise.
In circle wide, from strand to strand,
Around the huts the line is run;
Protecting squares the ditch command,
Which any prudent foe may shun.
The river, too, must be defended,
Against the swimmer and the fleet;
And soon the line is there extended;
And thus the circuit is complete.
A rag is on the maple hung—
The flag-staff of the citadel;
Defiance thus is boldly flung,
To Iroquois with loudest yell.
And now behold the cabin town,
A worthy theme for humble bard;
With battlement of high renown,
A new Parisian boulevard.
And yet by storms of later years,
And frequent culture of the ground,
The famous rampart disappears,
Till not a vestige more is found.

IX.

"And still," says worthy Che-to-waik,
"The wise will strong alliance make,
Although a confidence they feel;

Our clans, upon intelligence,
Will rally as for self-defense,
And bravely strike for common weal."
Says Ko-ko-ko-ho: "Quickly send
An embassy to every friend,
And every clan of kindred nation;
To rally for a final cast, —
To hurl the crushing thunder blast;
To carry death and desolation."
At once the embassies are sent,
The firm alliance to cement,
On every stream and every trail;
O-nun-da-no-ga, in the West,
Shall stir a mighty hornet's nest,
And woe to him who dare assail.
The Chippeway, and Kickapoo,
The Ottawa, and Huron too,
Miami and the Illinois; —
The Wyandots at once agree,
With vengeful Pottawattamie; —
All, all will fight the Iroquois.
And when begins the bloody fray,
The birds shall bear the news away,
To every cabin of the West;
And then the forest of the strait,
Shall ring with fierce Algonquin hate;
The tomahawk shall do the rest.

BOURDELAIS.

Recall again that dreadful hour,
That crushed the Huron's mighty power,
    Upon the distant Matchedash;
Ah, while there yawned a nation's grave,
No wakeful guard a warning gave,
    Of dread impending thunder crash.
Be wise in time. The foe may sweep
Upon the strong, the armed — asleep;
    And win by stealth and by surprise;
Then place the trusty sentinel,
To give the timely warning yell:
    Prevent a useless sacrifice.

X.

The chiefs again the counsel hear;
    And day and night the forest swarms,
With lynx-eyed watchmen, far and near,
    To notify of just alarms.
And now a painful, dread suspense,
    Each mind inspires, as grim as fate;
All feel the stake to be immense,
    And all the coming storm await.

TEUCHSA GRONDIE.

CANTO XXVI.

The Storm of War.

TO

GEORGE B. McCLELLAN:

THE SCHOLAR; THE GENTLEMAN;

THE SOLDIER; THE PATRIOT;

THE STATESMAN:

This Twenty-sixth Canto is respectfully inscribed, as a testimonial of the high esteem in which his private character, his distinguished attainments, and his great public services are held by many, and, among others, by

THE AUTHOR.

TEUCHSA GRONDIE.

CANTO XXVI.

THE STORM OF WAR.

A. D. 1665.

PREFATORY NOTE. Mi-no-sa-go-ink, the River Rouge, about four miles westerly from Teuchsa Grondie. It will be remembered that Pontiac held a grand war dance at the River Ecorce, some eight or ten miles westerly from Detroit, a short time before his attack on that village in A. D. 1763. In this Canto, as also in the next, it will be noticed that the town was twice indebted for its safety to Whippoorwill, the worthy wife of Wa-be-no-ka.

At the date of this Canto firearms had been in use for several years among the Iroquois.

I.

EXCITEMENT rises. On the green,
Heroic deeds, the braves proclaim;
Ancestral fame is loudly sung:
Wild dances night and day are seen;
The yells of war the chiefs inflame;
Defiance to the foe is flung.

And yet the cabin home is sad;
  The pappoose shrinks from loud alarm;
    The mother dreads the coming blow:
Ah, what is war? A nation mad:
  Ah, how can human slaughter charm!
    The mother's and the orphan's woe!
The stricken heart may quickly heal,
  The heavy losses, few deplore,
    The wounded nation onward bound;
And yet a people long must feel
  The strife that every fibre tore,
    That raised the lofty battle mound.
To hunters of the forest shade,
  Whose hut was oft in shoulder pack;
    To rovers of the western plain;
Fierce war a dreadful havoc made:
  The conquered flew on every track;
    Perhaps were never known again.

II.

The night was dark. Upon her mat,
The Whippoorwill in silence sat;
    Quick throbbed her breast in anxious care:
And as the gloomy moments fell,
She thought she heard a distant yell,
    In murmurs on the troubled air.
She quiet rose; she glided out;
She listened, eager, still in doubt;
    The clouds bespoke an angry sky:

The midnight hour was dark and chill,
But all was calm and peaceful still;
And yet she *felt* the foe was nigh.
She quickly to the river went;
She stooped, and to the surface lent
Her listening ear. A gentle roar —
A murmur crept along the shore.
Is it the foe — the warrior train,
In war-dance on the distant plain?
Before she yells the battle cry,
She first will prove the danger nigh.
She nimbly takes the western trail,
From whence the sounds her ear assail;
And tho' the midnight densely flings
Around her path his sable wings,
She yet familiar knows the way:
Here oft she tuned her childhood song;
Here trilled her merry roundelay:
Now, silently, she glides along.
Nor does her eager spirit shrink
To ford the Mi-no-sa-go-ink.
And now she more distinctly hears
The echoes that awoke her fears.
She also sees, reflected high,
The camp-fires on the cloudy sky.
She cautious winds the silent way;
Anon beholds, in bright array —
Upon the distant grassy plain,
In all the panoply of war —

In fury of the hurricane,
    The war-dance of the Iroquois.
And there is bloody Do-ka-tee;
    And there is gloomy O-to-quot;
And Tang-gu-shin, in fiery glee;—
    Like fiends of demon world begot.
The reeking scalp is upward flung;
    The tomahawk is flashing high;
The battle song is fiercely sung;
    The war-whoop echoes to the sky.

III.

Back flew the nimble Whippoorwill,
While all was dark and silent still;—
    Her chieftain told, in brief detail,
    Of foeman on the western trail.
The hasty counsel now to take,
They call the worthy Che-to-waik.
    The allied friends to notify,
    At once the trusty heralds fly;
That when the furious Iroquois
Shall hedge the town in storm of war,
    Upon his rear, in forest shade,
    A foe may spring from ambuscade.
The opening East is all aglow,
And yet no sign of coming foe.
    The day is past; the sun is set
    Ho-dé-no-sau-nee linger yet.
All night the chiefs a vigil keep;
    And as the morn awakes again,

A yell, like hoarse resounding deep,
Is heard along the western plain.

IV.

The foeman sees with much surprise,
The line that breathes impending fates;
And while his constant shouts arise,
For once he doubts and hesitates.
Behold the raging O-to-quot,
Around the works in fury stride;
To see if through unguarded spot
Could rush the overwhelming tide.
No point is found: For well combines,
The ditch and rampart everywhere:
Above, a crest of plumage shines,
And watchful eyes are gleaming there.
But Teuchsa Grondie trembles then;
Ho-dé-no-sau-nee now are nigh;
There swells the wrath of mighty men;
The war-cloud darkens in the sky.
And yet can Wa-be-no-ka quail?
Or terror-hurling Che-to-waik?
Na, na; let him who dare, assail;
They soon will bloody havoc make.

V.

The foe the mighty storm begin;
Fierce yells the haughty Tang-gu-shin;
A thousand voices swell the din;
The arrows sing along the sky:

And Teuchsa Grondie's worthy train
Send back the war-whoop shout again;
Their strong battalia firm maintain;
And whizzing shot for shot reply.
The battle groans along the ground;
The frighted forest roars around;
Responsive, distant shores resound;
The air is in commotion tost:
Keneú, imperial, circles high;
He downward throws his piercing eye;
Fierce battle pours in every cry;
"Onward," he screams, "at any cost."
The Iroquois, with demon glee,
Are seen to skip from tree to tree;
And whoop with all their energy;
And yet the arrow often hits:
Again, the strong, defensive foe,
The paint and plumage often show;
And many fall beneath the bow;
And yet his line he never quits.
The monk his loud devotion sings;
His cheering voice old Duroc flings;
And Whippoorwill the water brings,
To thirsty braves along the line:
And Wa-wa-tay-see, too, may vent
Precocious rage. The arrow spent
He gathers up. His mind is bent
In fields of glory far to shine.

VI.

But shall Oneida, distant fight?
Cayuga, not to charge incite,
Till fall again the shades of night?
    Was Mohawk ever known to fail?
Who shall the Seneca enchain?
O-nun-da-no-ga's arm restrain?
Shall proudest victors of the plain
    Before a forest village quail?
And where that haughty, ribald jeer?
That spirit, void of every fear?
That scorn to own an earthly peer?
    That overwhelming, fierce array?
"On!" yells the raging O-to-quot;
"We perish on this very spot,
Or else we here forever blot
    That village from the face of day!"

VII.

As rush the clouds along ethereal plain;
As roll the waves along the troubled main,
    High bounding to the angry sky;
So rush upon the foe the Iroquois,
And to the rampires bear the storm of war,
    With leap and shout and battle cry.
And does old Teuchsa Grondie frighted shrink,
As if already trembling on the brink
    Of woe and everlasting night?

She never does. From yells of Che-to-waik,
And all the rest, the very heav-ens quake;
No coward shuns the rushing fight.
As torrents down the mountain gorges leap,
Into the ditch Ho-dé-no-sau-nee sweep.
To mutual slaughter bow and bullet tend,
And heavy war-clubs on the brave descend.
Quickly the foemen mount the frowning moat,
While yells on yells in volleyed thunders float.
The tomahawk in circles cleaves the air,
And spectral Pauguk grimly hovers there.
And many fall. O-nun-da-no-ga braves,
Are sent in dozens to their honored graves.
Fair Teuchsa Grondie bleeds at every pore,
And blood, in rills, is creeping to the shore.

VIII.

The moat is carried. Fiercely mingle now
The hostile forces: Rage, on every brow.
The hatchets fly and fall like rat'ling hail;
The gleaming knives to mutual death assail.
The battle cries to shore and forest ring;
The war-club thunders in its mighty swing:
And many stately forms are lowly laid,
To land of dreams a gloomy masquerade.
And many foemen, grappled to the death,
Commutual slay and yield their flying breath.
Of hostile races, proud, the noblest blood
Is freely poured, an undistinguished flood.

Then worthy falls, amid the horrid din,
With other braves, the haughty Tang-gu-shin.
And Teuchsa Grondie mourns her Sub-be-kah;
And brave old Ken-na-beck and Shau-go-dah.
Fierce Wa-be-no-ka, like the comet burns,
And every foe and every danger spurns.
Wher-e'er the tide of battle thickest seems,
There towers his form and there his armor gleams.
And even Wa-wa-tay-see mingles then,
Among the manly acts of warrior men:
His flying arrows on the foemen tell;
And from his bow the lists of wounded swell.
And Whippoorwill; ah! what can mothers dare,
To guard their homes against the storm of war!
If Iroquois shall win the dreadful day,
In flames the happy town shall flee away;
And wives and mothers, fathers, children—all,
Beneath the hatchet, undistinguished fall.
The Whippoorwill, and every worthy maid,
And noble matron, eager lend their aid;
The weary to refresh, the water bring;
The arrow spent, and hatchet, quickly fling
To those that need: And when a foe is slain,
They make the welkin ring with shouts again.
And Duroc bravely mingles in the fray,
As also does the pious Bourdelais;
For if the village yields to haughty foe,
The monk and altar swift destruction know.

IX.

But will, at last, Ho-dé-no-sau-nee yield?
Nay, hope it not; their home is on the field.
As bends the forest to the sweeping gale,
The brave defenders now begin to fail.
And yet before an overwhelming tide,
For life the issue bravely they abide.
The swell of battle moves upon the square;
Beneath the maple: Many perish there.
As mighty foes on every side are met,
The sun of Teuchsa Grondie seems to set.
Ho-dé-no-sau-nee seem to clutch the prize;
Their shouts resound and roll along the skies.
Loud shrieks and groans in every cabin ring;
Despair is rife and hope is on the wing.
But hark! an echo! from the forest gloom!
No echo that; no sign of coming doom.
The war-whoop yell is ringing from afar;
See! No-ne-yah! in panoply of war!
See! Pottawattamie, in arms again,
Now pouring swift upon the battle plain!
See, how they stride in majesty and might!
See how they long to mingle in the fight!
See how their plumage dances to the sky!
What noble men, to conquer or to die!
From grief and wild despair hope springs anew,
As if inspired by guardian Manitou;
For warriors fresh, will horrid strife essay,
And turn the fortunes of the dreadful day.

X.

Think ye O-nun-da-no-ga, even now,
Will to a western clan submissive bow?
Na, na; to fiery tortures firm they'll go,
But never bow to any mortal foe.
And Do-ka-tee, and furious O-to-quot,
In terrors rage as if of Mars begot.
They quickly turn to Pottawattamie,
And yell and spring as if to jubilee.
Again the hatchets fiercely gleam on high,
And war-clubs circle in the frighted sky.
And many braves and worthy chief are slain,
And piles of dead are heaped upon the plain.
Like Grecian chiefs before the Trojan town,
The Iroquois sustain a just renown:
And yet with Wa-be-no-ka in the rear,
And No-ne-yah in front, unknown to fear;
Ho-dé-no-sau-nee must the battle yield,
And leave, in rage, a well contested-field.
With either host alone, the Iroquois,
Would quickly deal exterminating war;
In blood of every age would revel still,
And with unnumbered scalps their cabins fill:
But now, with fierce, with unabated ire,
Before superior force they grim retire.
The allies high the shout of triumph swell,
And Teuchsa Grondie echoes back the yell.
The forest nods to hear the cheerful roar,
And glad responds the distant vocal shore.

XI.

The sun is rushing to the West,
Glad tidings on the wing;
The skies, in richest purple drest,
Triumphant banners fling.
Brave No-ne-yah, invited guest,
Within the village lines retires;
And there the victors sink to rest:
The guard sustain the watchful fires.
Regardless of the chilling damp,
In forest shade, upon the ground,
The sullen Iroquois encamp,
Beyond the ancient burial mound.
As night advances, war-whoop yell
Is often heard, like distant horn;
It sounds a dismal funeral knell;
And all await the rising morn.

TEUCHSA GRONDIE.

CANTO XXVII.

Wa-be-no-ka.

To General WILLIAM T. SHERMAN:

Whose celebrated southern campaign was not only the *coup de foudre* to the southern armies, but was also the *coup de grâce* to the southern confederacy; and who has since exhibited many distinguishing qualities of the patriot and statesman, this Twenty-seventh Canto is very respectfully inscribed by

THE AUTHOR.

TEUCHSA GRONDIE.

CANTO XXVII.

WA-BE-NO-KA.

A. D. 1665.

PREFATORY NOTE. Shields of bark and of the skin of the bison were sometimes used among the Indians, as a defensive armor. Naval battles in bark canoes sometimes took place, though they were of rare occurrence. The disclosures, as related in this and in the twenty-fourth Canto, made by Ni-kan-no-kee, who, although an adopted Iroquois, was yet an Illinois, are regarded as entirely consistent with Indian character.

I.

A NIGHT upon the battle field,
Among the dying and the slain,
Will oft its frightful visions yield —
The horrid strife renew again.
The soul, in raging fury tost,
May every nerve to action string;
May fear the doubtful struggle lost;
Unconscious for the foeman spring.

How many visions, dark and dread,
Upon that bloody, frightful plain,
Again, the worthy foemen led,
To strike, among the ghastly slain!
How many jeebi 'round the nest
Of pappoose, in the cabin home,
Through wakeful or unquiet rest,
In spectral train were seen to roam!

II.

Brave Wa-be-no-ka, on his mat,
Of public danger thoughtful still,
In deep reflection calmly sat,
Beside his anxious Whippoorwill.

WA-BE-NO-KA.

Oh that I knew if Iroquois,
Were weary of this dreadful war!
Oh that their losses might induce,
A swift retreat or friendly truce!
Or that the blows he got to-day,
Might hold the mighty foe at bay,
Till other allies, far and near,
Could join us in the struggle here.

WHIPPOORWILL.

This day, this dreadful day is won;
And yet before the setting sun
To-morrow, terror-dealing foe,
May hurl a last — a fatal blow.

The night is foggy. I will ply
The office of the artful spy;—
    With cautious step his camp assail,
    To see what counsels there prevail:
To see if, ere the sun arise,
He plans a darksome enterprise;—
    To see if, on the coming day,
    He flies to home or battle fray.

WA-BE-NO-KA.

Na, na; here rest till morn return;
'Tis meet that I the danger spurn.
    I know each path of tangled ground,
    About, beyond the ancient mound.
I know each tree and bush to shun;
And if discovered, swift can run,
    Thro' covert wood to sure retreat;
I'll creep along in silent ken,
I'll probe the very lion's den,
    And learn his purpose in defeat.

III.

To be prepared for any sudden strife,
The hero took his hatchet and his knife.
He silent issued from the cabin shade,
And for the gloomy forest nimbly made.
The fog was dense; the darkness was profound:
A stench of blood arose from reeking ground:
And none but keenest, piercing, practiced eye,
Could any object, path or wood descry.

His foot is light; nor cat can lighter tread;
To listen, oft he stops, among the dead.
No sound is heard but of the distant owl;
Or farther still, of wolf, the dismal howl.
A form — a shade is seen! The practiced ear
Detects a footstep, cautious, drawing near;
And Wa-be-no-ka, silent, crouches low,
To learn if made by friend or skulking foe.
The step advances still; and gleaming eye
Is seen, like star athwart the hazy sky.
"Hist, hist!" says Wa-be-no-ka; "oh, I pray,
A wounded warrior safely bear away:
If till the morning dawn I here must lie,
By vengeful foe, an Iroquois will die."
The wary chief would thus the foe mislead,
If foe he be; and shun a mournful deed,
If on some secret mission, secret friend,
Might thus his steps towards the village bend.
"But what," he whispers still "thy worthy name?
For sure this act denotes established fame.
No niggard souls the Iroquois display;
And if they did, such would not now essay
The guarded lines." A whisper in reply
Is quickly heard: "Beneath the western sky,
I had my birth. I am an Iroquois:
I was a Chic-ta-ghick, — proud Illinois!
The change was wrought by fate — by firm decree;
My first, my only name — Ni-kan-no-kee."

WA-BE-NO-KA.

Hush, hush! Thou worthy chief. And can you keep
An early friendship—graven long and deep
Upon the soul? Ah, brave Ni-kan-no-kee,
Thy friend—young Wa-be-no-ka speaks to thee!

NI-KAN-NO-KEE.

I can, for I was once an Illinois;
Thus far I can defy the Iroquois.

WA-BE-NO-KA.

But why, on this obscure and heavy night,
Among the foemen, range the field of fight?

NI-KAN-NO-KEE.

I haste to tell, for soon I must return
To camp again; I snuff the early morn.
A sturdy, fearless band of Iroquois,
To yet retrieve the fortunes of the war,
Have stole above the town, to river side;
From whence, in boats, upon the gentle tide,
As soon as fully dawns the coming day,
And as the fog shall lightly float away,
They fierce intend to dash upon the strand;
And then, with tomahawk and blazing brand,
In one fell swoop, renew the battle fray:
Be wise the worst to meet; haste, haste away.

IV.

They part at once. The Illinois
Resumes his camp, an Iroquois;
And Wa-be-no-ka rapid threads,
The path that to his cabin leads.
The council meet upon the square,
At midnight's gloomy hour;
For threatened danger to prepare—
To meet a naval power.
A wise defense is quickly planned,
The foeman's fleet to brave;
And soon is formed a chosen band,
To meet him on the wave.
The worthy leader Che-to-waik,
To man the lines will undertake—
Whoever dares, will meet;
And Wa-be-no-ka, commodore,
In martial pomp, along the shore,
Commands the river fleet.

V.

At length the early morning cheers,
And yet no blushing East appears:
The town, the forest, river—all,
Is covered with a misty pall.
The eye can scarcely trace the view,
The length of cabin or canoe.
The forest weeps, and drops in tears,
The air a winding sheet appears.

A precious time for foe to spring,
And mighty column silent fling
  Against the line; the town essay,
  And turn, perhaps, the doubtful day.

VI.

The sun advances up the skies;
  The fogs, in circling eddies, lave
His face obscure. They slowly rise,
  And dim unfold the gliding wave.
As floats the misty screen away,
  The eyes, beneath the curtain, meet,
In naval pomp and firm array,
  O-nun-da-no-ga's martial fleet.
A shout from Wa-be-no-ka tells;—
  A deep surprise to O-to-quot;
And yet his anger fiercely swells,
  Despite the fatal counterplot.
The boats along the water sweep,
  As thirsty arrows eager sing;
The war-whoop rolls along the deep,
  Commutual death is on the wing.
Ho-dé-no-sau-nee bear the shield,
  Of hardened bark in rounded form;
The other, skins of bison wield,
  To guard against the arrow storm.
The navies mingle—fierce engage;
  Again the hatchet gleams on high;
The foemen throw the deadly gage,
  The war-club circles thro' the sky.

And man'y a graceful bark canoe,
In sorry fragments quick is torn;
And man'y a warrior sinks from view,
And down the current quick is borne.
Into the flood fierce Do-ka-tee
Is thrown by Wa-be-no-ka brave;
The Iroquois, with demon glee,
Drags Ko-ko-ko-ho to the wave.
They grapple fiercely — sink and rise;
They ply, in fury — each his knife;
They roll and writhe in deadly throe;
They dash the water to the skies;
They strangle, in the fatal strife;
They shoot to dismal realm below.
And O-to-quot but poorly makes
A naval warfare on the lakes,
With those that by the deep are bred;
He now retreats; he quickly lands;
A final hope — his dreadful bands,
To storm the lines will soon be led.

VII.

Brave Teuchsa Grondie now prepare,
The boldest feats of war to dare; —
The fury of the field to share;
The thunderbolt is poising high:
The wildest desperation, now,
Would stamp defeat upon thy brow —
To haughty victor make thee bow;
List — listen to the battle cry!

See O-to-quot, with lofty stride—
See Iroquois, in all their pride,
Approach, the issue to abide;
Themselves upon the line to fling:
Now Wa-be-no-ka, Che-to-waik,
With firm resolve your station take;
Once more Ho-dé-no-sau-nee shake;
Let eager arrows deadly sing.
They come, they come! like ocean swell;
The skies hurl back their mighty yell;
Now frightful blows will quickly tell;
Ah, hear the arquebuse resound!
Stand, brave defenders, firmly stand!
Meet, meet the foemen hand to hand!
Oh, strike for home and native land!
The line, the moat are hallowed ground!
The shelter Wa-be-no-ka spurns,—
In open view his whoop returns;
For war his every fibre burns;
In terror waves his plumy crest:
To hated foe he loud exclaims,—
"I wrapt your council-house in flames;
My yell awoke your sleeping dames;
I took your trophies of the West."
With this his hatchet rapid falls;
Proud Iroquois, the Pauguk calls;
The slaughter bravest hearts appalls;
And still his weapon reeks on high:
His war-club, with a mighty swing,
Is death itself upon the wing;

And foemen fall at every spring;
  O-nun-da-no-ga turn and fly.
The ditch, the hero quickly leaps,
And o'er the plain in terror sweeps;
The ground, with dead and dying, heaps;
His voice is like the howling deeps;
  He drives the flying foe amain:
He gleams, upon the plain afar,—
Saladin — with his scimetar;—
Æneas—in his whirling car;—
Ulysses—in the suitor war;—
  Achilles — on the Trojan plain.

VIII.

The field is won; and still the foe,
  To yet retrieve the fatal day,
Return and hurl a crushing blow;
  In havoc wield a dreadful sway.
Again the war-club thunders tell;
  On high the circling hatchet gleams,
And heroes, with a gasping yell,
  Affrighted, flee to land of dreams.
E'en now, O-nun-da-no-ga might,
May win the fortunes of the fight:
  E'en now, in triumph, bear away,
  The glories of the dreadful day.
At even hand with single foe,
The Iroquois no equal know:
  In arms they hold the argument,
  As well attest the continent.

And Teuchsa Grondie backward reels—
The mighty shock of battle feels:
    Loud, Wa-be-no-ka rings the cry,
    To nobly conquor, or to die.

IX.

What earthly comfort can compare,
    To that which comes on gilded wings,
As round us gathers black despair,
    And hope anew upon us springs!
Ah, listen! On the northern plain,
    Loud bursts the war-whoop from afar:
Ah, welcome, Kan-ne-tow again!
    Thrice welcome brave Tai-go-ne-ga!
The Hurons rush upon the field—
  The friends, of ruined Matchedash;
    And with them fearless Wyandot;
      A hero every man appears:
Ho-dé-no-sau-nee, die or yield!
  Now comes the final thunder-crash;
    Now tremble haughty O-to-quot!
      Ah, Teuchsa Grondie, quell your fears!
Nay, nay; expect not Iroquois,
To shrink from any doubtful war;
    As long as hope and chance remain,
    They fiercely brave the battle plain.
And now resounds the dreadful cry;
Hoarse thunders roll along the sky:
    The forest lends a deafening roar,
    That echoes to the distant shore.

Like stars that fire autumnal skies,
Intensely flash the foemen's eyes:
From side to side the hatchet gleams;
A crushing bolt the war-club seems.
Old Che-to-waik, wher-e'er he goes,
Makes ample room among his foes;
The valor of his youth returns:
Tai-go-ne-ga his vengeance takes,
A ghastly pile of foemen makes,
And still for slaughter fiercely burns.
And chieftains fall. Brave No-ne-yah,
Is hurled to waiting Po-ne-mah.
The worthy, fearless Kan-ne-tow,
Receives a deadly hatchet blow.
A brawny — giant Wyandot,
In fury drives at O-to-quot;
The Iroquois before him frowns:
Impelled as by a mighty spring,
Their tomahawks in fury swing;
The dreadful yell of death resounds.
They fiercely grapple; hand to hand;
A gazing circle 'round them stand;
By terror all are held apart:
The Iroquois, with ready knife,
Triumphant ends the horrid strife;
He drives it to the foeman's heart.

X.

And yet O-nun-da-no-ga, now,
Thy lofty form prepare to bow;

See swift advance that fiery brow;
The hero of the western plain:
With blood his war-club reeking teems;
The spirit of his father gleams
Around his head, from land of dreams;
Old Mus-ko-da-sa lives again.
"I bore your trophies proud away,"
Says Wa-be-no-ka: "Rue the day,
Ye brought the deadly battle fray,
Around these western village walls·"
His weapon sweeps upon the wing;
His battle shouts in thunder ring;
Down comes the blow with mighty swing,
And O-to-quot a ruin falls.
Triumphant whoops invade the sky;
Their tomahawks the victors ply;
Ho-dé-no-sau-nee turn and fly,
Pursued by yells and ribald jeers.
The victors gather up the slain,
To land of dreams an honored train:
Fair Teuchsa Grondie breathes again;
And freely sheds her grateful tears.

TEUCHSA GRONDIE.

CANTO XXVIII.

The Jubilee.

I DESIRE TO DEDICATE

THIS, THE LAST CANTO OF MY WORK,

TO THE

CITIZEN SOLDIERY

OF THE

UNITED STATES;

WHO,

FROM THE EARLIEST PERIOD OF OUR HISTORY, HAVE BEEN ABLE TO COPE WITH ALL ENEMIES;

AND WHO,

WHEN FINAL SUCCESS WAS GAINED, HAVE RETURNED, FREELY AND HONORABLY, TO THE WALKS AND DUTIES OF CIVIL LIFE.

TEUCHSA GRONDIE.

CANTO XXVIII.

THE JUBILEE.

A. D. 1665.

PREFATORY NOTE. The discussion in regard to the prisoners is intended to show the effect which the teachings of the missionaries may be supposed to have produced among the Indians at the date of this Canto.

It is difficult to determine when the Indians abandoned the site of Teuchsa Grondie; but as the place was unoccupied at the time Cadillac founded Detroit in A. D. 1701, and as La Salle does not report a village there at the time of his first voyage up the Lakes, in A. D. 1679, they are supposed to have done so sometime between 1665 and 1679, on account of the frequent and dangerous incursions of the Iroquois past their village to the upper lakes.

I.

FROM that disastrous, frightful day,
Repulsed, the foemen haste away;
They sullen flee to home afar—
To their own Ka-na-ta-go-dah.
The chiefs shall tell of western foes,
To frighted children, yet unborn;—
Of Wa-be-no-ka's mighty blows;
Nor brave Algonquin warrior scorn.

II.

At Teuchsa Grondie, on the public square,
The funeral rites the people now prepare:
While battle plains a nation's glory tell,
There, stricken hearts and deepest sorrow dwell.
While from the Lakes to distant Mexico,
Unnumbered tongues applaud the kindred foe —
That sent Ho-dé-no-sau-nee might and main,
To his Long House, discomfited, again;
Tho' victor name, upon a thousand wings,
Thro'-out the western forest loudly rings;
Yet far and wide, in every forest shade,
For worthy slain, a dismal moan is made.
And in the victor town, of many fears —
In every hut, are groans and floods of tears.
The fall-en braves in honored mound are laid,
And, circling round, is long procession made.
Among the rest are many neophytes,
For whose repose are said the Christian rites.
The solemn mass — impressive — grand display,
Is loudly sung by pious Bourdelais.
Nor does he fail to bless the heavenly power,
For safe deliv'rance in the dreadful hour: —
That France and Rome, in this a holy war,
Have England foiled with haughty Iroquois.

III.

And hapless, now, appear a captive band,
Expecting fire and torture at the hand

Of victor foes; yet firm as ocean rock,
To grim endure—defy the dreadful shock.
And shall these fearless, ever gallant foes,
In sad defeat, be overwhelmed with woes?
And must the victor, in the joyful hour,
Upon the brave, assert his brutal power?

BOURDELAIS.

It is enough to triumph in the field—
To make the haughty foe, or die or yield.
Ye worthy victors, would ye mercy find?
Then to unhappy braves be ever kind.
A vengeful foe perhaps ye thus disarm;
A generous act the hardest heart can charm.
The faith requires it; holy faith of God;—
To spare, like Him, the fierce avenging rod.

CHE-TO-WAIK.

Although to mercy I incline,
    And would the gallant warrior save;
Yet is not torture, here, divine?
    Ah, where is Mus-ko-da-sa brave!

TAI-GO-NE-GA.

For sudden, overwhelming crash,
Upon my own dear Matchedash;—
    For that exterminating blow,
    We, fiery tortures would bestow;
Yet Bourdelais, with earnest zeal,
And honest care for public weal,

Proclaims aloud, in holy cause,
A doctrine worthy of applause.

DUROC.

To bravely meet a worthy foe,
And deal the loud resounding blow,
Exalts the fame of any clan;
But mercy, in triumphant hour,
A glory sheds upon the power
That domineers the fall-en man.

WHIPPOORWILL.

My cabin home, with terror fraught,
As war was on the wing,
A gloomy frenzy highly wrought,
That leaves a painful sting.
Ah, how my fancy saw and felt,
I soon should cease to live!
How does my heart, in triumph, melt!
Oh, let us now forgive!

WA-WA-TAY-SEE.

Oh, let them live! I dread to see,
Their bodies in the flame;
Oh, loose their bands and let them flee,
To land from whence they came!

WA-BE-NO-KA.

A thousand ruling motives now conspire,
To ply the vengeful, all-consuming fire:

My father's torture in that council hall,
And fire and death, that stoutest hearts appall:
The mutilation of his honored form—
It stirs the soul to raging thunder storm:
The many friends, now flitting ghosts afar,
In land of dreams beyond the evening star:
Around our homes, in stern and dread array,
By these same men, the furious battle fray:—
All these the torture claim from victor band,
And vengeance waits from me the dread command.
And yet I now will show the Iroquois,
That we can soar above the chance of war.
To conquer such a foe—a glorious thing,
In future years to make the forest ring.
This battle field, the future shall proclaim—
A thousand echoes waken at the name.
Let foes be friends; let war's dread clamor cease:
Ho-dé-no-sau-nee, go; depart in peace.

IV.

The foe their grateful lot receive,
    In silence, held as by a spell;
They quiet take their final leave,
    And long of Wa-be-no-ka tell.
Among the rest a chief is seen,
Of lofty and imposing mien;
    As others go, alone he stays;
    And for the victors clear displays
A preference. He too, is free—
Our ancient friend, Ni-kan-no-kee.

A captive, in a former strife,
The victor spared his forfeit life.
He dropt his nation — Illinois;
Became a loyal Iroquois.
Again a captive, breaks the band,
That held him to adopted land.
His fate, by Wa-be-no-ka spoke,
Releases him from every yoke.
He soon will joyful see, again,
His home upon the western plain:
He soon again will draw the bow,
That lays the mighty bison low;
Perhaps will wage a vengeful war,
Against the distant Iroquois.

V.

And now the victor feast prepare —
The grand — triumphal jubilee;
Assemble, all, upon the square,
Around the ancient maple tree.
Bring forth the steaming sagamite,
The succotash of bean and corn;
Give fullest scope to appetite;
Let gayest dress the day adorn.
The people seated on the ground,
Beneath a now benignant sky;
Rare jokes and laughter free abound,
And happy souls are beating high.

By gallant leaders, one by one,
The dances, speeches, are begun,
From juvenile to warrior gruff;
And Wa-wa-tay-see leads the way,
He who the hero would display,
If this our song were long enough.
Each rises in the ample ring,
Of mighty deeds to loudly sing,
That may to distant ages reach;
And then, excitement to enhance,
He fiercely whirls in giddy dance;
And closes with a glowing speech.

WA-WA-TAY-SEE.

If I did not the foeman kill,
With arrows oft I wounded sore;
I showed the mighty chieftain's will,
And what could brave or chieftain more?

DUROC.

The implements of war I flung,
To braves that dealt the crushing blow;
And then the wildest song I sung,
To cheer them on against the foe.

NI-KAN-NO-KEE.

I seemed to ply my hatchet well;
My swinging war-club heavy fell;
With yells the battle plain I filled:

My task was difficult indeed,
To seem to fight and seem to bleed,
And neither kill or yet be killed.
Though born a brave of Illinois,
I now was bound an Iroquois;
To fate the chieftain sternly bends:
Yet could I earnestly engage,
And write a fratricidal page?
Ah, could I fight my ancient friends?

CHE-TO-WAIK.

What stronger force can nerve a blow—
Can more inspire a thirst for fame,
As fiercest storms of war appall;
Than, if o'ercome, to simply know,
That we shall perish by the flame;—
Extermination cover all!

WHIPPOORWILL.

Ah, how I trembled to behold,
And to and fro, the battle sway;
And many brave defenders yield!
What if our fate had thus been told—
Ho-dé-no-sau-nee, gained the day,
In triumph swept the bloody field!
How would he swell the victor cry,
And sport with every trembling life,
And thro' our village lordly stalk!

How would he fiery tortures ply,
  And wield his bloody scalping knife,
    And swing his crushing tomahawk!

TAI-GO-NE-GA.

My nation, on the distant Bay,
In one fell swoop was swept away;
    In broken, fragmentary bands,
    We wander far in stranger lands:
And yet this mighty victor blow,
Redeems a life of hapless woe.
    Ah, what can like the war-whoop ring,
    When fiery vengeance nerves the spring!

BOURDELAIS.

The Lord on high alone will vengeance take;
His were the bolts that made the mighty quake.
As loud the battle swelled upon the air,
The cross I raised upon the public square;
In lofty strain, revolving chant I sung,
And grateful incense round the altar flung.
In praise of God, let every heart abound;
Let vocal forests to His name resound.

WA-BE-NO-KA.

To God, or sprite, or guardian Manitou,
Whoe'er the sovereign be, the praise is due:
And yet with all, each warrior chieftain knows,
The triumph lies in heavy, crushing blows.

My brothers, all; ye did your duty well;
In distant ages high your fame shall swell.
Perhaps the birds, upon the joyful wing,
Thro' circling years, my honored name may sing;
Perhaps the forests catch the grateful strain,
And send the echoes over every plain.

VI.

"Now for the dance, your places take;
The whirling dance;" says Che-to-waik.
    Upon the square, on either side,
    The parties, ranged, the sign abide.
Aloud the choral voices swell;
On high resounds the festal yell:
    And to and fro at first they sweep;
    At first a steady movement keep.
But soon the wild excitement grows,
And every face with frenzy glows.
    The swinging arms are thrown on high;
    The plumage dances to the sky.
The steady measure soon forgot,
Each whirls and leaps upon the spot.
    The wild contortions, grim, affright,
    Like spectral demons of the night.
The mighty, troubled, bounding mass,
A den of furies might surpass;
    So fierce they every muscle play:
Their yells are like the ocean roar,
When billows lash resounding shore,
    And toss on high the cloudy spray.

But wild extreme, in any form,
Its own reaction will maintain;
And soon abates the festal storm;
The host are seated once again.

VII.

Tai-go-ne-ga arises now,
The vast assembly seated still;
Majestic is his manly brow:
He begs a song of Whippoorwill.
"Ah, sing the song of victory,
That soon will ring thro'out the West!
Oh, touch the cords of sympathy,
That vibrate in the human breast!"
She gently rises to the view;
A smile is beaming in her face;
She seems a guardian Manitou,
Endowed with every pleasing grace.
At once applause in thunder tells,
For her — the living power of song;
Upon her fixed is every eye:
And as her lofty stanza swells,
The chorus, loud, the host prolong;
It rolls along the vaulted sky.

SONG OF VICTORY.

1.

The foemen came, in dread array—
    The terror-dealing Iroquois;
The foe that holds a mighty sway—
That loves to storm in battle fray,
    In all the panoply of war.

CHORUS.

The mighty, terror-dealing Iroquois,
In all the dreadful panoply of war.

2.

The strong alliance then we sought,
    O-nun-da-no-ga clan to face;
Of chiefs that often bravely fought,
And deeds of signal valor wrought—
    The chieftains of Algonquin race.

CHORUS.

O-nun-da-no-ga's haughty clan to face,
The chieftains of the proud Algonquin race.

3.

On, onward comes the dreadful foe;
    He strides along the battle plain;
He twangs the mighty hunter's bow;
He deals the heavy, deadly blow;
    And yet we hurl him back again.

CHORUS.

He strides along the groaning battle plain,
And yet we bravely hurl him back again.

4.

He steals, obscure, upon the deep,
    A sore repulse to artful save;
But while he would upon us creep,
Our light canoes in fury sweep;
    We quickly drive him from the wave.

CHORUS.

A sore repulse he thus would artful save;
We bold assail, and drive him from the wave.

5.

Again he storms along the land;
    His war-whoop yell invades the sky;
We make a final—noble stand;
We grapple with him, hand to hand;
    Fly, fly! Ho-dé-no-sau-nee fly!

CHORUS.

His war-whoop yell invades the frighted sky;
Fly, fly! Ho-dé-no-sau-nee, turn and fly!

6.

Ah, look upon the battle plain!
    A dreadful charnel house it seems:
Ah! gather up the honored slain—
The braves that n'er shall fight again—
    That hasten to the land of dreams.

CHORUS.

A dreadful charnel house the battle seems;
Of braves that hasten to the land of dreams.

7.

Let every western forest wake,
    And ring triumphant with acclaim;
Let earth itself responsive quake;
Let river, prairie, rolling lake,
    Resound our never-dying fame.

CHORUS.

And ring triumphant with a loud acclaim;
Resound afar our never-dying fame.

8.

My song is ended. Happy home!
    We love thee, Teuchsa Grondie, still;
We love thee wheresoe'er we roam:
Then once for all, loud chorus, come—
    Respond again to Whippoorwill.

CHORUS.

We love thee, happy home; we love thee still;
And loud respond again to Whippoorwill.

MISCELLANEOUS POEMS.

BY

LEVI BISHOP.

PREFACE.

In the year 1864, the historical and personal incident entitled "Sir Bruin" was produced, that being the author's first serious attempt at poetical composition. After that, from 1864 to 1867, the pieces under the general title "Hours of Recreation," were written, to and including the one entitled "Science." In November, 1867, Teuchsa Grondie was begun. The tribute to the memory of young De Puy was composed in 1868. Teuchsa Grondie was completed in May, 1870. After that, the "Hours of Recreation" were resumed and continued in the order as they appear herein.

SIR BRUIN.

"BEWAR THE BAR."
WAVERLY.

The grim, taciturn bear,
The anchorite monk of the desert.
EVANGELINE.

These verses were suggested by the following incident: A short time before sundown of a pleasant afternoon in the autumn of 1844, the author was out shooting, near the Michigan Central Railroad, when that road entered Detroit on Michigan avenue. The evening train then happened to come in, and its noise aroused a full-grown black bear, just in the edge of the woods, about two miles from the City Hall, Detroit. In his fright, Sir Bruin started and ran directly for the city, and he passed through one field and far into another before he discovered his mistake. He then took a circuit, and, with several dogs yelling after him, bounded back into the forest. The incidents are fully related in the poem.

DETROIT, 1864. L. B.

Sir Bruin was a gallant lad:
The truth of history we relate;
To *fright* the game a taste we had,
Tho' game did rarely compensate.

The herds now hied them home to rest,
The milkmaid sung her rural song;
The sun was blazing in the West,
His evening beams he poured along.

'Twas Indian Summer—sweet November,
When fields were dry and leaves were yellow;
With gun, we ranged the copse and timber;
We met Sir Bruin—gallant fellow!

It seems Sir Bruin was inclined
  To leave his native forest home,
And take to city life refined,
  No longer in the wilds to roam.

And, sister cities of the West,
  Who rival greatness love to prate,
Sir Bruin's judgment gives the test,
  He chose the "City of the Strait."

Nor was it freak, or done in haste;
  His bearship gave it due reflection;
'Twas highly cultivated taste,
  That wisely gave him this direction.

He came within a mile or two,
  Where farm and forest then did meet;
He saw the city—full in view,
  The smoky air and dusty street.

He stopped and brushed his shaggy mane
  From sense of due propriety;
Then gaily started on again
  To join "Our Best Society."

'Twas near the Central Railroad track,
  The route it ran in former day;
So Bruin thought to mount its back,
  In hopes to find the better way.

Just then the pond'rous evening train,
  With fire, and smoke, and dust, and din,
Came whirling, rushing on amain,
  Came bounding, screaming, thund'ring in.

Doubt not, Sir Bruin, he had pluck,
For any ordinary plight;
For he could face the noblest buck,
And, as a pastime, give him fight.

A hundred crested gobblers gay,
Might strut and gobble in his track;
With beak and spur beset his way,
And he right soon would drive them back.

But what on earth could stand before
The fiery dragon in his wrath!
Enough, to gain his wilds once more,
With such a fury on his path!

As quick as thought he took to flight,
Nor took he well his bearings clear;
His brain it reeled; in such a fright,
He sprung for life, for life so dear!

He bounded on, as on a raid;
Beside the thundering train he went;
Forgetful of the course he made,
Directly for the city bent.

Fences he scaled, he swept the field,
As yet no slack was in his pace;
Nor would he to the fury yield,
In this his wild "two-forty" race.

The passengers all noted him,
As swift toward the goal he came;
A laurel crown they voted him,
With shouts, as in Olympic game.

Nimbly we raised our loaded gun;
  How tempting was the prize, how fair!
Oh! could we hit him on the run!
  If we could only bag a bear!

Too late; he's quickly out of range:
  And now his erring course he sees;
He sweeps around, that course to change,
  And all for life to forest flees.

And then the dogs the game espy;
  An ill-bred and uncivil pack;
And such a wild, discordant cry!
  Another fury on his track!

Sir Bruin to his forest flew,
  With heart as light as paws were fleet;
Nor further dare the curs pursue;
  It was a "masterly retreat."

And safe once more within his lair,
  All foam and dust from such a strife,
He feels content to be a bear,
  And seek no more for city life.

And yet, 'tis passing strange, I ween,
  That such a great variety,
Of these Sir Bruins oft are seen,
  All in "Our Best Society."

HOURS OF RECREATION.

INTRODUCTION.

I.

Celestial Muse! that still inspires,
And fans to flame poetic fires!
Thy kindly guidance now impart;
O touch this pen, and theme, and heart!
That numbers sweet, and truth, and ken,
And worthy thoughts, of things and men,
May deep impress our various song:
    The bold attempt be mine;
    The inspiration thine:
To Thee success and fame belong.

II.

But why thus on the muses call?
    And why this antique strain?
Must poets thus forever fall
    Into this path again?

The muses all, were but a dream,
    Illissus but a rill;
The Arno but a rapid stream,
    Parnassus but a hill.

Thus criticism surly growls
    At introductory rhyme;
So wise, so blind, like other owls
    To hoot in leisure time!

Know this — the strain of invocation,
  Which thus annoys the critic,
Is but a call on inspiration
  To lend the fire poetic.

III.

And, gentle reader, kindly share
  Our anxious toil and fears;
Unfriendly criticism spare,
  Grant sympathizing tears.

To us the rugged path of life
  Has rugged been indeed;
Yet never lacked we in the strife
  A friend in time of need.

O, now extend the friendly hand,
  For excellence was meant;
O, gently wave the healing wand,
  Approve the good intent.

We grant you all that you can say,
  For many faults are seen;
Then let them pass, let us we pray,
  Be our own Fadladeen.

IV.

This life abounds in charming pleasures,
But pain intrudes to mar them all,—
The base alloy in earthly treasures —
The doom of man since Adam's fall.

The pain, the anguish deep, all know them well;
And yet each tongue in glowing words can tell,
How dear each worthy triumph of the day—
The bright sunshine where storms beset the way.

In public and in private life,
  In civil sway, in war,
How sweet to conquer in the strife—
  To dash malignant star.

And when, with fearful odds, in battle fray
We meet, and stand, and face the stern array
Of numbers all undaunted; and we feel
Our firm resolve, though unrelaxed, yet reel
In doubt and in despair; then doubly sweet
To gain, unhoped, the victory complete.

Success! 'Tis varied, and for all
In some degree; the great, the small,
Sustain defeat. Our hopes, our fears,
Are drowned in joys or bitter tears.
To-day, we bear a rival's fling;
To-morrow, he will feel the sting.
To-day, repulse and gloomy sorrow;
We shout triumphant on the morrow.

V.

Shall we, in glowing verse, or ever soar
With Homer, Tasso, Akenside? who pour
From richest, purest fonts the sweetest streams
Of melody? whose stately measure gleams
  With heavenly light? who sound the deep,
  And ride the storm, and climb the steep,

Of purest contemplation? No:
How empty was the thought! But lo,
They guide our feet! Blazing afar,
We follow their auspicious star
Like Magi of the East. We sought
Not palfry pelf, but to be brought
In lowly admiration to their shrine;
Theirs the creative, the faint echo mine.
Their car of fire may dart celestial ray,
Like shooting comet or the milky way;
For theirs the lofty, ever glorious strain,
That mounts on high, by right divine to reign.

To genius humbly thus we sing,
Our lowly tribute thus we bring;
A tribute, ages pay, of every state;
That constant swells with rolling years,
Till fame is echoed from the spheres;
And time confirms the greatness of the great.

GIVE HIM HIS DUE.

NOTE.—In the fore part of the year 1865, the amendment of the federal constitution, for the abolition of slavery throughout the United States, was pending before the country. The author then wrote and circulated a pamphlet advocating the adoption of the measure. The following piece was composed about the same time.

These sentimental lines we write,
Make this deduction:
In sixty-five, when all unite
For "reconstruction."

The African is here, with sombre hue
In culture as in skin. Yet he was true,
E'en to oppressors, when, in deadly strife,
Millions went forth "to save a nation's life."

The danger, toil and death he shared;
He stormed the breach, his breast he bared,
In faith devout;
He stood as of a nation's brave,
And heard, while sinking to the grave,
The victor shout.

Then give him what is due; strike off his chain:
For blood like water poured, this much we gain:
Freedom we purge forever of the shame
Of bondage deep. We vindicate our name.
Then let him have his due. Let earth and sea
Echo the cannon's roar, and speak him free.
This much we may and should. He earned it well:
Then let his race, and now and ever tell
Of his deliverance. His lot at best
Is pitiful. His future is the test
How fast and far 'tis safe and best to go,
In lifting up a race now sunk so low.

But this we safely, justly, nobly can—
Proclaim, at least, and make him free;
Let him stand forth, as he was made, a man,
To swell the shout of victory.

THE WEST.

The West! The wild, the distant West!
Of Earth's domain the richest—best.
So fame would have us say, at least,
Of this luxuriant—natural feast;
Where moose, and wolf, and buffalo,
Have held their sway by streams that flow
Eternal to the Gulf; where rocks
And mounts are scarcely seen, but flocks
Abound, and game in plain and brake,
Roam far and wide to Northern Lake.

Of two proud races here we find;
The noblest of the human kind.
The White moves on from East apace,
A ruling and encroaching race.

Before his march the Red Man fast retires,
Like herds before the sweeping prairie fires;
He thus retires, but yet retires in vain,
He stands at bay before Pacific's main.

He struggles there a few short years,
Beside the "Golden Gate,"
And then forever disappears;
Thus speak the words of fate.

History records his gloomy story
Of robbery and wrong:
Poets embalm his name in glory—
In never dying song.

In this fair West, that teems with mind,
And all material things that bind
The race, and link the world in one,
But whose swift course is scarce begun,
Shall there be found whereof to fire
The generous breast, and to inspire
The lofty song? There shall indeed;
Whoever runs may freely read.

The wild flower and the eglantine;
The copper, lead and golden mine
With riches yet untold;
The plain, the mighty lake and river;
The gales that stately forests shiver;
The winter's sweeping cold:
The blade that shoots from every plain,
The waving fields of ripening grain,
The gathered corn in sheaf;
Refreshing showers of summer day,
The sweet perfume of new made hay,
The sear-autumnal leaf:
The smoke that curls from cabin home;
The Red Man, who as yet may roam,
In proud and fearless tread,
With knife at belt, and hunter's bow,
From British line to Mexico,
Among his mighty dead:
His war path, war whoop, mound and tillage,
His wigwam, wardrobe, mat and village,
His listless—idle life;
His partner drudge, beneath her pack,
Or with the pappoose at her back,
With only name of wife:
The gay cascade, the crystal fountain,
The Alleghany, Rocky Mountain—
Vast battlements on high—

That bound us on the east and west,
With gorge, and peak, and snowy crest,
Bold stretching to the sky:
All these and thousands more. And then,
Behold the crowning subject—men;
And women, too: The young and old
Of every name, of every mold:
Of every clime and every nation;
Of every rank and every station:
Of every mind and every passion:
Of every freak and every fashion:
With tastes and characters as various,
As best of fortunes are precarious.

And then the future: yes, the future West!
Its growth, its riches, power, who can foresee?
Its grand extent, from mountain crest to crest,
From lake to gulf; what is its destiny?

The central range of one vast continent,
It holds the balance firm of all the rest;
From teeming soil that never can be spent,
We feed the world as if it were a guest.

Here strangers swarm, a happy home to seek,
The waves rush on like ocean's swelling tide;
A few decades, and here shall millions speak
The law that shall a mighty empire guide.

Yes, poetry is all around us,
Enough, in truth, to well confound us.
The very air we breathe inspires our song;
The opening future years the strain prolong.

From wild Niagara's plunging flood,
To Minnehaha's distant wood,
The echoes rise, and swell, and gently fall;

They float upon the zephyr's wings—
As when sweet Philomela sings—
From "Pictured Rocks" to Montezuma's hall.

But who, of all, shall poet be
The Western harp to wake—
To sing in notes as bold, as free
As tempest on the Lake?

The songs that charmed the Grecian isles
Were echoed on Italian page;
Enchantments of Calypso smiles
Find counterpart in Dido's rage.

The Roman sway, unwieldy grown,
Is crushed beneath barbaric power;
Its mighty genius overthrown,
As northern blast will crush the flower.

The Crescent and the Turk assail
Byzantine Cross of Christian world;
Nor Rome's great name can aught avail,
Her Orient rule from place is hurled.

Majestic Muse of Greece and Rome!
From fierce destruction take Thy wing;
In Gaul and Britain find a home,
Again, in Western Europe, sing.

Nor wild Atlantic surges shun,
The gales shall bear Thee safely o'er;
The course of empire—with the sun,
Invites Thee to our western shore.

Responsive to the British lyre,
Our poets sing in sweetest strain;
But lend the West Thy native fire!
Here let Thine altars blaze again!

Then whose the genius, culture, might,
In all this western land,
To give its harp a worthy flight?
To touch it, whose the hand?

The instrument has strength and scope
For any earthly strain,
But untried hands can never hope
Its highest notes to gain.

"Great Spirit" of this garden World!
O genius of the West!
Let Thy proud banners be unfurled,
On Thee the work must rest!

DIGNITY OF LABOR.

"Is not this the Carpenter?"—MARK vi. 3.

Genius of toil! our verse indite,
And blaze along each line!
O, give it wing and give it might,
Creative power divine!

Thou source of plenty and of wealth,
Spirit of toil, now tune the lyre!
Fountain of peace, contentment, health,
Spirit of toil, our song inspire!

But can this humble theme, or ever dart
Celestial fires, or move or warm the heart?
Can sober fact, and dry detail
Of daily drudgery, avail
To raise the human mind, or soul
From earth towards its heavenly goal?
The Muses love heroic—battle songs;
But can they sing of bellows, coal and tongs.

In truth; for while in rich Homeric strain,
They sung Achilles on the Trojan plain,
They also sung, for that heroic field,
The work of Vulcan on Achilles' shield.
The process simple; glorious the design,
Such as can spring alone from hand divine.

Thus, while the heavy stone is laid,
And column, arch and beam—
Although for pile of lofty grade—
The toil may humble seem:

Yet as the work progresses high,
Held firmly by mechanic power,
The fair proportions charm the eye,
Of stately palace, dome or tower.

Nor stop we at the works of man,
In our poetic story;
Our theme extends to nature's plan,
To nature's lab'ratory:

At least, examples here it draws,
From nature's works and nature's laws.

The mellow tint, the blended shade,
Of leaf, and blade, and flower,
By fingers all divine are made—
By the Almighty power.

By work, the buds and blossoms shoot,
That load the autumn tree with fruit;
From natal to the mortal hour,
All nature feels mechanic power.

By work, the glorious sun was lit on high,
And hung resplendent in the blazing sky.

The planets whirling on their poles,
In system that forever rolls;
The ocean, air and sod;
The worm, and the leviathan,
His image — the immortal man,
Are master works of God.

By work, the comets blaze, and shoot, and flee;
By work, the earth was lifted from the sea,
The sky spread out so clear;
The mountain sprung from earth's convulsive throes,
By work divine the universe arose,
From chaos wild and drear.

Nor even here the glorious subject ends;
To moral, and religious, it extends.

By toil, and pain, and groan, and death,
Was man's salvation wrought;
In faith, by works, the preacher saith,
Must Christian life be fought.

The work is life-long, and from day to day,
In this, the sure, but straight and narrow way.
And in one universal plan,
'Tis work must form the moral man.

Yes, work may fire poetic pen,
And elevate its strain,
As well as aught of human ken,
In heaven, or earth, or main.

And who true happiness would know,
Or who would fill a worthy part,
In any place, or high or low,
Must work with body, mind and heart.

The intellect must lead the van,
The muscle must perform its share,
The heart must lead the social man,
For all affection centers there.

The cheerful swain,
That plows and sows his fields,
With hopes of plenty and of future gain,
Such as prolific nature yields;
Who tills the soil his God has made,
And toils at his command,
Goes whistling home at evening shade,
A monarch of the land.

Who plies a loom, or lays a keel,
Or makes a broom, or rims a wheel;
Or drives a team, or digs a ditch,
Or dams a stream, or takes a stitch;
Or lays a pipe, or "runs a mill,"
Or sets a type, or "drives a quill;"
Or swings a sledge or flail;
Or lays a brick, or tans a hide;
Or drives a screw or nail;
May lift his head in honest pride,
And boldly say:
I work, create, increase the solid wealth,
For which the idle play,
And win, by art, chicane, or stealth.

And yet, though strange, if well we scan,
His art may wrong the artisan.

With sooty—sweaty frock,
With heavy—callous hand,
He frames the cunning lock,
He molds the solid band—

That holds from toil, in rusty guard
Or vault, its fair and just reward.
The art, the skill, the taste, we may commend;
The fault, if fault there be, is in the end.
Nor artist blame in this assertion;
The blame is found in the perversion.

And furthermore; the hard-earned fruits of toil,
The golden streams of luxury, the spoil
Of business and of trade, before which all,
As to a charming goddess, bow and fall:
The shining merit of a prince or duke;
The very golden calf of Pentateuch;—
Whence comes it all? To whom does it belong?
To him who works, whatever else is wrong.
By craft the social system is deranged;
By working men that system may be changed.
However much their efforts may be slighted,
They have the power to see the system righted.
The social balance but adjusted well,
No miser, more, would golden counters tell.
Then equal all would public burdens bear,
And equal all the fruits of labor share.

And now, let's take a promenade,
And note of work a lower grade.

The humble—modest "hand"
That cleans the filthy street,
May proudly take his stand,
And worthily compete—

With him that rolls and spatters by,
So lordly seated, swelling high,
With livery, coach and four;
The one is honest poverty;
The other glittering bankruptcy,
All rotten at the core.

From labor all;
No matter what or where,
Or high, or low, or great, or small,
Or excellent, or base, or plain, or fair.
The ship that plows the ocean wave,
The palace that has seen a thousand years,
The lofty stone that decks the grave
And marks the spot once bathed in tears;
The creature comforts — luxuries of life,
The products of the teeming soil;
All come from weary strife —
From honest toil.

A term of years, let labor cease;
Let work be at an end;
Let those who live by wit increase,
Till all should thus depend.

Then how would swelling pomp and pride,
The strutting fop and painted fair —
Those floating bubbles on the tide,
Collapse to what they truly are!

The idle thousands, with their sordid gains,
The race itself, that honest toil sustains,
Would mourn, and weep, and wail;
Would rush by myriads into myriad graves,
O'erwhelmed beneath oblivion's chilling waves,
And no one left to tell the tale.

The man who justly views the scope of things,
And is not borne away upon the wings
Of ignorance, or prejudice, or pride,
Will take these sober maxims as his guide:

In labor, is true dignity.
In honest toil, benignity.

They touch our theme in all its ranges,
In its innumerable stations—
Its vast variety and changes,
In all its toiling occupations.

And from the ever working mass,
In social system all complex,
None are exempt of any class,
Or any rank of either sex.

Or if exempt, it still is but the drone;
Work, is the rule, from cottage to the throne.
Work, every station should embrace,
From skeptic to confessional—
In private and in public place,
The unlearned, the professional.

And women, too, the rule must share;
Her destiny is written there.

Woman! the fairest work of God!
Or servant, maid, or matron wife;
How sinks her heart beneath the load,
Of toilsome, painful, weary life!

But, says the lordly stoic, since the fall
We grant her no concession;
She justly sighs and suffers, one and all,
Because of her transgression.

But such is not her proper sphere;
Thus mournful speaks her nature, too;
Behold her, man, your mate and peer!
Yet sorrowful, she toils for you.

The implements of work to wield,
Was made the sturdy arm of man;
The gentler sex, that arm will shield,
From painful toil whene'er it can.

Lord of creation! proudly such,
Pity the sex, so tearful, sad;
Be not forgetful over much,
You have a mother, or you had.

Relieve her load, so heavy—weary;
Her frequent sufferings beguile;
And cheer her pathway—often dreary,
With kindly heart, and word, and smile.

Creative labor is of mind, and heart,
And soul, as well as of the hand;
And thought, reflection, letters, science, art,
Are brothers of a working band.

The one upon the other acts,
In generous co-operation;
Where theories unite with facts,
In ever-happy combination.
In union their perfection lies,
If aught is perfect 'neath the skies.

While muscle, mental, moral, thus we sing,
And from them all the fruits of toil we bring;
From works of Adam in his garden pent,
To those that proudly span a continent,
Where every blow is worthy of a line,
As kin to those that spring from hand divine;
Explore creation's utmost bounds, to find,
None can exemption claim, of human kind;
While thus we catch the soft angelic strain,
And gather flowers from all the golden train
Of pure intelligence; and virtue, too,
In ever charming smiles our verse may woo;
And while our theme, in each and every part,
Glows with the fires that move and warm the heart;
Yet blows of working men, now strike the lyre;
And these alone, may well the Muse inspire.

O then ye millions, ye who bow and sweat
Beneath your toil, for many a weary hour,
Stand forth — ye have not boldly stood as yet —
In all the grandeur, glory, of your power!

Let muscle, with the moral blend,
Improve the mind, improve the heart;
Let social to religious tend,
And fill on earth a worthy part.

The gifts of body and of mind,
Are lent by wisdom from above;
Aspire to be what God designed,
Let culture every gift improve.

This end to reach the way is plain;
From daily toil — an hour of leisure;
'Tis justice wrung from sordid gain,
A small per cent from bloated treasure.

The remedy pursue, be men!
Reduce your daily hours from ten
Of weary all-exhausting weight,
To healthy, cheerful, nine or eight.

Nor let these precious hours away be cast;
The sands of time are running — flying fast:
Eternal ages in the past are rolled;
Our lives, eternal ages, yet unfold.
The life of man — a point of time,
A note in one eternal chime.

Though health may bloom, the end is ever nigh;
Then well improve the moments as they fly.

And yet this life's a battle-field,
Of sturdy blows, and sighs and din;
Where sloth must to the active yield,
Where bad must lose and good must win.

Nor is it all — this life below,
To that to come — a short prelude,
Where all may rest from pain and woe
In glorious beatitude.
In time we find unerring test,
To fit us for eternal rest.

Then stand ye forth, I say again;
Be firm, but just, ye working men!

He who creates should ever hold command:
Then "league" your forces, all your powers combine;
In unity behold your strength to stand!
United "strike," success shall then be thine.

Industrial train! that saw the dawning ray
Of first creation; that, from age to age,
Has steady swept along the grand highway
Of circling years; where each historic page —

Is written o'er and o'er with hopes and fears,
And soothing smiles and bitter — burning tears!
How groan thy pond'rous cars beneath the freight
That toil produces! Vast — incumbent weight!
The richest streams from earth's remotest bound,
By thee are poured in one incessant round
Of sparkling beauty, 'mong the eager throng,
That share thy spoil, and would thy stay prolong.
Then still move on, with banner broad unfurled,
To feed, and warm, and cheer, and bless the world.

DIMANCHE.

(LA MI-JUIN.)

"O where shall rest be found—
Rest for the weary soul?"

Hail Sabbath-day! Of all the seven the best!
From six of bustling toil how sweet the calm!
A troubled sea, from surging waves, at rest—
To weary, wounded life, a healing balm!

The ever-circling hours upon the wing,
Are told by stately peals of morning bell;
In plaintive tone responding breezes sing;
The air seems laden with a solemn spell.

The home affairs of morn at first arranged,
For worship, parent, maiden, swain prepare;
From plain, to neat and gay, attire is changed,
In cabin, cottage, mansion—everywhere.

Now forth they issue on the rural way,
Or on the shady walk in cities swarm;
The sun looks down with mild, effulgent ray;
The twittering linnet lends melodious charm.

On every hand the "Earthly Courts" unclose;
Inviting calls the undulating chime;
In happy mood, while sipping every rose,
The wild bee hums response in gentle rhyme.

In "living green" the garden, forest, field,
The buzzing insect chants a solemn lay;
The locust blossoms sweetest incense yield;
All nature celebrates the sacred day.

The temple reached, the chimes their choral cease;
In beauty, fashion, shines the well-filled nave;
Yet all is pensive, for the Prince of Peace
Is here to bless, to sanctify and save.

And now the organ warbles softest notes,
Now gathers volume in its swell above;
Now bolder strain in vaulted arches floats,
And hearts are tuned to worship and to love.

In robes as white — as pure as faith is pure,
The priest advances now, sedate and slow;
And with a voice as calm as faith is sure —
"Arise I will and to my father go."

Impressive are the accents of the service — all:
The chant, the bow at Jesus' name, the air
And song of praise, to bended knee the fall,
The absolution, and the humble prayer;

The lessons, and the sermon — earnest — clear,
The creed, and that majestic litany!
In short, from "scripture moveth — brethren dear,"
To "Father, Son and Spirit — One in Three."

And then that fountain, full of mystery!
But which, to the devout, is all so plain;
That figures forth the passage through the sea,
"Of water-spirit, thou art born again."

And then the meeting of that little band
Of childhood years, whose plastic heart and mind
Are led and molded by the gentle hand,
And taught to lisp "The Saviour of mankind."

By hands laid on — confirmed baptismal vow;
Another solemn and mysterious rite!
Salvation's helmet — hope, reburnished now;
Another shield of faith for christian fight!

The innocence that "round the altar goes,"
    The "comfortable" wine and broken bread—
The broken body of the Man of woes—
    The risen Lord that brings to life the dead!

And then that nuptial form—ordeal severe;
    But yet, which covet all, in proper course;
That blends in one two loving hearts so dear,
    In life till death "for better or for worse."

And then the Herald, sent to distant lands,
    Where millions groan beneath the pagan rod;
Where superstition grim a monster stands,
    And gnashes vengeance on the man of God.

And then that safe retreat from want and woe,
    Which giver's heart improves in what is given—
The Hospital—a vestibule below,
    That smooths for honest poor the path to heaven.

And then the bed of sickness and of pain
    Where minutes--hours, are mark'd by sigh and moan,
O there, consoling thought! a Savior slain,
    Can soothe the anguish, sweeten every groan!

O yes, and e'en amid consuming fires
    That persecution lights—that blaze around
The martyr's head! E'en there the soul aspires
    To God, and with eternal life is crowned!

And then that solemn burial of the dead!
    Corruption incorrupt! Where ends the strife!
The immortality in Christ, the Head!
    "I am the resurrection and the life!"

The whole; how comprehensive and sublime!
    It covers life—the shortest, longest span;
Embraces all the wants and hopes of time;
    A boon of God, vouchsafed to fallen man!

It fits us for the race that here we run;
From earth to heaven it draws the soul and heart!
'Tis all a preparation, now begun,
For future world to which we soon depart.

Or true or false, let me believe it true!
Let not annihilation snatch my soul!
Let that soul live, eternal ages through,
And reach the blest abode, the happy goal!

Oh, when this weary life at last shall end,
Let not oblivion's ever gloomy wave
Roll o'er my sleeping dust! Great God! O lend
Thine own right arm, Omnipotent to save!

LA VILLE DU DETROIT.

Of all the cities of the plain,
Beside the river or the main,
How active or how fair;
Of rapid or of sluggish gait;
Give me the City of the Strait.
'Twixt Erie and St. Clair.

I love its budding, gushing spring,
Its ripening summer on the wing,
Its Indian Summer, too;
And e'en its wint'ry—snowy tides,
Its jingling bells and rapid rides,
Upon "The Avenue."

I love its cool, delicious shades,
Its water founts and promenades,
Its elegant hotels;

Its many men of worth and mind,
Its matrons — dignified — refined,
Its many pretty belles.

Its ladies; yes, I love to meet
Those fairy forms and tripping feet;
They come — they pass me now;
The angels condescend to smile;
I look, enraptured all the while;
I raise my hat and bow.

I like to meet the men I know,
And here and there — where'er I go,
A living, moving mass;
To shake the hand of young and old;
To tell the news or hear it told;
The "time o' day" to pass.

I like its spires and stately domes;
Its mansions and its princely homes,
Its social life within;
Its shops, its churches and its schools,
And e'en its fops and many fools,
And its incessant din.

I like its avenues so grand;
Yes, even those that Woodward planned:
I love that noble river —
So broad, so stately and so deep,
With that sedate and gentle sweep,
Majestic and forever.

I love to range the busy quay,
To see its thrift on autumn day,
To greet the sailor boy;
To see the boats that crowd the mart,
The graceful ships that come — depart;
"O, ho! A ship ahoy!"

I love to gaze at Britain's shore,
To stand and contemplate her power,
    And offer up the prayer,
That I may live the day to see,
When these our neighbors shall be free,
    With a Republic there.

I love its legendary story,
Its pioneer—historic glory,
    For much it has in store;
Its annals stretch much farther back,
Than gloomy days of Pontiac,
    Or Cadillac of yore.—

A new world springing into view,
At once the high ambition drew
    De Louis Quatorze—Le Grand;
His missions far the wild explore,
Coureurs des Bois from shore to shore,
    Hunt out the unknown land.

But whence and what that perished race,
Whose many footprints on the face
    Of western world are found?
That far advance in useful arts?
Those cities with extensive marts,
    Now deep beneath the ground?

With our own race was it the same?
Then how, and when, and why, it came?
    In barque with scanty freight,
Perhaps it strayed by accident;
Perhaps it fled from banishment,
    By way of Behring's Strait.

Thou silent tomb of ages past!
Must thy sealed book forever last,
    Nor yield its contents true?

How lived, and how, forgotten, died,
Those myriads in life's rushing tide?
Echo!! Our theme pursue.—

I like its French, with his good cheer,
Its German, with his lager beer,
Its burly Englishman;
Its Yankee—active, prying, "smart,"
Its warm and generous Irish heart,
Its Scot from Highland clan.

I like its healthy, steady thrift;
No ups or downs or bankrupt shift,
No fancy "bulls" or "bears;"
Its men of wealth, *own what they own*,
Nor is it small, as may be shown;
We have our *millionaires*.

I love its rich surrounding plain,
Where happiness and plenty reign,
In cabin life begun;
I love its glittering stars above,
Its mellow moonlight, too; I love
Its gorgeous setting sun.

To Paris or imperial Rome,
I it prefer, for it is home;
Our home, it has a spell:
I range the world, and yet I find
On my return, this home to bind
Me ever here to dwell.

Yes, lovely city of the West!
Here let me live, and die and rest,
When summons comes to go:
It is the place of places all,
Or rich, or proud, or great, or small;
A paradise below.

A "HOP" AT SARATOGA.

"On with the dance! Let joy be unconfined!"

The hall is ample; gilded arches shine;
Columns and decorated walls combine
To move the soul and swell the heart:
The guests are many; salutations gay;
And charms as lovely as the flowers of May,
As quick they fade, as quick depart.

Against the gorgeous lights suspended high,
The diamonds flash that rival maiden's eye:
In dress what medley shades! The green,
The black, the red, the violet, the blue,
The crimson, white and pink, all fashioned true
To native taste; a fairy scene:

And (speaking in a whisper) we may say,
Many a model bust *décolleté*,
And sweeping train and farthingale;
And "rats" and ample "water-falls" are there;
And glossy locks of false or colored hair;
And rouge to hide complexion pale.

Behold the forms! The tall as Teneriffe;
The medium—graceful as the dancing skiff
Upon the undulating tides;
The fleshy, robust, muscular and slim;
The dwarf; the short and thick, but neat and trim
As grace itself; the sylph that glides.

The faces! Broad and oval; laughing, plumpy;
The long, the "hatchet," and the short and stumpy;
The solemn, "lantern-jawed," and sainted;

The intellectual, with the look refined;
The "tallow," with the "stolid" well combined;
The merely plaster-paris painted.

The noses! From the bony, peaked, prim,
Through choicest model of the Grecian slim,
To purple, pugilistic "mug"
And from the Roman, boldly arching high,
Through flat and broad, or twisted all awry,
To short upturned, but jolly pug.

Tremendous whiskers! O ye Turkish race,
With shame behold, and shave thy hairy face!
The gray, the brown, the sandy, brindle;
The long and bushy, and the short and thin;
"Divine imperial" from the lip to chin;
The *moustache* twisted to a spindle.

The ties and chokers! Long the weary hours
He spent before his glass, and yet the powers
Prolonged the struggle ever new;
The hateful knot is tied and tied again,
And still he labors on with might and main,
Till full perfection springs to view.

The characters! From mincing, nipping miss,
With barely sense to simper — very — yes,
To scented fop with grinning glee;
The prude of forty with affected glances,
The matron with an eye to all the chances,
The bride that is, or is to be.

The coy advance of swain, sly ogle meets;
Young heart to beating heart responsive beats —
Leer not, ye roguish looker on; —
The lips disclaim, while hearts betray the sigh;
Consenting fathers turn aside the eye;
Avaunt, thou rival! Haste, begone!

But see that eye — that languish! That success
In curls and tints! Voluptuous loveliness!
Artfully artless smile — inspired!
Enthusiastic suitors swarm about her;
While envious rivals curl the lip and flout her;
How perilous — to be admired!

Such airs and affectations! Well, 'tis clear
As sun at noon, the fatal day is near,
When "Captain Snipe" and "Colonel Grand,"
With painted dolls may mince, and ape, and smirk,
And rush without restraint to — *a la Turque,*
Throughout this "broad and happy land."

Societies we organize, and lend
The means, and far away the mission send
The world to christianize and save;
While at our very hearths we should begin;
Here follies riot run, and social sin,
That drag to shame and to the grave.

But what avail in lofty tone to preach?
Or who, save high Omnipotence can teach
The Mississippi flood to stay?
The mighty shock of civil war is past;
Its dire effects in social life will last,
Till years on years have rolled away.

Begone the serious! Let the dance begin:
Softly the animating violin,
The warbling flute, the heavy bass,
The harp, unite in one voluptuous call,
To "Take your partners for cotillion," all,
Or in the dizzy waltz to chase.

With bow and winning smile, no pen can tell,
And "Will you dance with me, sweet mademoiselle?"
"O no, dear Sir, it cannot be;

I am engaged at least four sets ahead."
"Then say the fifth?" That face, how crimson red!
As she responds, "I—I—will see."

Now fairy forms, and sparkling eyes so bright,
And smiling faces, gaily all unite,
In one harmonious mazy chime;
And circling, bending, undulating swell
Of merry dance, with its bewitching spell,
Is beauty set to measured time.

And can we doubt that this enchanting scene
To virtue tends?—as blushing here between
The tender child and ripening years,
These happy loved ones ply their nimble feet,
And whirl, and laugh, and prattle on so sweet,
And banish care and all their tears.

Behold the graceful movements of the dance!
What other graces do they not enhance?
Exhilarating social pleasure!
Let cynics frown and bigots chide their fill,
The reason, common sense, approve it still—
That cheerful and majestic measure.

LOVE AND COQUETRY.

One only passion, unrevealed,
With maiden pride the maid concealed,
Yet not less purely felt the flame—
O, need I tell that passion's name!
LADY OF THE LAKE.

That tender passion! from its birth
So light and restless, like the leaf
In summer breeze;—so full of mirth
And ever glowing fancy, chief
Among the first, all know its name—
A spark, a flash of heavenly flame!

A flame that nestles in the heart;
That seems a self-ignited fire;
That scorns deceit and every art,
And every foe that may conspire;
True love!—a furnace heated well,
A passion language cannot tell.

It springs at times, like opening flower,
Like magnet trembles to its pole;
It bursts, at times, like evening shower,
And wildly rushes to the goal;
And yet, if e'er so quick or slow,
Effect the same—the flush, the glow.

Like softest ray of rising moon,
It steals into the tender heart;
Like melting beam of sun at noon,
It quickly shoots through every part;
Yet airy trifles drive it thence,
As chilling drops will steam condense.

But is it not a silly freak,
 An impulse of the passing hour;
A gush of feeling, fancy streak,
 A sudden sweet, as quickly sour;
A flitting meteor in the air,
That leaves no traces printed there?

And who can tell if love, in truth,
 Is basking in that heart sincere?
As thickly swarm those flattering youth,
 Must not the coquette then be near;—
To smile at one and smile at all,
Like smiling portrait on the wall?

It may be so; the social state,
 Suggests at times deceitful air;
And who politeness will berate,
 Although deceit be lurking there?
Or who, if part be acted well,
Can coquette from the lover tell?

Affection true, is often blind;
 And, let it never be forgot,
At times the heart, when truly kind,
 Would rather be deceived than not;
Thus pride is soothed and self-esteem,
By empty sighs that real seem.

The sources of the mountain stream
 That oozy lurk among the bogs,
Where strongest might of solar beam
 A contest wages with the fogs,
In doubt if bog, or mud, or lake,
Or stream, at last predominate;—

In silver thread at last are found,
 With murm'ring accents creeping slow,
Then rushing on with many a bound

Into the circling pool below,
Bright as the crystals of its bed,
Or as the rainbow o'er its head:

So love at first in maze obscure
The labyrinth of the heart may trace,
Nor feel its own existence sure,
And doubtful of a resting place;
Not knowing even what to say
To a proposal, yea or nay;—

But soon the current clear and strong
Of purest love is fully seen,
It swiftly bears the soul along
Through flowery meads of living green;
The crimson blush, the earnest stare,
Are proof conclusive love is there.

Two rivers on the mountain side,
In giddy turbulence may dash
From ledge to ledge in foaming tide,
And sparkle in the sunlight flash;
And yet, before their race is run
They calmly may unite in one:

So love, in wild, ecstatic glee.
May babble like the mountain brook;
Wring sighs from burning jealousy,
And daggers from the rival's look;
Yet truthful, loving hearts will tend
In one to mingle at the end.

The sweetest rose of blooming May,
That blushes at the sunbeam's kiss,
That showers its perfumes o'er the way,
And makes a heavenly world of this;
That in the evening's cooling shade
With zephyrs dances masquerade;—

To her sweet charms must ever yield,
    Whose blooming tints, at bright eighteen,
And flashing eyes are sword and shield;
    Who, to be loved need but be seen;
Whose guileless heart with love does burn,
Who loves and is beloved in turn.

As undulations of the lake,
    Obedient unto nature's laws,
When pebbles thrown, the surface break,
    Will circle round the central cause;
And even when the cause is spent,
Will still obey the impulse lent;—

So waves of pure affection roll—
    As free from guile as free from art—
With first vibration in the soul,
    In circles round the human heart:
O, whence the impulse—all benign?
One only source—'tis all divine.

THE CONTRAST.

—Our rash faults
Make trivial price of serious things we have,
Not knowing them until we know their grave.
ALL'S WELL THAT ENDS WELL.

"Earth has no hate like love to hatred turned,
And hell no fury like a lover scorned."

THE SUNNY SIDE.

Sweet is the nuptial morn. Now hearts are light,
From dreams of bliss in wedded life begun;
The altar now performs its solemn rite;
The mystic ring now links the two in one;
And longing hours of sentimental fiction,
An echo find in closing benediction.

"At home;" assembled now a brilliant throng;
Fair one, congratulations all are thine!
And wit and repartee and laugh prolong
The merry hours that swim in generous wine:
All hearts exclaim with every foaming tide:
Long life and health, thou lovely, happy bride!

Adieu, the time is up; the parting kiss,
For wedding tour, must close the festive scene:
How flies the train with flying hours of bliss!
How smiles the landscape in its dress of green!
'Tis night—'tis morn—a moment and 'tis noon,
For hours are minutes in the honey-moon.

Now varied objects gaily shine around;
In fond affection lost are all our fears;
In changing scene new pleasures yet abound;

In wild excitement now the world appears:
So light the heart, the step so light and free,
We scarcely touch, but skim along the lea.

That playful fondness meets the stranger's eye;
The soft contagion to his heart extends;
His breast is troubled with a heaving sigh,
And proudest mind to Cupid's sceptre bends:
Monarchs have toiled for universal sway,
But love, without an effort, gains the day.

Observed of all observers; and the side,
To which the busy tongue will ever tend;
For well the air content betrays the bride,
And courts congratulations without end.
Then let us grant them, cheerfully, to bless,
And swell the sum of human happiness.

How sweet, in modest home, the honey-moon!
Where pride is banished, and where wants are few;
Where pure affection, as a precious boon,
Is true, and constant, and forever new:
O where, but here, can Paradise be found!
'Tis heaven itself, begun on earthly ground.

The months, the years, in social order move;
The solid virtues crown the happy state;
And kindly voices echo wedded love,
And smooth the path of life, and banish hate;
Domestic altar! let me ever share
Thy love and peace, and worship ever there!

THE STORMY SIDE.

Now years have passed away, all years of toil
And struggle—pain, and death perhaps, and woe;
All years of sadness, sorrow and turmoil;

The buoyant heart is crushed, or nearly so:
The hopeful, joyful spring-time of affection,
Is all forgot, o'erwhelmed in deep dejection.

How many bitter, burning tears have worn
Deep in the soul, the ruts no time can heal!
Its very vital strings are wrung and torn
As by a tempest: Future woe or weal
Are recklessly defied, for black despair
Has left his footprints deep imbedded there.

Where now those gay, those happy, charming hours,
When friends their lively gratulations gave?
When pleasures came as come the summer showers?
Have they all sunk to an untimely grave?
How could such love become so lifeless — cold?
And was it truly love? or glitter — gold?

How many praised the "eligible match,"
And sent their costly "presents" for the name;
While others sneered and envied such a "catch,"
And "set their caps" for like or better game;
Assisted by those social pests — match-makers —
Detested matrimonial *undertakers*.

"Has it escaped so soon! Do people know it!
The very thought is crushing to the pride!
We had our 'spat,' but labored not to show it;
Did we not 'coo,' and 'love,' and 'dear' beside?"
'Twas all in vain; the world has read it all;
Nor thin, transparent forms could hide the fall.

"And what a life since rose that nuptial morn!
And what a hell our 'happy' home has been!
O, would to Heaven we never had been born,
Or that each other we had never seen!
Or would to Heaven that you or I had died,
Before deceitful tongue your heart belied!"

"Enough; we part! To meet again? No, never!
Who can endure this living desolation!
The proudest hopes are blasted, and forever!
Escape there is none but in separation!
These ill-assorted matches well suffice,
For those eternal torments yet to rise."

"Seek not, dear friends, to reconcile; 'tis all too late!
O that our friends as one had never seen us!
I fancied that I loved—but how I hate!
I brave the worst—put worlds on worlds between us!
Like disappointed love what can distress!
Oh! blot away that passionate caress!"

At last a full exposure—suit begun;
The double story must be told on paper—
To some a scandal, but to others fun,
Then dredge for gossip with a double scraper:
Details disgusting, but which all may see;
"O, let it end, and hasten the decree!"

But what decree? Each thinks the case is clear:
Perhaps the balance may the court perplex:
Where'er it falls the blow will be severe;
Then must it fall according to the sex?
Yes, let it fall, like gad on Balaam's pony—
Divorce *a vinculo* with *Alimony*.

TO A LITTLE NIECE.

Les rayons les plus doux
Brillent au levez de l'aurore.
HYPOLITE VIOLEAU.

So full of mirth, so full of play;
With mind and heart so light and gay,
And eyes that witchery betray;
And sprightly accents rolling on,
Like birds their merry matin song,
That sweet simplicity prolong:—
In all your little griefs and joys,
In all your sports among your toys,
In giddy romps with girls and boys;—
When dearest friends behold—admire,
And freely grant what you desire;
And touched as by a heavenly fire,
The highest, fondest hopes aspire;—
As life sweeps on its rapid stream,
And future prospects brightly gleam;
And love unfolds its morning dream,
That ripens to meridian beam,
And binds as by a law supreme;—
As years advance, and you shall see
The fading foliage on the tree—
The withered flowers upon the lea—
And, drawing near, by fixed decree,
The final bourne—eternity;
Then, little dove, REMEMBER ME!

LIGHT INFANTRY.

(SCENE—The front Piazza.)

The little ones will gather round,
  And play, and sit upon my knee,
And then will run, and hop and bound,
  And chirp and twitter full of glee.

And first there comes the little Posie,
  At roguish nine or more;
And then there comes the little Cosie,
  Just prattling into four;
And next *la petite enfante* Josie,
  So shy, and now but seven;
And last, the smiling little Rosie,
  Just blushing into 'leven.

But stay—here comes the little Lillie,
  Now five and full of tricks;
And with her also little Tillie,
  At restless number six;
And then the laughing little Fillie,
  Now eight and on the run;
And last the sprightly little Millie,
  Now ten and full of fun.

The innocents, how sweet they are!
How free from guile, how free from care!
But what their future? Who can tell?
Seek not to know; 't will all be well.

Let kindness ever hold the sway,
  And not the hardening rod;
Teach them to walk in virtue's way,
  And put their trust in God.

L'ALBUM D'UNE CANADIENNE.

Speak but one rhyme, and I am satisfied.
ROMEO AND JULIET.

'Tis thought, it seems, a pretty thing,
In rhyme to write, in song to breathe;
To climb Parnassus' height and bring,
To beauty's shrine poetic wreath.

Lady, the rhyme is all I boast;
The muse has ne'er inspired my heart;
Dull prose, its strength and beauty lost,
In form of verse, my humble part.

And yet the soul aspires to raise
A worthy note — of love divine,
Of hope, of friendship's balmy days,
Of — charms of mind and heart — like thine.

A strain to virtue: Born on high,
Our thoughts, affections, hopes, above
It raises. Who its praise deny?
Yet who are constant in its love?

Lady, adieu! If war again
Should shake "the border," and destruction,
With fiery, fierce and gloomy train
Assail us, this is thy protection.

Present it, and the ruthless hand
That dares to rise against thee, down
I'll strike it; this the charm — the wand
Thy sex to guard, the fair to crown.

THE CONSOLATION.

The liquid drops of tears that you have shed,
Shall come again transformed to orient pearl.
RICHARD III.

"Speak, mother—mother dear!
Ah! it is all in vain;
On earth I ne'er shall hear
The voice I loved again."
VIOLA.

In vain! O no; on zephyr's wings
Her voice salutes thine ear; she sighs
For those she left behind, but sings—
The tomb the pathway to the skies.

Her eye is in the moon-beam's glance;
The twinkling stars her crown adorn;
Before her suns and systems dance;
Around her smiles the risen morn.

She walks the sea of glass above,
She basks upon the heavenly plain,
Where all is peace and all is love,
And truth and God forever reign.

Celestial harps of sweetest strain,
Touch highest notes of rapturous song;
Their mingled echoes soft complain—
Viola, why your stay prolong?

THE MAPLE TREE OVER THE WAY.

The juicy groves
Put forth their buds, unfolding by degrees,
Till the whole leafy forest stands displayed
In full magnificence.

THOMPSON.

Of the queen of the forest we sing—
Of her robes and her royal array;
We hail the first buds of the spring,
On the maple tree over the way.

Next, the bloom of the summer is seen,
Tho' oppressive the heat of the day;
And clad in her foliage of green,
Is the maple tree over the way.

Then, the frosts of the autumn appear,
When nature prepares for decay:
And robed in her rich golden sear,
Is the maple tree over the way.

Then comes the drear season at last,
With the storms of the chill winter's day;
And they spare not, exposed to the blast,
The maple tree over the way.

A lesson from this may be drawn:
The life that is blooming to-day,
Very soon will be withered and gone,
Like the Maple Leaves over the way.

THE DEATH OF A FRIEND.

SIT TIBI TERRA LEVIS.

Daughter of faith, awake, arise, illume
The dread unknown, the chaos of the tomb.
PLEASURES OF HOPE.

Again the enemy hath bent his bow;
Again we mourn a friend's untimely fall;
Again we feel the oft recurring woe;
Again we contemplate the end of all.

The place he filled shall know him never more;
Silent that voice, those lips nor smile or move;
We cherish, now, his many sufferings o'er,
The ever dear memorials of his love.

His faults and failings we forget; the tomb
Shall hide them all; but, shining as the sun,
His many solid virtues shall illume,
And cheer our path till life's short race is run.

Thou King of Terrors, let the loved ones stay!
Ah! why so partial to the shining mark?
Is life so long that we must haste away?
Why glory in destruction—gloomy—dark!

And why may not those genial hearts, that blend
In love and lasting friendship, that bestow
On life, the charm that nothing else can lend,
Escape that fatal, final, dreaded blow?

Friendship and love are Paradise begun;
A bliss that mortals with the angels share;
Thus linked with those above, may we not shun
The grave? Just God! Thy NO is written there!

THE SPAN OF LIFE.

Yet bright success awhile
I give thee.
COWPER'S HOMER.

I give thee one illustrious day,
One blaze of glory ere thou fadest away.
POPE'S HOMER.

The rays that first salute the morn—
That scatter pearls along their way,
Are dim, like future yet unborn,
But hopeful of the rising day:
Thus gems, and future promise too,
Are dimly seen in childhood's years;
They shoot from indications true,
But still are wrapped in hopes and fears.

The sun that tells meridian tide—
That sits enthroned in purest light—
That darts his beams on every side,
Is full of majesty and might:
Thus, who to middle life belong,
May fling to view what first began
In early hopes—be wise, and strong,
And good, and true to God and man.

The sun that shoots to western main,
With blazing banners full unfurled,
And plunges there, to rise again,
Bequeaths a lesson to the world:
The man that sinks at last to rest,
With ripened virtues full in bloom,
Like sun that sinks beneath the West,
Shall spring to life beyond the tomb.

"THE BURDEN OF A SIGH."

RESURGAM.

An angel's arm can't snatch me from the grave;
Legions of angels can't confine me there.
YOUNG.

When we on earth have run our race,
And earthly visions flee;
And we are called upon to face
That dread eternity:

As we lie down, o'erwhelmed with pain,
And feel the ebb of life;
And care and human skill are vain,
And flesh gives up the strife:

As flickering lights more dimly grow,
And stifled is the breath;
And feeble pulse more languid flow,
And feel the chill of death:

As vain is found each earthly trust,
Unworthy of the name;
And these poor frames return to dust,
To dust from whence they came:

As to that resting place we go,
That narrow house of gloom;
And weeds, and grass, and wild flowers grow,
On that forgotten tomb:

Then lift Thine arm, Almighty God,
And stretch it forth to save!
Oh, let not Thine avenging rod,
Be felt beyond the grave!

SATURNALIA.

Quelle guerre intestine avons-nous alumée!

IN OMNIA PARATUS.

Marshal each band thou hast, and summon more;
  Of war's fell stratagems exhaust the whole;
Rank upon rank, squadron on squadron pour,
  Legion on legion on thy foeman roll,
And weary out his arm, thou canst not quell his soul.
VISION OF DON RODERICK.

The sweetest calm man e'er beheld
  Since first creation rose,
We saw, when faction madly yelled
  For war's convulsive throes.

Peace, plenty, comfort—all were here;
  We felt no chastening rod;
And yet the dreadful scourge was near,
  Of an avenging God.

And States are rocked by agitation,
  And threatening clouds appall;
And we must drink, this happy nation,
  The wormwood and the gall.

As Saturn madly would devour,
  His own dear progeny;
Columbia thus, in frenzy's hour,
  Her sons—the brave, the free.

And blame is here, and blame is there;
  Some more, some less to blame;
Yet all the deep distress must share;
  If shame, the burning shame.

Our thirty millions one must stand—
United stand or fall;
Once civil war invades the land,
It must envelop all.

Shall we sink down in degradation,
O'erwhelmed with taunts and jeers?
Never! Pour out a full libation,
Of blood and burning tears!

Far sounds the call, loud beats the drum,
The nation's heart rebounds;
The strife—the crimson strife is come,
The clash of arms resounds.

The spirit of the fathers wakes,
From Independence Hall;
Earth with the crash of battle quakes,
The bravest, noblest fall.

How vast the stake! Ho, ye that would be free,
Now bravely strike for nationality.
An infant late we stood, with hopes and fears,
And then in youth, and then in riper years;
And yet, tho' strong, our strength we did not know,
Till twice we grappled with the parent foe.
And still another test; that strength to show
In foreign land, we strike at Mexico.
Nor yet, with all had we the trial had
Of rupture, treason, half the nation mad.
But we have tried this fiery test at last;
Headlong we went, in boiling caldron cast.
Mountains on foes in Heaven's war were hurled,
So States on States in this our lower world.
The nation reeling, to and fro, we see,
And tremble oft for nationality.
But sure, at length, to cheer the patriot's eyes,
Behold her proud proportions pierce the skies!

The strife was gloomy, terrible and drear;
The storm once past, serener skies appear.

We calmly now may count the cost,
And what is gained, and what is lost.

What though our men in arms were millions!
With thousands upon thousands slain;
What though the cost we count in billions!
The heavy loss may yet be gain.

Our prowess, now, no mere suggestion,
Or hint, or boast, to be denied;
Come, world in arms! and test the question,
The fiercest storm we have defied.

On thousand battle plains, and gory,
Have freemen bravely fought and fell;
'Tis mournful, but they tell the story,
And who but says they tell it well!

And now the fearful shock is o'er;
The land that bled at every pore,
Again with peace is blest;
Though myriads fell amid the gloom.
They quiet fill the honored tomb;
Oh, peaceful may they rest!

The arch of triumph, let it rise:
Mount up, proud column, to the skies;
Their deeds commemorate!
Forget them! No, eternal shame!
Blaze forth their each and every name;
Their fame perpetuate!

And freedom has outlived the storm,
In fearless spirit and in form;
Though sacrilegious hands,

Have dared to touch its sacred shrine,
Not fearing man or wrath divine:
  The Constitution stands.

And could it in the deadly strife,
Like Eden's flaming sword of life,
  Defend each vital part?
Preventing each and every blow,
If aimed, or by a friend or foe,
  From reaching to the heart?

It could; it did; it ever can,
Defy the wrath and power of man,
  Their worst to hate or do:
Note, who despotic scepters sway;
Freedom shall live and rule the day,
  If wise, and brave, and true.

Nor from those dark and angry waves,
In mockery of those patriot graves,
  Has despot rose to power:
The storm abates and leaves us free;
We still may boast our liberty,
  In this the peaceful hour.

Note, despots of the earth, again:
Behold those armies on the plain—
  See how they strike and die!
But let them once unite their blows,
And hurl them upon foreign foes;
  Such foes shall quickly fly.

Our wish, our policy is peace,
That this good land may yet increase—
  This land so broad and fair;
Our friendship ever true shall be,
But terrible our enmity;
  Then rouse it ye who dare.

The Union stands, above domestic foes;
It pales not, snaps not, from domestic throes;
  It stands as firm as ever:
The bold — the wild fanatic shakes it not;
Determined — fiery southron breaks it not;
  It shakes, it breaks, no never.

Then let us gather round the fallen brave,
And cast our garlands on his hallowed grave;
  Let incense there arise!
And, as we chant aloud the victor strain,
That all may hear — and earth, and rolling main,
  And those above the skies; —

Let 's swear, by help of Him whom we adore:
This Union — from the ocean shore to shore,
  From pole to tropic sun —
This mighty Union of the States shall last,
Till worlds on worlds are into ruin cast:
  THE UNION EVER ONE!

SERENADE.

  The bright stars are gleaming above;
The moon sails along in her glory —
          Arrayed in her glory;
And yet thou art sleeping, my love —
          Art dreaming, my love —
Ye hear not a lover's sad story —
          A true lover's story!
Oh, dream of thy lover's sad story!

How fresh and how balmy the air;
My locks the soft breeze is caressing—
So sweetly caressing;
And yet I am wild with despair—
I die with despair;
And shall I despair of thy blessing—
Or hope for thy blessing?
Oh, lend the sweet charm of thy blessing!

Awake thee, nor true heart despise;
Art risen! The spell now is broken—
The dark spell is broken;
I now catch a glimpse of thine eyes—
A gleam of bright eyes,
And throw thee a kiss as a token—
Thy true lover's token;
Oh, send me a kiss for a token!

And now I must bid thee adieu;
The curfew has told the long numbers—
Now tells the short numbers;
Oh, bid me my visit renew—
My song to renew;
Then sink to thy soft dreamy slumbers—
The sweetest of slumbers;
Oh, dream of me in thy soft slumbers!

THE OBSTACLE.

Oceans of bliss around us gently roll,
When love sincere in all its power is felt;
When mind and plastic heart, and very soul,
Of two in one together fondly melt.

How cruel! if malignant star, or pride,
Parental will, or fixed pre-occupation,
Presents itself to check the genial tide—
To bar the final—happy consummation.

SHADOWS OF CRIME.

La crainte suit le crime, et c'est son châtiment.
VOLTAIRE'S SEMIRAMIS.

I'll haunt thee like a wicked conscience still,
That mouldeth goblins swift as frenzy's thoughts.
TROILUS AND CRESSIDA.

His early youth was formed in virtue's way,
Nor tempting vice e'er led his feet astray;
Swiftly his years in happy quiet flew,
Nor spot of leprous crime e'er felt or knew.
And songs of praise are his, and pious thought,
And offerings to the sacred altar brought;
And, fixed in firm resolve, his earnest soul
Can sin withstand, though floods around him roll.
As free from guile as saint or angel blest,
He thinks of crime but only to detest.
Of earthly goods he has enough, and more,
He covets not his neighbor's gold or store.

Perhaps his portion is the humble cot,
Yet sweet contentment is his happy lot;
Or, if in princely affluence he leads
A life of ease, 'tis marked by worthy deeds.

In evil, fatal hour the tempter came—
To touch, to taint, to load with endless shame;
To blacken innocence with crime and lies,
To blast the hopes that reach beyond the skies.
The purest fountain of the mountain top,
Is quickly curdled by the poison drop;
And once impregnate with the fatal grain,
The dark solution wanders to the plain;
From thence around with foul, malarious breath,
'T will spread and widen to the gates of death.

The tempter comes: the first dim thought of crime,
Disturbs the quiet of that soul sublime.
He feels an agitation—tremor—dread,
As if already to the prison led.
The deepening shades collect around his soul;
The darkening, turbid waters round him roll.
He fears himself; he fancies others read
His troubled thoughts, and watch the coming deed.
His early virtues oft revive, but feel
The tempter grasping with his hooks of steel.
He struggles oft in tears and deepest grief,
And dreads the never dying brand—A Thief.
He reasons, doubts, resolves, but to the goal
He steady moves, with loosened self control.

His neighbor's store secure before him lies,
He furtive looks about him, takes, and flies.
A chill, a shudder darts through all his frame;
He hates the light, he hates his very name.
In every breeze he hears the *hue and cry*;
He flies, and from himself he fain would fly
His eye is often o'er his shoulder cast,

With horror stricken face and look aghast.
His shadow keeps his steps in measured time,
The ever present witness of his crime.
His consciousness of guilt will quickly trace
Suspicion of his crime in every face.
Each unexpected touch — electric shock;
"I'm not the man," he cries, to striking clock.
The evening stars are but a hateful light,
That drag his guilt to dreaded human sight.
The smiling moon a mocking demon seems;
His sweetest slumbers are but fitful dreams.
Handcuffs and bolts and bars and shackles loom,
From every quarter of his haunted room;
And specters, hydras, march before his eyes,
As panting, stifled, on his couch he lies.
"Avaunt!" he mutters with affrighted tone;
He springs, he wakes — to find himself alone.
He wakes as from suspended animation;
He wipes the heavy drops of perspiration.
"O, never dying worm, I pray depart,
Or strike at once and sting me to the heart."

Now darker shadows flit across the room,
And fill his troubled soul with frightful gloom.
The tuneful cricket, innocent and kind,
Shouts black perdition to his tortured mind.
If silence reigns, its terrors but display
The awful thunders of the judgment day.

"A knock! I'm tracked and found! It is the knell,
That breaks the terrors of this midnight spell!
To prison — dungeon — horrible relief!
The fear is past — I know the worst: A thief!
These solid walls and rays of light so pale,
Are real now; they tell the heavy tale.
Oh, that this narrow cell, so full of gloom,
Were but the rest and quiet of the tomb!
Oh come, thou grim destroyer, end the strife!

Stretch forth thy bony fingers — clutch my life!
To mortal, sunk in crime, no tyrant thou!
I gladly would embrace thee, here and now!"
In vain; exposure — witness — proof of guilt —
The verdict — sentence — all must yet be felt;
No burning tears of sorrow aught avail,
As prying eye and curling lip assail.

Perhaps the crime was murder — first degree;
"Hold, hold my reeling brain! Behold that sea
Of human gore that floats and curdles round me!
Its sickening, damning odors well confound me!
See through its reeking mists — the beam — the halter!
Toward the fatal drop I walk — I falter!
A broken law with thunders rends the air;
Around me gather clouds of black despair.
Beneath my feet a yawning pit — the brink
Invites my step — the step I take — I sink!!
As being fails, as night invades mine eyes,
One ray alone I see from angry skies;
The ray that shone to thief upon the tree;
Oh, Star of Bethlehem, remember me!"

* * * * * * * *

Now motion, sense, vitality are past;
The mantle of the tomb is on him cast.

THE ALBUM.

> If sometimes in the haunts of men
>   Thine image from my heart may fade,
> The lonely hour presents again
>   The semblance of thy gentle shade.
>
> BYRON.

I take your book — of autographs:
I take a look — at photographs.

You here in happy order range,
  Your many friends, forever dear —
For fleeting time and restless change,
  A precious, lasting souvenir.

Permit me, too, to write my name;
  But where? with Jennie or with Mattie?
    With Katie, Minnie, or with Pollie?
No matter where, 'tis all the same,
  Whether with Nellie or with Hattie;
    Then put it here along with Mollie.

The partial act no one can blame;
  All petty jealousy may cease;
Admiring all, we thus proclaim,
  A preference for a lovely niece.

The memory of tender years —
  Those years that quickly fly,
So full of hope, so free from tears,
  Can never, never die.

Though far apart we wander,
  As time shall roll away;
Our hearts no space can sunder,
  Our love can ne'er decay.

GIDEON'S BAND.

He plays o' th' viol-de-gambo.
TWELFTH NIGHT.

Oh, what is this unearthly noise,
  That sends affright thro' all the city!
They call it music—jovial boys,
  Just throwing off a lively ditty.

The coach a sorry dragon seems;
  The grays their every rib may tell;
Ill-favored kine of Phar'oh's dreams,
  Would scarce be found a parallel.

The idle crowd will stand and gaze,
  The untied horses start and run;
The dogs will howl as in a maze,
  The wags pronounce it best of fun.

A din of sounds—a wild confusion,
  From horn and trombone madly flung;
To quiet life a rude intrusion,
  Yet "b'hoys" must "go it" while unhung.

Then lash the horses to a trot,
  And bang away in loudest thunder—
No matter who is pleased or not—
  Till every ear is split asunder.

Let stunning echoes rend the air,
  Let every pipe send forth a bray;
Blow hard, no matter how or where,
  For every dog must have his day.

INTRODUCTORY AND VALEDICTORY:

Spoken at the Annual Examination of the

BISHOP UNION SCHOOL,

DETROIT, JUNE 28, 1867.

INTRODUCTORY.

OUR PATRONS ALL! In form of simple lay,
We bid you welcome on this closing day.
  We now recount the labors of the year—
  Our earnest toil, in this the humble sphere.
The germ of mind we here present to view,
The swelling bud and fragrant blossom too.
  Our course of study here is various,
  As business life is multifarious.
Of letters, arts and science, here we trace
The outline—here we sweep the solid base.
  Here sweetly open on the minds of youth,
  The genial rays of elemental truth.
'Tis like the rising moon upon the eye,
When darkness flees and light invades the sky;
  Or like the cooling draught so rarely won,
  Amid the sands beneath a tropic sun:
We quaff the waters of the sparkling pool,
And bless the teacher of the public school.
  At times we deem ourselves already wise,
  And play the *inkhorn* with pedantic cries;
And for one mighty self all wisdom claim,
As if already on the rolls of fame;
  The many dry details of books we spurn,
  And coolly ask, what more there is to learn.
The cure for this may be applied at once;

The pointed question sinks us to the dunce,
  Suffused with blushes of the deepest hue,
  To see how small the sum of all we knew.
When thinking minds in friendly contest meet,
The truth revealed will banish self-conceit.
  No exclamation, then, how fast we grow!
  But simply this, how little do we know!
And thus with patient effort press we on,
Till many weary days and weeks are gone.
  Though oft discouraged, earnestly we tell
  The plodding round, and in the end excel.
As cities by the spark are set on fire,
So from electric flash our minds aspire.
  Those simple letters, twenty-six in all—
  Ah, how the untaught urchin they appall—
Are elemental powers, unbounded, vast,
In which a Webster's solid fame was cast.
  We learn to dot the "i" and cross the "t";
  We sometimes try a task at poetry;
But while in unpretentious rhyme we sing,
The soul may rise as on the eagle's wing.
  Here we may count the seconds of the years;
  Here we may trace the orbits of the spheres;
Here we may weigh a world, divide a fraction;
Here learn the proper end of human action.
  And yet, dear friends, we see and deeply feel
  Our nothingness; and now to you appeal.
Thrice welcome then, your happy smiles and cheers;
Your sympathy removes our anxious fears.
  We pass the test of this examination,
  If we can win your kindly approbation.

VALEDICTORY.

INDULGENT FRIENDS! Our yearly work is done;
The goal we touch, the victory is won.
  Strong was the hope and strong the moving cause,

To reach that goal with honor and applause.
Defects are the exception, not the rule,
In any well conducted Union School.
Perhaps you would prefer it more "select."
The child from "vulgar contact" to protect;
But child, to manhood grown, will soon be hurled,
Against an unselect and heartless world.
This point we hold, refute it if you can,
The public school 's the place to make the man.
How broad the field that here before us lies,
Where thoughts in never ending progress rise!
A never ending work of new creations,
A vast, a boundless range of combinations!
By patient thought true knowledge we coerce;
'Tis simple thought that rules the universe.
Where'er in life successful men abound,
There thoughtless men are rarely to be found.
We grant misfortune may perform a part,
Depress the resolution, chill the heart;
With gloom and darkness shroud the future life,
And make the prize seem hardly worth the strife:
Yet still, success is mainly in the man;
Whoever says he will, will find he can.
Say you, not all can rank among the great?
They need not; virtue this may compensate.
The laws of worthy action, and of mind,
And heart and body—all are here combined.
We test the truth by process analytic;
We re-adjust the parts in mode synthetic;
The whole—a happy order of induction—
The true Baconian method of instruction.
A varied social life we here embrace;
See true politeness beam in every face;
And see in every scholar, if you scan,
The little lady—little gentleman.
And higher culture here is unconfined;
The drawings on the walls adorn the mind.

The moral, too, is not neglected here;
In proper case, the right, the wrong appear.
  From golden rule, the wrong we here eschew;
  We learn the just, we learn the good and true.
In public spirit, too, our souls aspire;
We feel the glow of patriotic fire.
  While other sterling virtues here expand,
  We learn to love our own, our native land.
Its manly freedom here we learn to cherish;
Oh, far the day when liberty shall perish!
  Inspire, Oh gentle Goddess! every heart,
  In thy defence to act a worthy part.
And higher still our daily teachings tend;
They show the pathway to the happy end.
  The law divine is ever kept in view,
  In all the various studies we pursue:
They gently flow like sweet Siloa's stream,
Fast by the radiant light of heavenly beam.
  The jarring discords of the sects they shun,
  But point unerring to th' Eternal One.
While thus the subject vast before us lies—
From center earth to yonder vaulted skies;
  While we the harvest proudly gather now,
  Like tempting burden on the autumn bough;
Yet, patrons—friends! Your gracious presence here,
Has crowned the many labors of the year.
  Their fruits upon the future age shall tell;
  Oh, may you live to see them!—

FARE YOU WELL.

JULY FOURTH.

1867.

Spoken at the Annual Examination of the Cass Union School;
Detroit, June 28, 1867.

Awake, anew, Columbia's anthems!
  Let future ages catch the strain;
Hail, sons of freedom, hail ye millions!
  The nation's birth-day dawns again.

Now hear the loud artillery booming;
  Hear church-bell, clarion, fife and drum;
See rockets, bonfires; grand commotion!
  For lo! our jubilee is come.

To Seventy-Six cast back the vision;
  Behold that brave, devoted band!
With what heroic, firm decision,
  Like men, like demi-gods they stand!

That gloomy night of revolution,
  With all its terrors grimly cast!
Weak hearts may shun the dread solution,
  But stout ones brave it to the last.

Tho' Britain threat the traitor's halter,
  And spread a fierce, consuming fire;
Her foes are men that never falter,
  To fame immortal they aspire:

In darkest hour of tribulation,
  They grasp the future, grand and free;
Of many States—one mighty Nation:
  Come, celebrate our jubilee!

"Press on to greatness and to glory,"
Upon the stars and stripes unfurled,
Foretells a proud but simple story,
To friends of freedom thro' the world.

This broad domain is truly ample,
The richest that the world has known;
And July Fourth a bright example,
To such as still in fetters groan.

Our freedom was our own creation;
The fathers gained it, we maintain;
Maintain, though tossed by agitation,
Like barque upon the rolling main:—

Maintain, though sectional defection
May thirst and strike for brother's blood;
True hearts shall be its firm protection,
Through raging tempest, sweeping flood.

The storm may threaten desolation—
Spread wild destruction far and wide;
And yet the work of restoration,
Shall rise above the surging tide.

To God of Armies let us render,
The glory, honor, lasting praise;
He is our Rock, our sure Defender,
To him our highest song we raise.

Then strike anew Columbia's anthems!
The nation's birth-day dawns again;
On each return, Oh, shout ye millions!
Let distant ages swell the strain.

BATTLE AT THE RIVER RAISIN,

January 22, 1813.

Spoken at the Annual Examination of the Barstow Union School;
Detroit, June 28, 1867.

Now gleam and thunder, from afar,
The threatening clouds of savage war;
The war-whoop and the wild hurrah,
Proclaim the rising gloom.

Now waves on high the savage crest;
Revenge now heaves the savage breast;
His race now send their high behest—
The white man's bitter doom.

And yet that small but fearless band,
Is there, with firm resolve, to stand,
The bulwark of their native land,
Whatever may betide.

Then let the deadly bullet fly—
The arrow sing along the sky:
They echo back the battle cry,
The issue they abide.

Now sweep the red men o'er the plain,
And Proctor's columns charge amain,
And rifles rattle, and again,
The deafening cannon boom.

And Raisin's banks are heaped with dead,
And Raisin's flood is dyed with red;
Brave warriors find a lowly bed—
The soldier's honored tomb.

Though victory we cannot boast,
Yet hold the field at any cost;
Oh, yield it not till it has lost,
Its very last defender!

That fearful shout, that fiendish yell!
As from the very gates of hell!
Alas! too plainly they foretell,
The folly of surrender.

Enough; the vanquished yield the strife,
Assured of safety and of life;
'Gainst tomahawk and scalping knife,
The Briton's faith is given.

That faith is not an empty sound?
Then where shall treachery be found?
Speak! whitening bones, above the ground,
Denied for months the burial mound,
Is Britain's honor riven?

Victors! the torture, slaughter, ply!
All your infernal engines try!
Wring out the deep, the cursing sigh!
Call down the vengeance of the Sky!
Just retribution now is nigh—
Defeat and burning shame.

Ho! Chiv'lry of the West, awake!
Your country calls, the plow forsake,
The victor's vaunted power to shake;
Beside the Thames his ranks shall break;
Avenge the torture and the stake!
And forest, prairie, river, lake,
Shall swell your lasting fame.

THE TINY HAT UPON THE BROW.

1867.

That elfin crown, so light and neat,
  Might well a fairy queen endow;
With flower or plumage all complete—
  The tiny hat upon the brow.

It rides the *chignon* lifted high,
  Like regal bonnet on the prow,
Triumphantly; yet some decry,
  This janty *chapeau* on the brow.

The crusty cynic we may see,
  Bent fiercely on "domestic row,"
Who calls it, in his fiendish glee,
  A cabbage leaf upon the brow.

Ah, what a stupid cabbage head,
  That to perfection will not bow!
Could he admire, so vulgar bred,
  This true perfection on the brow!

Its color—texture—delicate,
  Like bloom of summer on the bough;
Behold, the prince of courtly state—
  This bloom of roses on the brow!

Thou snowy cap of alpine peak,
  That glitters in the sunlight now,
To rival this no longer seek—
  This beacon light upon the brow!

Like crest upon the foaming tide;
  As evanescent all allow;
Yet when it decks the lovely bride,
  Oh, bridal garland on the brow!

The use need not our souls perplex;
  Its taste no one can disallow;
Enough, it crowns the gentler sex—
  A crown of glory on the brow.

And yet that blooming cheek below,
  Far, far outshines it all avow;
No art can rival nature's flow,
  Not diadem upon the brow.

THE WHISTLE OF THE TRAIN.

The time is up, the friends are near,
    To bid adieu again,
As soon as we again shall hear,
So welcome to the waiting ear,
    The whistle of the train.

Impatient now we long have stood,
    To catch the cheerful strain,
That echoes from the distant wood,
And fills the air as with a flood,
    The whistle of the train.

They come! the whirling smoke we see,
    As in a hurricane;
And yelling in ecstatic glee,
So wild, and shrill, and bold, and free,
    The whistle of the train.

A moment only now to stay,
    For naught can here detain;
A word is all that we can say;
A parting kiss; it calls away—
    The whistle of the train.

The air is calm, the day is bright,
No sign of gloomy rain;
And like the arrow is our flight,
To instant death, perhaps, despite
The whistle of the train.

'T were wiser far to check our pace,
Our eagerness restrain;
If "switch" or "draw" be out of place,
It sounds a knell, in frightful race,
The whistle of the train.

The gentle kine are on the way;
Put on the "brakes" amain;
"Cow-catcher" will quick work essay,
Unless they instantly obey,
The whistle of the train.

The nimble deer is on the track,
His forest to regain;
He springs as from pursuing pack,
And distant leaves behind his back,
The whistle of the train.

On every side the whirling land,
The hamlets of the plain;
The rural village is at hand;
They wait, that crowd upon the stand,
The whistle of the train.

While thus from home we travel far,
For pleasure or for gain;
We take, at night, the "sleeping car;"
Then howls, our slumbers to debar,
The whistle of the train.

And when in nightly shadows deep,
We long have restless lain;
And heavy hours upon us creep;
How mournful, in a fitful sleep,
The whistle of the train!

We dash among the mountains high,
And hear that wild refrain;
From ledge to ledge the echoes fly;
It starts the eagles in the sky—
The whistle of the train.

It sounds as from the burning throne;
Of Pluto's gloomy reign;
Or like a giant's deepest groan,
From depths of mortal anguish blown,
The whistle of the train.

And yet how pleasant is the yell,
And free from every pain,
When "home, sweet home," it deigns to tell,
And rings it out through gorge and dell—
The whistle of the train.

We have it when the trip is o'er,
The whistle "on the brain;"
Like motion of the ship, ashore;
We hear that oft recurring roar,
The whistle of the train.

SCIENCE.

To learn the laws
Of nature, and explore their hidden cause.
DRYDEN'S OVID.

"Harp of a thousand strings," awake,
And fling thy melodies afar!
For theme, the world of science take,
From center earth to blazing star.

"Proud Science!" wonders hast thou wrought;
Inventions to perfection brought;
The curious brought to view;
And powers and combinations latent,
Hast well displayed and crowned by patent,
As if for something new.

See how unerring laws, in nature's plan,
Are clear unfolded by the Artisan!
Proud Mathematics, with a stretch sublime,
Would touch the utmost verge of space and time.
Says Archimedes, "give whereon to stand,
I raise the seas, the mountains and the land."
Invoked by Chemist in his lab'ratory,
See plastic Nature tell her simple story!
The fruits of science are on every hand;
They well improve and beautify the land;
And yet with all the wealth they now have told,
Far greater still the future shall unfold.

Mount Cenis well may beg for grace,
The gnawing worm is at his base;
The engine and the whirling car
Shall soon defy the Alpine bar.

Pacific Railway! That stupendous plan!
  With proud expectant banners broad unfurled!
A work that shall the Rocky Mountains span,
  And change the trade and commerce of the world.

The bridge, across that mighty river,
  That proudly bears Victoria's name,
With base and strength to stand forever,
  May well bespeak a world-wide fame.

Pass up that rapid tide,
    Ontario—pass it o'er,
And take your stand beside
    Niagara's deafening roar.
Look through those misty showers;
    That eddying surge behold;
And see those lofty towers,
    Upon those banks so bold.
The master-work of man!
    Look at it, never fear;
See in that graceful span,
    Triumphant Engineer!
Behold the slender strands,
    The net work and the bow!
Can they maintain their bands,
    Above that flood below?
And see that train—that goes—
    Majestic—o'er the deep!
One thread—it snaps—suppose—
    Ye gods! The horrid leap!

The Telegraph—the chief of wonders:
The lightning's flash without its thunders.
  Distance, what is it? Next to naught;
  And weeks are into seconds brought.
At once a fact or thought has birth;

This nervous system of the Earth,
Will dart it forth, and far and wide;
And e'en across the ocean's tide.
For be it known, we shall be able,
Ere long to lay Atlantic Cable:
We have! The victory is won!
In Sixty-Six the work is done.

And next in wonder and in worth,
The Power of Steam stands boldly forth;
With bit and rein, like foaming steed,
The loom, the forge, the ship to speed.
With heavy car and thund'ring train,
It dashes wildly o'er the plain;
And ledge and forest, gorge and dell,
All stand affright to hear its yell.

Now harnessed for the rapid flight,
And belching fire and smoke,
It comes — 'tis here — 'tis out of sight,
Like flash of sabre stroke.
A train ahead! Switch out of place!
Or draw in bridge — so rash!
It plunges on in frightful race —
A shriek! A murd'rous crash!
And now the Coroner is seen,
With his devoted twelve,
To sit him down with gravest mien,
Into the facts to delve.
They seem to know their office well,
'Tis simply not to see;
Or if they see, 'tis not to tell,
And let the matter be.
"The dead are mute, their friends are far;
Then why should we berate,
And place within the felon's bar,
The influential great?

The proofs are clear — before our face,
Yet verdict all the same; —
This was an accidental case;
We find — NO ONE TO BLAME."

Proud Science, too, with line and pendant lead,
Surveys the deepest, darkest ocean bed;
Explores the valleys, tells where mountains rise,
That seem, beneath the flood, to pierce the skies·
Detects the treacherous sands, the island curves;
The varying currents carefully observes:
Familiar chats with myriad finny train —
With pearls, and wrecks o'erwhelmed beneath the main.

Science, again, amid the furious strife,
Of wind and wave, that threatens every life,
Erects, above the all-devouring flood,
The bow of hope — the promised boon of God.

And Science, too, with slim and lengthened probe,
Has pierced the solid strata of the globe; —
Those strata that unnumbered years have told,
For hidden streams of wealth and shining gold.
The Earth shall ever yield the rich increase;
The surface will respond the "Golden Fleece"
To honest toil; the mine will also bring,
The Israelitish calf, the glittering King,
To avaricious throng, with pomp and glare,
For high, and low, and base, who worship there.

And Science swings his tube on high,
And sweeps his view across the sky,
And clear unfolds to human eye,
Infinity sublime;
And whirling planets, far and vast,
On axis and in orbits cast,

Whose music shall forever last —
A glorious — heavenly chime.
Say — Astronomic Devotee!
Can you not stretch enough to see,
The Great — Eternal — One in Three,
Upon His starry throne?
Ah, no! your vision multiply
Into itself, and still you try
In vain; and yet His reign is nigh;
'Tis everywhere alone.

Alas, Great God! what puny worms we are!
The flitting mote; the very dust; yet dare
We oft, Thy mighty 'venging arm laid bare,
When nothing else can save:
As we among the whirling planets soar,
And comets blazing far, let us adore
Thy wond'rous power and goodness evermore;
And live beyond the grave!

TRIBUTE TO THE MEMORY

OF

CHARLES VINE DE PUY:

Suggested by a visit to his grave, at Addison, Steuben County, N. Y., August 12, 1868.

Sleep on, brave boy! In quiet sleep;
  No battle storm disturbs thee now;
The drooping pines around thee weep—
  Above that fevered, pallid brow.

Upon the Rappahannock shore;
  In Sherman's legions firmly set;
Thou heard'st the battle's deafening roar,
  Undaunted every foeman met.

The harmless bullet past thee flew,
  And harmless burst the gleaming shell,
As dark the storm of battle grew,
  And thousand braves around thee fell.

And yet the miasmatic damp,
  The wet, the chill, of nightly bed,
In ill supplied, uncovered camp,
  Have numbered thee among the dead.

Thy country's cause was also thine,
  When duty called thee to the war:
Sleep on, brave boy! Thy name shall shine,
  In honor's roll like evening star.

Above thy dust the rose shall bloom;
  The breezes rock thy soul to rest:
Thy mem'ry casts a sweet perfume,
  As from the kingdom of the blest.

AN OLD SAW NEWLY RENDERED.

Although nor wise nor deep in thought,
A maxim we present that none may scorn;
The maxim this, of wisdom fraught:
Who would success in life be taught,
Must row his own canoe and toot his horn.

Are you at school in younger day,
With obstacles unnumbered full in view?
Where lessons interfere with play?
Would you surmount the weary way?
Then toot your horn and row your own canoe.

Are you a doctor, wise and deep?
And yet unknown, in poverty, forlorn;
With practice rare, or low, or cheap?
Would you to reputation sweep?
Then row your own canoe and toot your horn.

Perhaps the trader is your lot;
Would you with golden flowers your path bestrew?
Avoid the bankrupt's heavy blot?
Retire, with troubles all forgot?
Then toot your horn and row your own canoe.

Perhaps the artisan you toil;
Perhaps the farmer — to the manor born:
And would you gather golden spoil?
Gain richest fruits from rugged soil?
Then row your own canoe and toot your horn.

Do you, a briefless lawyer, trudge,
And mourn that merit never finds its due?
Submit to frowns of surly Judge
And all that your success begrudge?
Then toot your horn and row your own canoe.

Are you a scholar, deeply read,
With culture that would any place adorn?
And do you lack your daily bread?
And other wants and sorrows dread?
Then row your own canoe and toot your horn.

Would you in social circle shine,
A strutting coxcomb, vulgar parvenu?
Sublimest ignorance combine
With golden calf in lofty shrine?
Then toot your horn and row your own canoe.

Perhaps to office you aspire,
From public crib to draw your daily corn;
Then quiet pull the secret wire,
Nor shun the name of cheat and liar;
And row your own canoe and toot your horn.

Perhaps in death you still are mad,
And at the tomb your pride would bring to view?
On marble write, however sad,
The virtues that you never had?
Then toot your horn and row your own canoe.

SELF CONTROL.

A worthy triumph; one that shines afar,
We oft may gain, in raging civil war
Of self with self. Is provocation sent;
Or slight affront; or word by malice lent,
Or drop't in innocence and misapplied;
A — nothing, or to nothingness allied:
Do we sustain the hateful, random fling
At birth or rank; or bitter word, to sting
The self esteem: Is humble occupation
Reviled or slurred — a deep, a sore vexation:
Does trivial thing annoy, however slight,
In life's great drama: suffer we a blight
In fondest hopes: Are trials lent to test
The power of self-control; and kindly, lest
We fail in virtue: Then we quickly dash
Contentment by. The eager lightnings flash.
The calm gives place to rolling thunder clouds,
And tow'ring fury, darkly, fiercely shrouds
The whole existence: Every fibre feels
The raging tempest: Reason quakes and reels
To gain the mastery. Ah! then behold,
Unruly passions in rebellion bold
Against their Lord! The sequel wait: And will
The traitors yield, or brave the contest still?

Oh yes, they yield at last,
  The Ocean swell subsides;
The storm so fierce is past,
  Now still the surging tides.
Many the battle sore and long,
  That poor, weak man has won;
But vict'ry o'er himself, so strong,
  Is virtuous life begun.

In satisfaction calm, the victor smiles:
The foe within has played his artful wiles;
And, in the wild excitement of the hour,
Has bid defiance to the ruling power.
But now the traitor and the treason yield,
And surly quit the well-contested field.
The vanquished, in the storms of future day,
May still the sway of reason fierce essay;
Yet reason may, in empire of the soul,
Its rule assert, sublime in self-control.

BREVITY.

How many strive for the sublime,
And volumes write in prose or rhyme,
Nor thoughts or words condense
Forgetful that the long essay,
Can seldom live to distant day,
Though loaded down with sense.

We therefore try a shorter section;
And this, upon mature reflection,
And not from levity.
And here perhaps it ought to end—
To lengthen out does not amend,
This happy brevity.

Behold of spicy verse,
This rare example;
And of this writing terse,
A simple sample.

And terser still,
  No loose excess;
Behold the skill!
  The rare success!

If wit the point supply,
  In brief expression;
How heavy, tedious, dry,
  Is long digression!

Then ye who speak or write or teach,
And all who argue, sing or preach,
  This merit is the chief;
And do not let enthusiasm,
Or oratoric cataclysm,
  Prevent your being brief.

The task is difficult, we know;
The subject will upon us grow,
  But still the promise keep:
To say direct what you've to say,
And let the hearers go away,
  Before they fall asleep.

THE FUNERAL.

Nothing speaks grief so well as to speak nothing.
CRASHAM.

There is a pang that spurns all soothing cares:
The pang the mourner feels. It matters not
If worldly goods and social worth be there,
Refinement and the cultivated man.
The case they meet not. Strong but tender cords,
That link the heart to heart, the soul to soul,
Are rudely snapt; and this by Hand that gives
And takes at pleasure. When His rod afflicts,
And He the trembling soul wrings from the lump
Of vanquished clay, and dark and desolate
The scene, nor tears nor moans nor magic wand
Can change the stern, the final dread decree.
In vain our sympathetic nature weeps;
And all that we can say or do is vain:
Dead silence is by far the better part.
The heart that still survives is struck as with
The hand of death. In moans and tears it may
Relief obtain, but comfort none; no more
Than can the pulseless heart for which it sighs.
The rupture far too deep for aught but balm
That comes from God direct. 'Tis He alone
Can soothe our woe; and He can soothe it well.
Who thus can wound, the pain can well allay;
And time, in power to heal, stands next to Him.
His instrument is time: and this He wields
For wisest purposes. And time, old time
Eternal is, except so far as He
Shall cut it short. And time shall bear away
Our woes, our pains, our sufferings, our name,

Our memory—all, as on a gentle, sweet,
Delicious stream, to dark oblivion.
And as we thus glide on, the pangs we felt
We feel them less and less. The wounds are healed
To rigid scars; and all by kindly means
Which God vouchsafes and sends to our relief.
Forever more adored His holy name!

THE REGRET.

To Georgie Cowley, Addison, N. Y.

If inclination ruled the hour,
  My heart would fly away;
Impelled as by resistless power,
  To see the wedding-day.

And yet tho' distant far I seem
  I'm present none the less;
O, may there spring from bridal dream,
  A world of happiness.

Ever truly yours,
LEVI BISHOP.

Dated Detroit, June 2, 1869.

TO REV. W. H. MILBURN.

Dear friend, we guide thee to the altar,
To worship there on bended knee;
And tho' thy step may never falter,
Ye touch our warmest sympathy.

Those eyes that once like sapphires burned,
In vain they ope, in vain they rise;
And yet thine eye of faith is turned
To future home beyond the skies.

To that calm voice of prayer so clear,
The saints in glory seem to bend;
The God of mercy, drawing near,
A listening ear will kindly lend.

As glowing words the arches fill,
And richest imagery abounds,
The heart and soul with rapture thrill;
We seem to hear angelic sounds.

Ah, sweep that heavenly chord again!
Salvation is the worthy theme;—
Salvation; yes, a Saviour slain,
Us, sinful mortals to redeem.

Oh, if these lines shall greet thine ear,
Alas they cannot meet thine eye!
Oh, may you find in them to cheer,
To smooth your pathway to the sky.

There no dim light shall intervene;
Nor tear is there, nor sigh or moan;
There you shall see as you are seen;
There all shall know as they are known.

JULY 4, 1870.

Our jubilee! Forever blest!
To day we all are one:
To-day this nation of the west,
The rights of freedom to attest
Its grand career begun.

Then, clouds and darkness gloomy hung,
Above the infant state;
And yet our flag on high we flung,
And songs of freedom loud we sung,
This day to celebrate.

At last the mighty struggle came,
That bravest might appall;
And tho' the hero struck for fame,
Still higher was the patriot's aim—
His country, all in all.

Now rages, dread, the storm of war,
The fiercest lightnings play;
And yet the tattered flag, afar,
Is gleaming high a radiant star;
Columbia gains the day.

And peace within our border dwells,
And plenty everywhere;
Unbounded energy impels;
The nation's greatness rapid swells;
And all, the blessing share.

Where peace and freedom jointly reign,
    Intelligence the guide; —
Where equal laws the right maintain,
And vice and tyranny restrain,
    True glory must abide.

Red civil war is on the wing;
    The friend to foeman turns;
See brother for his brother spring!
Their bosoms to the carnage fling!
    A demon fury burns.

Again, the storm has died away,
    The bow is in the sky;
And brighter gleams from bloody fray,
The gladness of the peaceful day;
    Sad recollections die.

Like Anteus again we rise,
    Renewed, from mother earth;
On high the union banner flies;
Loud hallelujahs rend the skies,
    As for a second birth.

May God in mercy still preside,
    And shape our destiny;
Confirm and strengthen, far and wide;
Thro' every danger safely guide,
    As one and ever free.

THE OYSTER.

Beneath the water, near the strand,
Retired as in a cloister;
Upon the gravel, rock or sand,
The bay or river near at hand,
Is found the growing oyster.

The iron rake, or tongs, or hook,
Or other means shall raise them;
And as they drip and seem to look,
And seem to call for ready cook,
The epicure shall praise them.

With salt and pepper on the shell,
I cheerfully will take them;
The opener storms the citadel;
My tongue, it waters like a well;
They vanish ere I wake them.

You recommend the dainty pie,
The fanciful escalop;
You urge the stew, the mealy fry;
Then down they go, as all we try,
As if upon a gallop.

No matter what the form, I ween,
For spoon, or fork or platter;
Just let the appetite be keen,
And soon we sweep the table clean,
Amid a lively clatter.

Away with salad, gobbler, quail,
In quiet, or in royster;
Nor can the ortolan avail;
They all must soon ignobly fail,
Beside the luscious oyster.

THE BAR.

"Strive mightily,
But eat and drink as friends."
TAMING THE SHREW.

I.

When bards the Lybian desert sing,
And thence the fragrant breeze invoke;
Then flowers of poesy may spring,
From barren Tidd and quaintly Coke.

II.

Say ye, of active life and strong,
Ye who have toiled severe and long;
Ye who have stood and nobly stand,
The first of this forensic band;
Is there in life in all its stations,
In all its varied occupations —
Is there a calling, yea or no,
That taxes like it here below?

III.

A new herculean task each litigation;
New facts, new law, or new in application.
The work is long, the toil is ever dreary;
The goal has charms, the way is ever weary.
Explore we must in books however musty;
No precedent ignore however rusty;
Pursue an endless round of technic drudgery,
And wisdom seek beneath a load of fudgery.

IV.

How many quickly turn astray,
  Unable to endure the pain;
How many falter in the way,
  With over-loaded, shattered brain.

V.

Ye anxious student, would ye gladly learn,
Why some by magic skill, can always turn
To good account, full all they chance to know,
And vastly more? Why every reckless blow
They random give, brings on them as by stealth,
A dazzling fame, and wide renown, and wealth?
And why so oft, as chance of two is equal,
And both are eager for the golden sequel,
    The one is sure to bear away,
        While scorning all digression,
    The glories of a doubtful day,
        In this our law profession?
    And this perhaps by merest play,
        Or cool "adverse possession;"
    Or, as may sneering rival say,
        By reckless, bold aggression?
    And why on one alone shall swell,
        The popular applauses?
    'Tis simple all, so fame would tell —
        'Tis that he gains his causes.
    The other may as well retire,
        To any place he chooses;
    In law, 'tis useless to aspire,
        Because he always loses.
    Or if he chance to gain a case,
        At heavy — double, treble cost,
    He does it with so bad a grace,
        The crowd believe that he has lost.

VI.

Behold that something all can see —
That off-hand manner, always free,
  Yet full of shrewdest guile:
In proper place, the smile, the pun;
The serious air, the touch of fun;
  The happy lawyer style.
Nor can success be well foreseen;
The future is behind a screen,
  Like range of future life;
The man himself must lift the veil;
In difficulties never quail;
  The proof is in the strife.

VII.

But why is failure seen so oft,
  Where culture, education,
In nothing end, or end in soft
  Professional negation?
The reason plain, or plain may seem,
  That causes this vexation;
Nor need it wound the self-esteem,
  'Tis want of adaptation.
Here influence, and taste refined,
And wealth, and graces well combined,
  May dance around ambition;
If adaptation want, beware;
See disappointment written there;
  He lacks the one condition.

VIII.

Nor can this work discouragement, I ween;
For whose conceit at blooming, bright eighteen;
Does not in self, in mighty self detect,
A wondrous prodigy of intellect?

The tyro can in modest rival trace,
The failure and professional disgrace;
While yet he deems himself a chosen star,
To rise and blaze and glitter from afar.
And thus the way is open, free to all;
Ambition rings aloud the stirring call;
    And well the noble mind may try it:
Let all aspire, and let him win who can;
But let the race bespeak the worthy man:
    Dread ye a failure? No; defy it.

IX.

The law profession; worthy field!
    A truly noble calling!
When vice it shuns and does not yield,
    To pettifoggers' bawling.
When aspirations run not low,
    E'en in degenerate day:
Nor oft succeed *les Chicaneaux*,
    Les Petits Jeans so gay.
When high its aim, not sorded pelf,
    A virtuous power to wield,
It has for others and itself,
    The helmet, sword, and shield.
Then boldly for the right it stands,
    And throttles what is evil;
It strikes with honest men, the hands,
    Nor fears to face the devil.

X.

And in a nation's worthy cause,
    When agitation shakes the State,
The lawyer may proclaim the laws
    Above the rage of factious hate.

His very life, the air he breathes,
 Are law — the vital form of right;
If wrong above the right he sees,
 He for the law will boldly fight.
The advocate may quell the wrong,
 May soothe the anguish, dry the tear;
Protect the weak against the strong,
 And to the just his name endear.
And such a calling well may claim,
 The mind and heart of gen'rous youth;
For then its practice is the same,
 With love of justice, love of truth.

XI.

Nor this is all: reflective mind
 May soar above material things;
May dash all sordid pelf behind,
 And mount upon celestial wings.
Released from labors of the day,
 The soul may tune the lyre and sing:
May gather flowers along the way;
 May sip the clear Pierian spring.
It may be verse or measured prose,
 It may be solemn, gay or witty;
And yet the muses well may close,
 A heavy day of Kent or Chitty.

XII.

And is it true, perhaps ye ask,
 That hours of lofty meditation,
May quiet crown the daily task,
 And that as pleasant recreation?
Yea, doubt it not; apply the test:
 As Logic drags the heavy hour,
Imagination, Fancy, rest,
 Then spring in turn to active power.

Another force is brought in play,
  That Logic may regain its might;
The powers of mind that dormant lay,
  Are fresh for wing and lofty flight.
Though active mind, from daily round
  Of endless toil, may weary be,
It springs elastic at the sound,
  Of soul inspiring melody.
To Fancy's flight no bounds are set;
  The richest fields before us lie,
Where thoughts may other thoughts beget,
  In freely rolling reverie.

XIII.

Then let the man of law aspire,
His eyes upon the heavenly choir,
  Till not a cloud shall intervene:
In mental culture never tire,
Till every dross shall feel the fire,
  And final judgment close the scene.

BLATHERSKITE.

Spoken in character by —— at ——.

A burden rests upon the mind,
Of which the wise and good may write;
The mighty subject is to find,
And clear unfold to dull and blind
The proper sense of blatherskite.

To start with beasts: The surly dog,
That growls and snaps as if to bite;
The stubborn ox upon the bog;
The nag that holds the tedious jog;
May each be termed a blatherskite.

The girl and boy that idly shun,
Where truth and culture free invite;
A wicked race have thus begun;
Will soon a race of sorrow run;
Will soon become the blatherskite.

The crafty beggar that by stealth,
His tale of want can grim recite;
And pity claim; and yet has wealth
In ample store; and strength and health;
Expose the cheat — the blatherskite.

The miser, with a heart of ice,
Whose very smile is chilling blight;
Whose coffers are his paradise;
Who blooms in every sordid vice;
Oh, blast the blasted blatherskite!

The would-be critic; ever wise
In self conceit, yet seldom right;
A lump of venom in disguise;
A chronic grumbler; ah despise
And kick the sneaking blatherskite.

Who social circle ape to lead,
Without the solid requisite;
Where high pretension is the creed,
And every look betrays the breed;
Avaunt, ye vulgar blatherskite.

Behold the swelling parvenu,
The uninvited parasite;
Who tawdry flaunts in public view;
To baser instincts ever true;
In every place a blatherskite.

The ever happy, smiling home—
A theme we know is always trite;
Who mar it; or neglectful roam;
Its present peace and that to come
Destroy; Oh, brand the blatherskite.

Shall we a stanza, brief, essay,
Of theme that shuns the ear polite?
Let wild suggestion freely play?
No; no; the fashions of the day,
Court other name than blatherskite.

Ye who, with eye and ear intent,
Behold us here so gaily dight;
The real scamp to represent;
Ye soon may guess the skitey meant,
And silent name the blatherskite.

A dozen rhymes we thus have made,
And some perhaps the muse will fright;
Have run a word in every shade;
Who likes it not, the renegade,
May write himself a blatherskite.

EASTER ANTHEM.

Dedicated to Rev. T. C. Pitkin, D. D.
Detroit, April 9, 1871.

Sing the loud anthem o'er land and o'er sea;
The Savior is risen, his people are free.

Strong was the tomb, but its fetters are broken,
And from its dark slumbers He rises to save:
Oh, vain were its terrors! of sin the dread token!
Emmanuel conquers the tyrant—the grave.

Strike the loud cymbal o'er land and o'er sea;
The Savior has risen, his chosen are free.

Praise to the Victor! He dies not again:
Now o'er his dominions in justice shall reign.

Who can be silent! Oh, tell the glad story,
Of loud hallelujahs to swell the full tide!
For Jesus the slain now comes forth in his glory,
And all that reject him shall fall in their pride.

Shout the loud anthem o'er land and o'er sea;
Jehovah has triumphed, his kingdom is free.

PIONEERS OF DETROIT.

Introductory poem read before the Pioneer Society of Detroit, by the President, Levi Bishop, Esq., on May 4, 1871, and published at the request of the Society:

In ancient days, on every hand,
The West, without compeer,
Inviting smiled a promised land
To hardy pioneer.

The call we heard, obeyed it well,
Unknown for weal or woe;
And yet, with all, we rarely tell
Of fifty years ago.

From nearly every state and nation,
To western land we came;
Our each profession — occupation,
Records a worthy name.

We found a home, by choice or fate,
Beside this noble river;
The lovely "City of the Strait,"
We cherish now and ever.

The forests, rivers, azure skies,
Then lent their charming mood;
Now, cities — palaces arise,
Where once the cabin stood.

The pioneers of other climes
In quiet here we found; —
Adventurers of other times;
Now both as one are bound.

And time the flying years has told,
And long has been our toil;
We gather now, from days of old,
The rich but withered spoil.

The fatherland, the early home,
Our recollections fill;
And though we left them far to roam,
We oft re-visit still.

The past we love to ponder o'er,
The memory to cheer;
We note the fast receding shore,
That soon will disappear.

And many, too, have left the scene,
In silver locks and sear;
We'll drop beside their evergreen,
The sympathizing tear.

As former days we here recall,
In reminiscence cast;
In course we also soon must all
Be numbered with the past.

May He that kindly led us here,
A far exploring band,
Still guide us, when the end is near,
To His own happy land.

ALEXANDER J. FRASER, Esq.

The parents' lament upon his early death.

Oh, sad was the lot of the child we loved dearly,
  The son — only son, that from us now is torn;
And short were his years, tho' the spring time was cheerly,
  The bright early promise untimely we mourn.

Whatever seemed worthy, of care and of culture,
  Was freely bestowed, with refinement and taste;
Yet all now has vanished, as if the stern vulture
  Had pounced on the garden and left it a waste.

We counted upon him, as age was declining,
  The evening of life to sustain and solace;
Alas, he is gone, and, in fruitless repining,
  We mourn with the loved one he left in his place.

His grave we will moisten with fountains of sorrow;
  There wither the hopes that were lately in bloom:
With flowers we will strew it, and wait for the morrow,
  The morrow that springs from the sleep of the tomb.

WIFE IS AWAY.

Soliloquy of a Lonely Husband.

Oh welcome, lone cricket, thy song,
Tho' never so dull be thy lay;
Oh linger, thy music prolong,
For now the dear wife is away.

The hall and the kitchen are mute,
Where Bridget of late had her say;
Nor even the clock will dispute,
That the mistress of all is away.

The dining-room, cosy and neat,
Is shrouded in gloom and dismay;
We miss that dear social retreat,
Whenever the wife is away.

The parlor is lonely and drear,
In spite of its tasteful display;
It has not a smile or a cheer,
So long as the wife is away.

The pictures that hang on the wall,
Are now but a dismal array;
The dear, charming picture of all—
The wife—is away, far away.

The evening her curtain may spread,
The beams of the noon to allay;
The flowers their sweet odors may shed,
Yet still the dear wife is away.

Then heavy must be our refrain—
A sigh in the brief roundelay,
Until she returns once again—
The wife who is far, far away.

www.ingramcontent.com/pod-product-compliance
Lightning Source LLC
LaVergne TN
LVHW021241110826
845150LV00002B/374

* 9 7 8 1 4 2 5 5 6 1 5 4 3 *